LEITH'S
CONTEMPORARY
COOKING

LEITH'S CONTEMPORARY COOKING

More than 200 Meatless Recipes

by
Prue Leith
Caroline Yates & Alison Cavaliero

BLOOMSBURY

Acknowledgements

We have had great fun writing this book and preparing it for publication.

We cannot, in a short Acknowledgement, adequately thank those who have helped us. Caroline Waldegrave inspired and encouraged us, read the first draft and made numerous suggestions and improvements. She knows, without this formal thanks, just how grateful we are to her for her support.

On the production side, we would specially like to thank Hilaire Walden, the editor; Andrea Heselton, the photographer; Sue Russell, the food stylist; and Puff Fairclough, the home economist. We are filled with admiration for their painstaking attention to detail and their professionalism.

We would like to thank Mary Spyromilio for the Greek recipes.

Finally, we would like to thank our husbands, who have not only been willing guinea-pigs but also stoically put up with the stresses and pressures caused by disasters and deadlines.

We believe that the recipes in this book are new, except where we have stated otherwise. However, we live and work in a world of food, read and eat widely, and it is simply not possible to claim that all the recipes are entirely original. There are, after all, only a limited number of ways of cooking a cabbage.

First published in Great Britain in 1994
Bloomsbury Publishing Limited, 2 Soho Square
London W1V 5DE

Copyright © 1994 by Leith School of Food and Wine Ltd

The moral right of the authors has been asserted

A CIP catalogue record for this book
is available from the British Library

ISBN 0 7475 18017

10 9 8 7 6 5 4 3 2 1

Typeset by Hewer Text Composition Services, Edinburgh
Printed in Great Britain by
Butler & Tanner Ltd, Frome and London

Photographer: Andrea Heselton
Assisted by: Marcus Potts
Stylist: Sue Russell
Home economists: Puff Fairclough, Caroline Yates
Line drawings by: Kate Simunek

CONTENTS

FOREWORD

Cooking is both driven by fashion and comfortably impervious to it. Look at the pictures in any cookbook more than ten years old, and they will seem dated and dreary (or pretentious and silly); but study the recipes and you will find that the same great traditional flavour combinations go on and on – fish and lemon, eggs and herbs, cheese and tomato, pasta and garlic.

However, there has been a general, increasing shift in our tastes – a move towards healthier food, or vegetarian food, or simple 'homely' food. The move has been going on steadily for a decade, and has been particularly noticeable in fashionable restaurants with young British chefs at the stoves, in women's magazines and in the delicatessen departments of supermarkets – but rarely, I think, in cookbooks, which are often written by famous chefs who use ingredients that no-one else can afford, let alone find, or by designers who concentrate on beautiful pictures and then scrabble about for recipes to fit.

This book, I strongly believe, fills the gap. Caroline Yates is an unrepentant foodie who will happily test and re-test an idea until the result matches the original concept, and Alison Cavaliero, who provided much of the background information on the ingredients in the book, is an unswerving advocate of meat-free cooking.

All the recipes work. They should. There are fifteen teachers at Leith's School of Food and Wine, and recipe-testing and tasting is a lunch-time event in the staff room. Successful dishes go past the more rigorous hands (and tastebuds) of ninety-six exacting – not to say extremely fussy – students.

Leith's Contemporary Cooking is not entirely vegetarian, nor entirely healthy, nor entirely anything. But it is the sort of food that keen cooks long to prepare, and that enthusiastic diners want to eat. It is gastronomy for today.

Prue Leith

INTRODUCTION

This is not a vegetarian book, although none of the recipes in it makes use of flesh (meat or fish) as a main ingredient. Today, meatless cookery has overcome its 'bland, brown and cranky' label. This book contains new recipes for both meat-eaters and vegetarians who want an opportunity to cook contemporary, exciting and different dishes.

Leith's Restaurant, awarded a Michelin star in 1994, has noted that 20 per cent of its customers select dishes from their vegetarian menu. According to surveys, approximately 10 per cent of the population in the United Kingdom prefer not to eat meat. These facts suggest that meatless dishes that are attractively described, cooked and presented have a wide appeal, and that at least one guest around the table at home is likely to prefer to eat good vegetarian food. It is impractical to make a different dish just for the non-meat-eater, and yet a lot of vegetarian recipes are dull and unacceptable to carnivores. We hope to have given some inspiration and shown how easy it is to overcome this problem.

This is not a book with a message: we are not trying to convert anyone to vegetarianism, and certainly not to suggest that it is a more healthy way of life. Our sole objective has been to share some of our own recipes with people who enjoy good food and are prepared to believe that a meal without flesh is not bound to be boring.

The eggs used in the recipes are size 3, and where spoon measurements are given, we have used level, standard measuring spoons. All herbs are fresh, and all vegetables are medium-sized, unless specified otherwise.

For the strict vegetarian, we should point out that

(a) we use gelatine as a setting agent. However, we have given advice about the use of agar agar as an alternative;

(b) we have used anchovies, anchovy essence and Worcester sauce in some recipes; these are optional and can be omitted, though the finished dish will not taste the same.

The aim has been to produce a book with sophisticated recipes for entertaining, but there are recipes for day-to-day eating too. Some of these may have long lists of ingredients but they are not complicated because of this. There is something for both the skilled and the not-so-skilled cook.

All the products we have used are readily obtainable and we have included a list of suppliers for those who do not have ready access to the better supermarkets.

Conversion Tables

The tables below are approximate, and do not conform in all respects to the conventional conversions, but we have found them convenient for cooking. Use either metric or imperial measurements. But do not mix the two.

Weight

Imperial	Metric	Imperial	Metric
¼ oz	7–8g	½ oz	15g
¾ oz	20g	1oz	30g
2oz	55g	3oz	85g
4oz (¼ lb)	110g	5oz	140g
6oz	170g	7oz	200g
8oz (½ lb)	225g	9oz	255g
10oz	285g	11oz	310g
12oz (¾ lb)	340g	13oz	370g
14oz	400g	15oz	425g
16oz (1lb)	450g	1¼ lb	560g
1½ lb	675g	2lb	900g
3lb	1.35kg	4lb	1.8kg
5lb	2.3kg	6lb	2.7kg
7lb	3.2kg	8lb	3.6kg
9lb	4.0kg	10lb	4.5kg

Australian cup measures

	Metric	Imperial
1 cup flour	140g	5oz
1 cup sugar (crystal or castor)	225g	8oz
1 cup brown sugar, firmly packed	170g	6oz
1 cup icing sugar, sifted	170g	6oz
1 cup butter	225g	8oz
1 cup honey, golden syrup, treacle	370g	12oz
1 cup fresh breadcrumbs	55g	2oz
1 cup packaged dry breadcrumbs	140g	5oz
1 cup crushed biscuit crumbs	110g	4oz
1 cup rice, uncooked	200g	7oz
1 cup mixed fruit or individual fruit, such as sultanas	170g	6oz
1 cup nuts, chopped	110g	4oz
1 cup coconut, desiccated	85g	3oz

Approximate American/European conversions

Commodity	USA	Metric	Imperial
Flour	1 cup	140g	5oz
Caster and granulated sugar	1 cup	225g	8oz
Caster and granulated sugar	2 level tablespoons	30g	1oz
Brown sugar	1 cup	170g	6oz
Butter/margarine/lard	1 cup	225g	8oz
Sultanas/raisins	1 cup	200g	7oz
Currants	1 cup	140g	5oz
Ground almonds	1 cup	110g	4oz
Golden syrup	1 cup	340g	12oz
Uncooked rice	1 cup	200g	7oz
Grated cheese	1 cup	110g	4oz
Butter	1 stick	110g	4oz

Liquid measures

Imperial	ml	fl oz
1 ¼ pints	1000 (1 litre)	35
1 pint	570	20
pint	425	15
½ pint	290	10
⅓ pint	190	6.6
¼ pint (1 gill)	150	5
4 scant tablespoons	56	
2 scant tablespoons	28	
1 teaspoon	5	

Australian

250ml	1 cup
20ml	1 tablespoon
5ml	1 teaspoon

Approximate American/European conversions

American	European
10 pints	4.5 litres/8 pints
2 ½ pints (5 cups)	1.1 litres/2 pints
1 pint/16fl oz	1 pint/20fl oz/5.75ml
1 ¼ cups	½ pint/10fl oz/290ml
½ cup plus 2 tablespoons	¼ pint/5fl oz/150ml
¼ cup	4 tablespoons/2fl oz/55ml
½ fl oz	1 tablespoon/½ fl oz/15ml
1 teaspoon	1 teaspoon/5ml

Useful measurements

Measurement	Metric	Imperial
1 American cup	225ml	8fl oz
1 egg, size 3	56ml	2fl oz
1 egg white	28ml	1fl oz
1 rounded tablespoon flour	30g	1oz
1 rounded tablespoon cornflour	30g	1oz
1 rounded tablespoon caster sugar	30g	1oz
2 rounded tablespoons fresh breadcrumbs	30g	1oz
2 level teaspoons gelatine	8g	¼ oz

30g/1oz granular (packet) aspic sets 570ml (1 pint) liquid.

15g/ ½ oz powdered gelatine, or 3 leaves, will set 570ml (1 pint) liquid. (However, in hot weather, or if the liquid is very acid, like lemon juice, or if the jelly contains solid pieces of fruit and is to be turned out of the dish or mould, 20g/ ¾ oz should be used.)

Wine quantities

Imperial	ml	fl oz
Average wine bottle	750	25
1 glass wine	100	3
1 glass port or sherry	70	2
1 glass liqueur	45	1

Lengths

Imperial	Metric
½ in	1cm
1in	2.5cm
2in	5cm
6in	15cm
12in	30cm

Oven temperatures

°C	°F	Gas mark	AMERICAN	AUSTRALIAN
70	150	¼	COOL	VERY SLOW
80	175	¼	COOL	VERY SLOW
100	200	½	COOL	VERY SLOW
110	225	½	COOL	VERY SLOW
130	250	1	VERY SLOW	
140	275	1	VERY SLOW	SLOW
150	300	2	SLOW	SLOW
170	325	3	MODERATE	MODERATELY SLOW
180	350	4	MODERATE	MODERATELY SLOW
190	375	5	MODERATELY HOT	MODERATE
200	400	6	FAIRLY HOT	MODERATE
220	425	7	HOT	MODERATELY HOT
230	450	8	VERY HOT	MODERATELY HOT
240	475	8	VERY HOT	HOT
250	500	9	EXTREMELY HOT	HOT
270	525	9	EXTREMELY HOT	VERY HOT
290	550	9	EXTREMELY HOT	VERY HOT

MENU PLANNING

Deciding what to cook is a major step towards serving successful meals. However, making the decisions can be a daunting task. So here are a few hints to help you.

1. Avoid repeating the same ingredient in a menu: if serving tartlets for a first course, do not give your guests strudel for pudding. However, it would be perfectly acceptable to start with a red pepper soup and then serve black olive polenta with warm Mediterranean vegetables (including the red peppers).

2. Try to devise a meal that is colourful. This is particularly important with vegetarian food as it can be very 'brown', and especially when planning a buffet party.

3. Think about the texture. If the first course is soup or pâté, do not serve mashed potato or puréed parsnips with the main course, or stewed apple for pudding. The methods of cooking are too similar.

4. Vary the cooking methods. If serving plain, boiled vegetables to accompany the main course, do not serve poached fruit for pudding.

5. On the whole sauces are popular so be generous with them.

6. Try not to have too many 'main' flavours in one menu. The flavour of fresh ingredients can sometimes be drowned by too strong a sauce. Also, serve only one sauce at any one course. As with wine, go from light flavours to stronger tastes. Do not start a meal with a highly seasoned dish and follow it with something with a subtle flavour. Rather, serve a full flavoured main course too. Follow this with something light and sharp.

7. We would always recommend serving a simple salad with any rich meal. With careful choice of ingredients, good preparation and elegant presentation, a green salad will always go down well. A good dressing helps clean the palate.

8. Make the food relevant. Giving a rugger XV grilled aubergines with pesto would be as inappropriate as serving mustard molasses bean hotpot to a ladies lunch party. And although it is not set in stone (and could be got around with care) it is safer to stick with one style of food. Leaping from Italy to Southern France, to Southern Spain, i.e. Mediterranean food, is fine, but it would not work to serve a tricolour salad, followed by black bean chilli, followed by pecan pie.

9. Although we have become accustomed to many vegetables and fruits being available all the year round, try to keep menus as seasonal as possible. The flavour of vegetables and fruits is unquestionably better when they are **meant** to be harvested.

10. Balance a meal in terms of its nutritional composition (see p. 207). However, it is not necessary to be too extreme about this for one event.

11. Give interest to dishes by adding a clever garnish. Keep these simple, keep them relevant and keep them fresh.

There is always much discussion at Leith's about the order in which courses should be served. In England we serve the pudding after the main course, and before the cheese. In France, the cheese is served after the main course – the theory being that the red wine is finished before a sweet white wine is served with the pudding. We rather like the French approach for both its wine appreciation factor and its practicality; the hostess can go into the kitchen and give last minute attention to the pudding.

Finally, a menu should not be too ambitious. Three hot courses is going to make a hostess feel successively more flushed with each one.

A cold pudding made the day before is one less thing to worry about on the day; so prepare as much as possible in advance. We strongly advise making a time plan for the preparation of the meal, and **sticking** to it.

FOOD PRESENTATION

If food looks delicious, people are predisposed to think that it tastes delicious. If you have spent a long time cooking, it is a shame just to dump the food on a plate. At Leith's School we have gradually developed a set of rules which can be used as guidelines when presenting food. Fashion may dictate the method – be it stylish nouvelle cuisine or chunky country food – but the guidelines are the same.

1. Keep it simple
Over-decorated food often looks messed about and no longer appetizing. The more cluttered the plate, the less attractive it inevitably becomes.

2. Keep it fresh
Nothing looks more off-putting than tired food. Salads wilt when dressed in advance; sautéed potatoes become dull and dry when kept warm for hours, and whipped cream goes buttery in a warm room, so don't risk it.

3. Keep it relevant
A sprig of fresh watercress complements most things nicely. Scratchy sprigs of parsley, though they might provide the colour, are unpleasant to eat. Gherkins cut into fans do nothing for salads, tomato slices do not improve the look of a platter of sandwiches. It is better by far to serve a dish with a couple of suitable salads to provide the colour and contrast than to decorate them with undressed tomato water-lilies or inedible baskets made out of lemon skins and filled with frozen sweetcorn.

4. Centre height
Dishes served on platters, such as meringues or profiteroles are best given 'centre height' by arranging the food so it is higher in the middle with sloping sides. Coat carefully and evenly with the sauce, if any.

5. Overloading
Do not overload serving platters as it makes serving difficult. Once breached, an over-large pile of food looks unattractive.

6. Contrasting rows
Biscuits, petits fours, little cakes and cocktail canapés all look good if arranged in rows of one variety, rather than dotted about. Pay attention to contrasting colours, taking care, say, not to put two rows of chocolate biscuits side by side, or two rows of white sandwiches.

7. Diagonal lines
Diagonal lines and diamond shapes are easier to achieve than straight ones. The eye is more conscious of unevenness in verticals, horizontals and rectangles.

8. Not too many colours
As with any design, it is easier to get a pleasing effect if the colours are controlled,

for example, just green and white, or just pink and green, or chocolate and coffee colours or two shades of any other colour. Coffee icing and hazelnuts give a cake an elegant look. Adding multi-coloured icings to a cake, or every available garnish to a salad, tends to look garish. There are exceptions of course; a colourful salad Niçoise can be as pleasing to the eye as a dish of candy-coated chocolate drops.

9. Uneven numbers

As a rule, uneven numbers of, say, rosettes of cream on a cake, or baked apples in a long dish, look better than even numbers. This is especially true of small numbers. Five and three invariably look better than four, but there is little difference in effect between eleven and twelve.

10. Contrasting the simple and the elaborate

If a serving dish or bowl is elaborately decorated, contrastingly-simple food tends to show it off better. A Victorian fruit *épergne* with ornate stem and silver carving will look stunning filled with fresh strawberries. Conversely, a plain white plate sets off pretty food design to perfection.

11. A generous look

Tiny piped cream stars, sparsely dotted nuts, or mean-looking chocolate curls on a cake look amateurish and stingy.

12. Avoid clumsiness

On the other hand, the temptation to cram the last spoonful of rice into the bowl or squeeze the last slice of pâté on to the dish leads to a clumsy look and can be daunting to the diner.

13. Overlapping

Sliced foods look best if they are evenly overlapping. This way, more slices can be fitted comfortably on the serving dish than if they are placed side by side.

14. Best side uppermost

Usually the side of the food that is grilled or fried first looks the best, and should be placed uppermost.

FOOD SAFETY

Vegetable cookery does not present the same food safety problem as meat cookery, but there are important precautions that should always be remembered.

1. There may be earth on vegetables and herbs. *Clostridium perfringens* (a bacterium which is a common cause of food poisoning) is often present in soil. It is therefore sensible to wash vegetables thoroughly, even if they are going to be peeled.

2. Listeria is commonly found in many foods but *listeriosis* is very rare because most people's immunity copes well. However, it is wise for pregnant women, those with impaired resistance to infection and babies to avoid soft, ripened and blue-veined cheeses.

3. Good kitchen and personal hygiene is important.

4. Bugs like warmth, moisture and time, so avoid giving them these conditions.

5. Refrigerate perishable food, and never leave it on the side in the kitchen waiting to be used. To avoid the risk of re-infection with bacteria, do not leave cold, cooked food at room temperature for more than 1 hour.

6. Cool food as quickly as possible without any covering; open food cools quicker.

7. Never put hot food into a refrigerator: it raises the internal temperature of the fridge and may encourage the growth of bacteria.

8. Reheat food thoroughly right through to the middle. Do not mix hot food with cold food unless it is to be reheated at once.

9. If there is no alternative but to keep food warm, make sure that it has been thoroughly heated to kill any bacteria, then keep it really hot, not lukewarm.

10. Do not consume large dishes cooked from frozen without making sure that the centre is piping hot.

    Thaw food in a refrigerator or in a leak-proof plastic bag under cold water. Do not try to speed up the process by using hot water or a warm oven. Defrosting in a microwave is safe because it is very quick. Never refreeze thawed food without cooking it first.

WINE AND FOOD

None of the recipes in this book uses poultry, game, beef, lamb, pork or fish, so the usual conventions for matching wine with food, such as red wine with red meat and white wine with fish, cannot be applied. Wines to suit our recipes may be chosen strictly according to taste, without any concerns about being 'correct'. Obviously, the wine should 'go' with a dish, in the sense that it should complement the food rather than spoil or be spoilt by it. For guidance, at the end of each appropriate savoury recipe, there is a wine which, in our opinion, would go with it. In the end, however, the choice is personal.

The starting point when choosing the right wine is to identify the essential characteristics of both the wine and the food. The factors which influence the character of a wine are numerous: for example, grape variety, colour, country of origin and region (the soil conditions and climate), age and vinification. In combination, these give the wine its appearance, bouquet, taste and alcohol content. As an extremely loose guide the hotter the climate, the heavier and fuller the wines – both red and white: a cooler climate will produce a lighter, more acidic wine. Modern technology is, of course, trying to change all this. Wines are often described in conventional terms such as fruity, dry, acidic, crisp, smokey, light, medium or full-bodied. Thus, a wine such as a Beaujolais (red: the Gamay grape) might be described as 'light and fruity'; a Tokay (white: the Pinot Gris grape) as 'crisp and dry'; a Soave (white: the Garganega grape) or a Sancerre (white: the Sauvignon Blanc grape) as 'dry and acidic'; a Rioja (red: the Tempranillo grape), a Barolo (red: the Nebbiolo grape) or Chablis (white: the Chardonnay grape) as 'medium-bodied'; New World Chardonnays, which have been matured in oak barrels, as 'smokey' or 'oakey'.

There are many good, very readable and unstuffy wine books which explain more fully how wines get their character. Wine merchants usually employ staff who have knowledge of the subject and of the products in their shop, while most supermarkets give information about wines through the labelling on their shelves. The labels on wines from Eastern Europe and the New World often contain information about the principal characteristics of the wine, in addition to identifying the grape variety and alcohol content (expressed as a percentage).

As with wine, the taste and texture of food is a direct result of the ingredients used and the way they have been prepared and cooked. Food and recipes might be described as oily or dry; smooth or rustic; rich or strong (or hot); acidic or mild; delicate or bland.

A full, rich wine, such as a Côtes du Rhone, will overwhelm a delicate recipe, like asparagus filo tartlets (see p. 45). Conversely, a rich or oily dish, such as vegetable feuilletées (see p. 70) will overpower a light delicate wine, for example Soave, whereas a Chablis or other more acidic wine will cut through the same dish and be the perfect complement. Wines with low acidity will taste dull if drunk with acidic foods, e.g. lemons, oranges and tomatoes, or dishes containing vinegar, for example a salad with a vinaigrette dressing.

If more than one wine is being served at a meal, we suggest that, as a general rule, it is better to start with a light wine (even as an aperitif carried through to the first course) and progress to something heavier; move from dry wines to sweet wines low in acid to those with higher acidity, fresh, young, fruity wines to wines which are mature and dry. This is likely to fit in well with the choice of food because a strong, heavy first course would drown a light delicate main course. A light first course followed by a heavier main course will, therefore, encourage compatibility between the food and the wine.

European wines evolved to complement food and, in our opinion, do taste better drunk with a meal. New World wines, on the other hand, are easy drinking and taste delicious on their own.

These are just our suggestions and are not intended to create a set of rules for wine with meatless food.

STYLE OF FOOD	STYLE OF WINE	SUGGESTIONS
NIBBLES	Light dry whites	Frascati, Chablis, Moselle, Soave
	Sparkling Whites	Champagne, Cava, Crémant de
	Kir Royale (a sparkling	Bourgogne, Saumur, New World
	white with crème de cassis)	Sparkling
	Dry Sherry	Manzanilla, Fino
	Madeira	Sercial, Verdelho
1ST COURSES		
Soups	Dry Sherry	Manzanilla, Fino
	Crisp dry whites	Sancerre, White Burgundy, Soave
Egg Dishes	Medium dry whites	Vouvray, Vinho Verde, Moselle
	Light fruity reds	Beaujolais Nouveau, Zinfandel
Salads with dressing	Dry acidic whites	Soave, Sauvignon Blanc
	Dry light reds	Valpolicella, Beaujolais, Loire reds
Vegetable terrines/	Medium dry whites	Moselle, Vouvray, Orvietto
Pâtés	Light dry fruity reds	Beaujolais Nouveau, Merlot

STYLE OF FOOD	STYLE OF WINE	SUGGESTIONS
MAIN COURSES		
Smoked Food	Oakey whites	New World Chardonnay
	Sparkling whites	Champagne
Pasta	Dry light whites	Frascati, Sancerre
	Light fruity reds	Young red Burgundy
	Medium reds	Chianti Classico, Vino da Tavola
Fried foods	Dry whites with good acidity	White Burgundy, Sauvignon Blanc wines, some Alsace Pinot Gris
Casseroles/Tagines	Full-bodied reds, fruity or acidic according to the richness of the sauce	Claret, Chianti Classico, some Riojas
Spiced dishes	Full bodied dry red	Chianti Classico
	Full 'oaked' reds	New World Cabernet Sauvignon, Clarets, red wines from southern Rhone, Shiraz
	(Beer)	
Sauces	Light wines for light sauces	
	Heavier wines for richer sauces	
CHEESE		
Soft/cream/fresh	Full-bodied whites with good acidity	White Burgundy
	Medium/full reds	Chianti, Rioja, red Burgundy
Blue	Sweet whites	Sauternes and sweet Loire
	Full-bodied reds	New World Cabernet Sauvignon
	Port	Vintage, Tawny, Ruby
	Sweet sherry	Oloroso
Hard, mature	Dry full-bodied whites	New World 'oaked' Chardonnay
	Sweet whites	Barsac, Sauternes
	Full-bodied reds	Burgundy, New World Cabernet Sauvignon
	Sweet reds	Banyuls
	Port	Vintage, Tawny, Ruby
	Sweet Sherry	Oloroso
Goat	Full-bodied whites	Aged Chardonnay (Burgundy or New World)
	Sweet whites	Barsac, Sauternes
	Madeira	Bual, Malmsey
	Dry Madeira	Sercial, Verdelho

COOKING WITH WINE

The use of wine in cooking is almost as important as what is drunk. Resist the temptation to slosh any old wine into a casserole or sauce in the belief that it will improve it. Indeed, misusing wine in cooking can spoil a dish that would have been better without any wine at all.

Here are a few points to remember:

1. Think about a wine's colour and taste. To flavour a white sauce with red wine would obviously not be sensible, whereas a white wine could be used in a dark sauce, although the sauce would lack the depth and richness achieved by using a red wine. Similarly, a Sauternes would not be suitable in a savoury white sauce, even though it is a white wine. If the recipe is titled 'Bourgogne' or 'Bourguignonne', try to use a Burgundy.

2. If a recipe requires the wine to be added at the end of the cooking process, boil the wine for 5 minutes to eliminate the alcohol otherwise the sauce will taste raw and sour.

3. Wine may be added to recipes which are not cooked, such as sorbets, jellies and ice creams, although it should be remembered that alcohol has a low freezing point and will prevent dishes to which it has been added from freezing completely, at the usual temperature.

4. Wines can be used as a marinade to flavour and tenderise meat before it is cooked. Vegetables do not need this treatment so in this book 'marinading' is done *after* cooking, when the softened vegetables are left in the wine to soak up the flavours.

5. Do not use the old leftovers of an opened bottle. Wine turns to vinegar after it has been exposed to the air for between 24 and 48 hours, depending on the age and quality of the wine (the better quality the wine the quicker it sours). Wine which has turned to vinegar will become concentrated as the water evaporates during cooking, making the dish or sauce unacceptably sour and acidic.

6. Any leftover wine for which there is no immediate use can be stored in a bottle from which the air has been removed by one of the effective proprietary devices on the market. Alternatively, pour the wine into a smaller bottle with a tight-fitting cap, or a lidded glass jar, and keep somewhere dark and cool. Better still, drive off the alcohol by boiling the wine for 5 minutes in a non-aluminium saucepan, allow it to cool and then freeze in ice cube trays. It can then be used at any time in any suitable recipe.

SOUPS

Almond Soup
Red Lentil and Coconut Soup
Spiced Chick Pea Soup
Ginger and White Radish Soup
Fresh Corn-on-the-cob Soup
Parsley and Spinach Soup
Butternut Squash and White Stilton Soup
Red Pepper Soup
Summer Courgette and Mint Soup

Almond Soup

Almond soup is traditionally made with bread to thicken it. This is a lighter version and very good.

SERVES 4

225g/8oz unblanched almonds
55g/2oz butter
2 onions, chopped
4 sticks of celery, chopped
110 ml/4fl oz dry white wine
1.1 litres/2 pints vegetable stock (see p. 172)
salt and freshly ground white pepper
1 teaspoon orange flower water
290ml/10fl oz milk
150ml/5fl oz single cream (optional)

1. Place the almonds in a blender or food processor and, using the pulse button, mix until they look like coarse breadcrumbs (do not over-grind the nuts, but do not leave any unpalatably large bits either). Alternatively, chop the nuts by hand. Set aside.
2. Melt the butter in a saucepan, add the onion and celery and cook gently until soft but not coloured.
3. Add the almonds and stir well. Cook for 2 minutes.
4. Add the wine and stock and bring to the boil. Season, cover and simmer for 30 minutes. Allow to cool for a few moments.
5. Pour the soup into a blender with the orange flower water and mix until velvety smooth. Return the soup to the rinsed pan. Thin to the required consistency with the milk and single cream, if using. Taste and season if necessary.
6. Before serving, reheat gently but do not boil, otherwise it will curdle.

◆ ◆

Red Lentil and Coconut Soup

SERVES 4

1 tablespoon groundnut oil
1 onion, finely chopped
1 chubby red chilli, seeded and finely chopped
1 teaspoon peeled and grated fresh ginger
pinch of freshly grated nutmeg
2 red peppers, seeded and diced
110g/4oz red lentils, soaked for 10 minutes and
    drained
290ml/10fl oz vegetable stock (see p. 172)
110g/4oz creamed coconut, chopped
475ml/17fl oz hot water
salt and freshly ground black pepper

1. Heat the oil in a large saucepan and cook the onion over a low heat for 10 minutes or until transparent. Add the chilli, ginger and nutmeg and cook for a further minute.
2. Add the peppers and lentils and stir to mix.
3. Pour in the stock, bring to the boil and simmer gently for 10 minutes.
4. Put the coconut into a measuring jug and make up to 570ml/1 pint with the hot water. Stir to melt. Add to the soup. Continue to cook until the peppers are soft. Remove from the heat.
5. Pour the soup into a blender and mix until smooth. Return the soup to the rinsed saucepan, season to taste and reheat.

Spiced Chick Pea Soup

This is a good hot, spicy soup and perfect for a cold day. It can be made as hot or as mild as required by adjusting the quantity of chilli.

SERVES 6

2 tablespoons groundnut oil
225g/8oz onions, finely chopped
2 cloves of garlic, crushed
1 teaspoon ground allspice
1 teaspoon ground cumin
1 teaspoon ground coriander
½ teaspoon chilli powder
110g/4oz tomato purée
½ small green chilli, seeded and finely chopped
110g/4oz chick peas, soaked overnight and drained
1.1 litres/2 pints vegetable stock (see p. 172) or
    water
1½ teaspoons sugar
30g/1oz spaghetti, 5cm/2 inches long

1 tablespoon finely chopped parsley
1 tablespoon chopped mint
juice from ½ lemon
salt

TO SERVE:
lemon wedges

1. Heat the oil in a large saucepan and cook the onion and garlic for about 10 minutes, or until soft and lightly browned.
2. Stir in the ground spices and tomato purée and cook for 1 minute.
3. Add the green chilli and cook for 2 minutes.
4. Add the chick peas, stock or water and the sugar and simmer for 45 minutes.
5. Add the spaghetti and cook for 10 minutes, or until the spaghetti and chick peas are cooked.
6. Before serving, stir in the herbs and add lemon juice and salt to taste.
7. Serve garnished with lemon wedges.

◆ ◆

Ginger and White Radish Soup

SERVES 4

2 tablespoons peanut oil
1 large onion, chopped
3 cloves of garlic, crushed
7.5cm/3 inch piece of fresh ginger, peeled and
    chopped
2 large white radishes (mouli), peeled and
    roughly chopped
570ml/1 pint vegetable stock made with white
    vegetables only (see p. 172), or water

20 large coriander leaves, finely chopped
55ml/2fl oz medium dry sherry
1½ teaspoons clear honey
about 1 tablespoon light soy sauce
freshly ground white pepper

TO GARNISH:
2 spring onions, thinly sliced diagonally

1. Heat the oil in a large saucepan and cook the onion and garlic over a low heat for about 10 minutes or until soft and transparent. Do not brown.
2. Add the ginger and white radishes and cook for 2 minutes, stirring.

3. Pour in the vegetable stock or water, bring to the boil, reduce the heat and simmer gently for a further 20 minutes or until the radish is soft.

4. Purée the soup with the coriander in a blender. Return to the rinsed saucepan and add the sherry, honey, light soy sauce and pepper to taste. Reheat gently.

5. Serve garnished with a few slices of spring onion.

◆ ◆

Fresh Corn-on-the-cob Soup

There is no substitute for the taste of fresh corn-on-the-cob, so do not be tempted to make this with canned sweetcorn. This is a thick and satisfying soup, but can be made into a finer, more sophisticated version by sieving it after stage four.

SERVES 4

45g/1½ oz butter
2 onions, finely chopped
2 cloves of garlic, crushed
4 large corn-on-the-cob, cooked
4 yellow tomatoes, peeled and chopped
1 yellow pepper, seeded and coarsely chopped
1 teaspoon oregano
860ml/1½ pints water
salt and freshly ground black pepper

TO GARNISH:

4 tablespoons corn kernels (see method)
butter
4 sprigs of oregano

1. Heat the butter in a large saucepan and cook the onion and garlic over a low heat for about 10 minutes, or until soft and transparent. Do not allow to brown. Remove from the heat.

2. Scrape the kernels from the cobs with a sharp knife, reserving about 4 tablespoons for garnishing. Add the corn, tomatoes, yellow pepper and oregano to the onion and cook for a few minutes, stirring.

3. Add the water, bring to the boil, reduce the heat and cook gently for a further 10 minutes. Season to taste.

4. Purée the soup in a blender, and pass through a sieve, if liked. Return the soup to the rinsed saucepan and reheat.

5. Put the reserved corn into a small pan with a little butter and sauté until just beginning to brown.

6. Serve the soup hot, garnished with the corn and sprigs of oregano.

Parsley and Spinach Soup

SERVES 4

FOR THE PARSLEY AND GARLIC
CROÛTES:
½ French stick
110g/4oz butter, softened
4 cloves of garlic, crushed
2 tablespoons chopped parsley

55g/2oz butter
1 fat leek, white part only, chopped
1 tablespoon plain flour
570ml/1 pint vegetable stock (see p. 172) or
    water
450g/1lb spinach, cooked
110g/4oz parsley, stalks chopped
juice of ½ lemon
salt and freshly ground black pepper
150ml/5fl oz double cream (optional)

1. Make the parsley and garlic croûtes:
preheat the oven to 200°C/400°F/gas
mark 6. Cut the French stick diagonally into
2.5cm/1 inch thick slices. Mix the butter,
garlic and parsley together in a small bowl,
and spread thickly on the bread.

2. Meanwhile make the soup: melt the
butter in a large saucepan, add the leek, and
stir to coat with the butter. Cover and cook
over a low heat for about 5 minutes. Do not
let the mixture brown.

3. Stir in the flour and cook for 1 minute.
Gradually add the stock or water, stirring all
the time, and bring to a boil. Season with
salt and pepper. Cook for a further 5
minutes but no more.

4. Purée the spinach, parsley leaves and
stalks and the leek 'soup' in batches in a
blender, until completely smooth. Sieve, if
liked, for a particularly fine, smooth soup.
Pour into the rinsed saucepan.

5. Put the croûtes on a baking sheet and
bake on the middle shelf of the oven for 10
minutes or until golden brown.

6. Reheat the soup carefully over a low heat,
add the lemon juice and season to taste.*
Stir in the cream if using. Serve immediately
with the croûtes.

NOTE:
* Any bright green soup will lose its colour if left
over heat for too long and should be made on the
day it is to be eaten.

Butternut Squash and White Stilton Soup

SERVES 4

55g/2oz butter

225g/8oz leek, white part only, chopped

450g/1lb butternut squash, peeled, seeded and
    cut into chunks

2 cloves of garlic, crushed

pinch of freshly grated nutmeg

1 teaspoon paprika

570ml/1 pint vegetable stock (see p. 172), or
    water

2 ripe tomatoes, peeled, quartered and seeded

55g/2oz white Stilton, crumbled

4 tablespoons double cream (optional)

salt and freshly ground pepper

TO GARNISH:
chopped chives

1. Heat the butter in a large saucepan, add the leek and butternut squash and cook gently for about 10 minutes.
2. Add the garlic, nutmeg and paprika and cook for a further minute. Do not allow to brown.
3. Add the vegetable stock or water, and the tomatoes. Season with salt and pepper and simmer for 20 minutes.
4. Purée the soup in a blender with the Stilton. Return the soup to the rinsed saucepan, season to taste and add the cream, if using. Reheat. Serve garnished with chopped chives.

◆ ◆

Red Pepper Soup

SERVES 4

2 tablespoons olive oil

1 onion, finely chopped

1 leek, finely sliced

225g/8oz carrots, sliced

2 red peppers, quartered, seeded and diced

salt and freshly ground black pepper

1.1 litres/2 pints vegetable stock (see p. 172) or
    water

Tabasco sauce

1. Put the olive oil, onion, leek, carrots and red peppers into a large saucepan and season with salt and pepper. Cover and cook over a gentle heat until the onion is soft and transparent.
2. Add the vegetable stock or water and bring to the boil. Reduce the heat and simmer for 20 minutes or until the vegetables are cooked.
3. Purée the soup in a blender, then sieve it into the rinsed saucepan. Add Tabasco sauce and season to taste.
4. Reheat before serving.

Summer Courgette and Mint Soup

SERVES 4

1 tablespoon olive oil
1kg/2lb courgettes, sliced
1 onion, sliced
1 clove of garlic, crushed
1.1 litres/2 pints vegetable stock (see p. 172)
salt and freshly ground black pepper
1 tablespoon coarsely chopped mint

1. Heat the oil in a large saucepan, add the courgettes, onion and garlic and cook gently until softened.
2. Add the stock, bring to the boil and then simmer for 10–15 minutes. Do not cook for longer as the courgettes will lose their colour. Season to taste and add the mint.
3. Purée the soup in a blender and return to the rinsed saucepan.
4. Serve warm* or chilled.

NOTE:
* Reheat the soup carefully over a low heat. Any bright green soup will lose its colour if left over heat for too long.

FIRST COURSES

Fresh Tomato Puddings with Tomato Vinaigrette
Fresh Tomato and Mascarpone Tartlets
Spinach and Olive Panzerotti
Patties of Diced Vegetables with Soured Cream
Mini Caesar Salads in Toasted Baskets
Poached Fennel Hearts with Light Provençal Sauce
Poached Ricotta and Feta Dumplings
Deep-fried Ricotta and Feta Dumplings
Twice-baked Goats' Cheese Soufflés
Baked Sweet Potato Soufflé
Roast Red Peppers with Tapenade and Mozzarella
Grilled Aubergines with Pesto
Onion Tart
Sage and Corn Pancakes with Field Mushrooms
Mushroom Pâté
Melitzanosalata (Aubergine Salad)
Guacamole
Broad Bean Pâté
Spiced Broad Bean and Yoghurt Timbales
Asparagus Charlottes
Asparagus Filo Tartlets
Artichoke and Green Olive Rillettes
Saffron Rice Balls with Dolcelatte and Peas
Deep-fried Croûton Balls
'Scotch' Quail's Eggs
Baked Squash with Spiced Yellow Split Peas
Roast Garlic
Water Chestnuts and Chinese Mushrooms with Deep-fried Lentils
Lentil, Caper and Parmesan Patties
Fresh Beetroot Ravioli

Fresh Tomato Puddings with Tomato Vinaigrette

The idea for these little puddings is based on the traditional summer pudding. They are wonderfully easy because they require no cooking.

SERVES 4

FOR THE TOMATO VINAIGRETTE:

1 ripe tomato, chopped
reserved seeds from the beef tomatoes (see below)
4 tablespoons oil
1 tablespoon raspberry vinegar
small pinch of English mustard powder
small pinch of sugar

FOR THE PUDDINGS:

12 slices of stale brown bread*, rolled thin
6 large ripe beef tomatoes, skinned, seeded and
  finely chopped, and the seeds reserved
1 small clove of garlic, crushed
1 small shallot, finely chopped
4 large basil leaves, finely sliced
2 good sprigs of thyme
dash of chilli sauce (optional)
about 1 teaspoon tomato purée
pinch of sugar (optional)
salt and freshly ground black pepper

1. Make the vinaigrette: mix all ingredients in a blender until well emulsified. Push through a sieve and set aside.

2. Make the puddings: brush four ramekins with oil and line the bottom with a disc of greaseproof paper cut to fit.

3. Cut two discs from two slices of bread* to fit the bottom and the top of a ramekin, using a pastry cutter of the right size. Remove the crusts from another slice and cut three strips to go round the inside of the ramekin. Repeat with the remaining bread and ramekins.

4. Either dip the discs and strips of bread quickly in the vinaigrette, or brush it on with a pastry brush. Line the ramekins with the bread. Set aside.

5. Mix the tomatoes, garlic, shallot, herbs, chilli sauce, if using, and enough tomato purée to give some colour. Add the sugar (if the tomatoes are ripe the sugar may be omitted) and season to taste.

6. Pack the tomato mixture into the ramekins. Dip the remaining four bread discs into the vinaigrette, or brush it on. Cover the puddings.

7. Stand the ramekins in a dish. Press a coffee saucer or small plate** on top of the puddings and place a 450g/1lb weight on top. Leave in a refrigerator overnight.

8. To unmould: remove the saucer or plate and the weight from each, run a rounded knife round the edge of the ramekin, invert a plate over the top and turn both over together. Give a sharp shake or two and when the pudding has dropped free, remove the ramekin (ease out with a knife if necessary and smooth over any damage). Remove the paper disc. Spoon over some of the tomato vinaigrette and serve with a sprig of basil.

NOTES:

* Use stale bread as fresh bread becomes doughy when rolled, and therefore will not absorb the vinaigrette or tomato juices.

** If no small saucers or plates are available, cut stiff cardboard discs to fit. Cover the puddings with cling film, place the cardboard discs on top and then weight.

*** For another dressing use a virgin olive oil which has been infused with the herbs used in this recipe.

**** The remaining bread scraps can be baked at the bottom of the oven the next time it is on, and then processed to make dried breadcrumbs.

DRY SHERRY

◆ ◆ ◆ ◆ ◆ ◆ ◆ ◆ ◆ ◆ ◆ ◆ ◆ ◆ ◆ ◆ ◆ ◆ ◆ ◆

Fresh Tomato and Mascarpone Tartlets

Some advance preparation to the tomatoes is required, so start a day before the tartlets are needed.

MAKES 12

1 quantity of thyme pastry (see p. 186)

FOR THE TOP:

12 ripe plum tomatoes, skinned, seeded and cut into eighths
salt

FOR THE FILLING:

250g/9oz mascarpone cheese
110g/4oz Cheddar cheese, grated
55g/2oz Parmesan cheese, freshly grated
2 tablespoons finely chopped oregano
4 tablespoons water
salt and freshly ground black pepper

TO GLAZE:

1 tablespoon tomato purée
1 tablespoon olive oil or sun-dried tomato oil

TO GARNISH:

salad leaves

1. Prepare the top: lay the tomato quarters in rows on several thicknesses of paper towels on a tray. Sprinkle with salt, cover with several more layers of paper towels and leave for at least 6 hours, preferably overnight, to extract the maximum amount of moisture.

2. Roll out the pastry thinly on a floured surface and use to line twelve tartlet tins. Chill in the refrigerator for 30 minutes (this prevents shrinkage during cooking).

3. Make the filling: combine the filling ingredients in a bowl. Add the water to soften the mixture. Season to taste.

4. Preheat the oven to 200°C/400°F/gas mark 6.

5. Line the tartlet cases with greaseproof paper and bake 'blind' (see p. 183) for about 10 minutes. Remove from the oven, lower the temperature to 180°C/350°F/gas mark 4. Scoop out the 'blind beans' with a metal spoon, and put the tartlet cases back in for a further 5 minutes or until they have dried out but are not completely cooked. Cool on a wire rack.

6. Divide the filling equally between the tartlet cases. Smooth the top with a knife.

7. If the tomatoes are very salty, rinse them quickly under running cold water and pat dry thoroughly with paper towels. Trim the segments to fit the tartlets and fan them neatly on top of the filling.

8. Before serving, place the tartlets on a baking sheet and heat gently for 8–10 minutes or until the cheese mixture has begun to melt and the tomatoes are warmed through. Remove from the oven and allow to cool slightly.

9. Mix the tomato purée with the oil to produce a spreading consistency and glaze the tomatoes, using a pastry brush. Serve immediately, garnished with mixed salad leaves.

CRISP DRY WHITE

◆ ◆

Spinach and Olive Panzerotti

Panzerotti are traditionally crescent-shaped, bite-sized puffs.

MAKES ABOUT 20
double quantity of puff pastry (see p. 174) or
   450g/1lb frozen puff pastry
beaten egg for sealing
oil for deep-frying

FOR THE FILLING:
225g/8oz fresh spinach, cooked and roughly
   chopped (see p. 182), or 110g/4oz frozen
   spinach, thawed and cooked until dry
110g/4oz black olives, pitted and chopped
1 small clove of garlic, crushed
1 tablespoon capers, coarsely chopped
1 small shallot, coarsely chopped
55g/2oz walnuts, coarsely chopped
15g/½oz Parmesan cheese, grated
pinch of freshly grated nutmeg
1 egg, beaten
salt and freshly ground black pepper

1. Roll out the pastry as thinly as possible on a floured work surface. Cut out as many 7.5cm/3 inch diameter circles as possible. Place on a tray and refrigerate.

2. Make the filling: put the ingredients into a food processor* and, using the pulse button, process until the mixture resembles coarse breadcrumbs. A bit of texture, especially with the nuts, is essential. Season to taste. Add more Parmesan if necessary.

3. Place 1 tablespoon of the filling on one half of each pastry disc, leaving a rim of 1cm/½ inch. Brush this with beaten egg, fold over the other half of pastry and seal carefully. Mark with a fork if wished. Prick the tops and refrigerate for 1 hour. (They can be frozen at this stage and can be deep-fried straight from the freezer.)

4. Heat the oil in a deep saucepan over a moderately high heat until a cube of stale bread starts to sizzle immediately it is added.

5. Deep-fry a few panzerotti at a time for 5–8 minutes until golden brown and puffed up. Remove with a slotted spoon, drain them on paper towels and sprinkle lightly with salt. Spread out on a baking tray and keep warm.

NOTES:
* If a food processor is not available, chop the spinach, olives, garlic, capers, shallot and walnuts finely then mix them with the cheese, nutmeg, egg and seasoning.

** Panzerotti are nicest when freshly made, but they reheat very well; allow 10 minutes in a moderate oven. They are also good when cold and make ideal picnic food.

CRISP DRY WHITE

Patties of Diced Vegetables with Soured Cream

These little patties are quite delicious. They look better if the vegetable dice are all the same size and elegantly small.

SERVES 4

½ cucumber, seeded and finely diced
salt
1 avocado
juice of ½ lemon
1 red pepper, peeled, seeded and finely diced (see p. 181)
170g/6oz waxy potatoes, cooked and finely diced
1 shallot, finely chopped
1 teaspoon very finely chopped parsley
1 tablespoon chopped chervil or thyme
1 tablespoon mayonnaise (see p. 114)
salt and freshly ground black pepper

FOR THE TOP:
2 tablespoons soured cream
1 teaspoon creamed horseradish
lemon juice
cayenne pepper

TO GARNISH:
French dressing (see p. 114)
1 tomato, peeled, seeded and finely chopped
chervil leaves

1. Put the cucumber into a sieve, sprinkle with salt and leave for 30 minutes. Rinse carefully (taste to make sure the salt has gone) and dry very thoroughly on paper towels. Put into a large bowl.
2. Peel and stone the avocado and cut into fine dice. Toss in the lemon juice to prevent discolouration.
3. Place the red pepper on paper towels and pat dry, changing the towels as often as necessary until the dice are quite dry. Add to the cucumber.
4. Drain the avocado thoroughly before adding to the pepper and cucumber mixture.
5. Add the potato, shallot and herbs to the other ingredients and combine with as much mayonnaise as is required to bind. Season to taste.
6. Make the top: mix all the ingredients together in a small bowl. Take care with the lemon juice as the mixture should be thick.
7. To assemble: put a 5cm/2 inch pastry cutter on a serving plate and pack it tightly with a quarter of the vegetable mixture to within 1 cm/½ inch of the rim. Top with a quarter of the soured cream mixture and smooth with a knife. Carefully remove the pastry cutter. Repeat three times.
8. Serve with the French dressing and garnish with chopped tomato and chervil leaves.

NEW WORLD WHITE WITH GOOD ACIDITY

Fresh Beetroot Ravioli

BAKED FENNEL WITH SUN-DRIED TOMATOES AND GOAT'S CHEESE

Poached Ricotta and Feta Dumplings

ASPARAGUS FILO TARTLETS

RICOTTA AND HERB FILO TART

Fresh Pasta Cannelloni

CRISP PASTA CAKE WITH GARLIC MAYONNAISE

Mini Caesar Salads in Toasted Baskets

Mini Caesar Salads in Toasted Baskets

If a jar of sun-dried tomatoes in oil is available, use the oil to give the baskets a delicious flavour (top up the jar again with more olive oil).

SERVES 4

4 large slices of white bread, crusts removed
150–290ml/5–10fl oz sun-dried tomato oil, or
  olive oil
55g/2oz rocket
55g/2oz corn salad
a few radicchio leaves
yellow part only of a frisée lettuce
225g/8oz piece Parmesan cheese
3 anchovy fillets, soaked in milk (optional)
6 quail's eggs
1 quantity French dressing (see p. 114)

1. Make the baskets: preheat the oven to 170°C/325°F/gas mark 3. Roll out the slices of bread thinly. Trim the corners with scissors so that the slices are rounded. Brush both sides of each slice with sun-dried tomato or olive oil.

2. Make four shallow shapes by pressing the bread into the moulds of a deep patty tin. Line with greaseproof paper and weight with 'blind beans'.

3. Put the patty tin on to a baking sheet and put on the middle shelf of the oven. Bake for about 10–12 minutes. Remove the 'blind beans', take the baskets out of the patty tin, turn them upside down on the baking sheet and return them to the oven for 8–10 minutes until pale golden brown; any browner and they will be unpleasantly hard

to eat. Take out of the oven and cool on a wire rack.

4. Wash the salad leaves and dry carefully. Tear the leaves into small pieces, keeping a mini 'leaf' shape if possible. Put into a plastic bag or container and refrigerate until required.

5. With a 1cm/½ inch melon baller, scoop out about 28 little balls from the piece of Parmesan. Put into a bowl and cover.

6. Take the anchovies, if using, out of the milk and pat dry with paper towels. Cut the fillets into fine strips with a sharp knife. Take care not to tear them. Set aside.

7. Boil the quail's eggs for 3 minutes. Remove and put them into a bowl of cold water to prevent further cooking. Peel and leave them in cold water until required.

8. To serve: place a toasted basket on each of four plates. Toss the salad leaves in as much dressing as is needed to coat them, and fill the baskets. Put two strands of anchovy on top and a few of the Parmesan balls. Drain the quail's eggs and pat dry. Cut into quarters lengthways and put on the plate beside the baskets with some extra Parmesan balls, and small salad leaves.

NOTES:
* The baskets can be made well in advance and stored in an airtight container for up to 2 weeks, or frozen for 3 months. Refresh in a warm oven for 10 minutes and allow to cool before using.
** The baskets can be assembled up to an hour in advance provided the salad leaves have not been dressed. Store, covered, in a cool place and drizzle with the French dressing just before serving.

LIGHT ACIDIC WHITE

Poached Fennel Hearts with Light Provençal Sauce

This recipe was entered by Tessa Strickland, one of our students, for an olive oil competition held at the school. It is perfect for a light lunch.

SERVES 4
4 large bulbs of fennel
4 tablespoons olive oil, plus extra for brushing
salt
1 focaccia (see p. 155)

FOR THE SAUCE:
1 egg yolk
1 clove of garlic, crushed
1 tablespoon water
4 tablespoons olive oil, plus extra for brushing
juice of half a lemon

1. Remove any damaged outer leaves of the fennel bulbs, trim the stalks and cut the bulbs into thick slices. Cut out the heart from each slice, leaving enough to keep the slice intact. Put the fennel in a sauté pan, add the oil and just enough salted water to cover the fennel. Poach over a low heat for about 10 minutes or until completely soft. Drain and set aside.
2. Make the sauce: put the egg yolk, garlic and water into a blender and mix until beginning to thicken. With the motor running, gradually add the olive oil and the lemon juice through the feed hole in the lid until a light but thick consistency is obtained. Transfer to four small ramekins.
3. Preheat the grill to its highest setting.
4. Cut four slices from the focaccia and halve each slice to make eight pieces. Brush both sides of the bread with olive oil and place under the hot grill until golden brown and crisp. Keep warm.
5. Grill the fennel for about 5 minutes a side, or until brown.
6. Serve immediately on a warm plate with the warm toasted croûtes and a ramekin of sauce.

LIGHT ACIDIC WHITE
DRY SHERRY

◆ ◆

Poached Ricotta and Feta Dumplings

We have suggested serving these dumplings with tomato sauce, but robust mushroom or watercress sauce (see pp. 120 and 121) are equally good. The dumplings can also be served cold with tomato vinaigrette (see p. 114) spooned over, as shown in the photograph.

SERVES 4–6 (12–18 DUMPLINGS)
250g/9oz ricotta cheese
200g/7oz feta cheese
1 tablespoon Parmesan cheese, freshly grated
2 eggs, separated
1 teaspoon freshly grated nutmeg
2 tablespoons finely chopped parsley
30g/1oz fresh white breadcrumbs
freshly ground black pepper

TO SERVE:

melted butter

tomato sauce (see pp. 117 and 118)

chives

1. Put the ingredients, except the egg whites, into a large bowl, and mix together thoroughly with a wooden spoon. Season well with black pepper as poaching will dilute the flavour.

2. Whisk the egg whites until stiff but not dry. Mix 1 tablespoon of the whisked egg white into the cheese mixture and then fold in the rest with a large metal spoon.

3. Fill a large shallow pan or sauté pan with 7.5cm/3 inches of salted water and heat to a gentle simmer. Turn the heat right down so that the water is barely moving.

4. Drop in 3–4 spoonfuls of the cheese mixture and cook for 5–6 minutes on each side. Remove with a slotted spoon, drain through the slotted spoon onto paper towels, then put on to a warm plate. Cover and keep warm. Repeat with remaining mixture. Keep topping up the pan with boiling water so that the dumplings never touch the bottom of the pan.

5. Put three or five dumplings on each warm plate, drizzle with melted butter and serve with 2 tablespoons tomato sauce. Garnish with long chives.

LIGHT RED

MEDIUM-BODIED WHITE

♦ ♦

Deep-fried Ricotta and Feta Dumplings

These dumplings should be made a day in advance.

MAKES 12–18 DUMPLINGS

1 quantity of poached ricotta and feta dumplings
(see p. 34)

2 egg whites

about 170g/6oz dried white breadcrumbs

oil for deep-frying

TO SERVE:

mixed leaf salad

tomato vinaigrette (see p. 29)

1. Make the dumplings as described on p. 34 from step 1–4. Leave in the refrigerator, covered, overnight.

2. Beat the egg whites lightly to break them up. Put the breadcrumbs into a bowl. Dip the chilled dumplings in the egg white and then cover them evenly with the breadcrumbs. Chill for 30 minutes.

3. Meanwhile, heat the oil in a deep saucepan until a cube of stale bread starts to sizzle immediately it is dropped in.

4. Deep-fry in batches for 2–3 minutes until pale golden brown. Remove with a slotted spoon and drain on paper towels.

5. Deep-fry once more for 1–2 minutes before serving.

NOTE:

* The dumplings are best served straight after the second frying, but in order to avoid cooking smells, they can be completed in advance and reheated in a moderately hot oven for about 8–10 minutes just before serving; they will be nearly as good.

WHITE LOIRE

Twice-baked Goats' Cheese Soufflés

These soufflés can be cooked a few hours before dinner and then re-baked at the last minute. For a richer version, serve with seasoned single cream instead of the roast tomato sauce.

SERVES 6

55g/2oz butter
290ml/10fl oz milk
1 slice of onion
45g/1½oz flour
110g/4oz strong, hard goats' cheese, grated
pinch of fresh thyme leaves
3 eggs, separated
salt and freshly ground white pepper
1 quantity of roast tomato sauce (see p. 118)
1 tablespoon grated Cheddar cheese
1 tablespoon dried white breadcrumbs

1. Preheat the oven to 180°C/350°F/gas mark 4.
2. Melt the butter in a saucepan and use enough to grease six ramekins generously (the rest of the butter will be used for the soufflés).
3. Heat the milk slowly with the onion, leave to infuse for 15 minutes. Strain.
4. Stir the flour into the remaining melted butter. Cook, stirring, for 1 minute. Remove from the heat and gradually pour in the milk, whisking until smooth.
5. Return the pan to the heat and bring to the boil, stirring continuously. Simmer for 2 minutes, stirring. Remove from the heat, add the cheese, thyme, and egg yolks and season to taste.
6. Whisk the egg whites to the soft peak stage. Fold 2 tablespoons into the cheese mixture with a large metal spoon, then fold in the remaining egg whites.
7. Spoon the mixture into the ramekins until two-thirds full. Stand in a roasting tin of boiling water to come half-way up the sides of the ramekins, and bake on the middle shelf of the oven for 15 minutes or until set.
8. Remove the ramekins from the roasting tin and leave to cool and sink.
9. Run a knife round the soufflés to loosen them. Turn them out onto the hand, giving the ramekins a sharp jerk. Put them, upside down, onto a heatproof serving dish.
10. Twenty minutes before serving, preheat the oven to 220°C/425°F/gas mark 7.
11. Warm the roast tomato sauce in a saucepan and then pour around the soufflés.
12. Combine the Cheddar cheese and breadcrumbs and sprinkle over the soufflés. Place them on the top shelf of the oven for 10 minutes or until brown and crisp. Serve quickly before they sink.

FULL-BODIED WHITE

Baked Sweet Potato Soufflé

SERVES 6

55g/2oz Parmesan cheese, freshly grated
750g/1½lb sweet potatoes, baked in their skins
55g/2oz butter
1 onion, finely chopped
1 large clove of garlic, crushed
45g/1½oz plain flour
150ml/5fl oz milk
4 eggs, separated
2 egg whites
55g/2oz Gruyère cheese, finely grated
½ teaspoon freshly ground allspice
salt and freshly ground pepper

1. Butter a 1.1 litre/2 pint soufflé dish and dust inside with the Parmesan. Turn upside down, tip out the surplus cheese and reserve.
2. Scoop the flesh from the potato skins, mash it slightly and push through a sieve.
3. Preheat the oven to 180°C/350°F/gas mark 4.
4. Melt the butter in a thick-bottomed saucepan, add the onion and garlic and cook for about 10 minutes or until transparent and soft. Add the flour and cook over a gentle heat for about 3 minutes, stirring all the time. Draw the pan off the heat, pour in the milk and mix well.
5. Return the pan to the heat and cook, stirring continuously, for 10 minutes. The sauce should be the consistency of thick double cream, so add water if necessary. Allow to cool.
6. Beat the egg yolks and add to the sieved potato with the Gruyère cheese. Mix in the sauce and season generously.
7. Whisk the egg whites to the soft peak stage. Mix 2 tablespoons into the potato mixture with a large metal spoon, then fold in the remaining whites.
8. Spoon the mixture into the prepared soufflé dish. Sprinkle with the reserved Parmesan.
9. Place the soufflé dish in a roasting tin, surround with enough boiling water to come half-way up the side of the soufflé dish and put on the middle shelf of the oven. Bake for 50 minutes or until risen and brown on top. Serve immediately.

NOTES:
* This soufflé will not rise as high as a cheese soufflé.
** The soufflé will serve four for a main course.

MEDIUM RED WITH LOW ACIDITY
MEDIUM DRY WHITE

Roast Red Peppers with Tapenade and Mozzarella

SERVES 4

FOR THE TAPENADE:
110g/4oz pitted black olives
1 tablespoon capers, preferably dry-salted
4 anchovy fillets (optional)
1 large clove of garlic
2 tablespoons virgin olive oil

4 red peppers with stalks, halved through the
    stalk and seeded
oil for brushing
2 yellow peppers, seeded and thinly sliced
    lengthways
2 green peppers, seeded and thinly sliced
    lengthways
225g/8oz mozzarella cheese, cut into 8 slices

1. Make the tapenade: put the ingredients into a food processor or blender and mix until blended, occasionally scraping down the sides of the bowl or goblet with a spatula. Add a little more oil if necessary to keep the mixture on the move. The sauce should be neither too smooth nor too oily.
2. Preheat the oven to 190°C/375°F/gas mark 5.
3. Brush the cut surfaces of the red peppers with oil and coat the inside with the tapenade, using the back of a teaspoon. Fill with slices of yellow and green peppers. Put on a baking sheet and bake on the top shelf of the oven for about 25 minutes or until soft.
4. Place a slice of mozzarella on the top of each pepper and bake for a further 5 minutes until the cheese has melted but not browned. Serve immediately.

MEDIUM-BODIED RED
FULL-BODIED WHITE

◆ ◆

Grilled Aubergines with Pesto

SERVES 6
2 aubergines, sliced
salt
2 teaspoons French mustard
1 quantity of French dressing (see p. 114)
parsley pesto (see p. 119)

1. Sprinkle the aubergine slices liberally with salt and leave in a colander for 30 minutes.
2. Add the mustard to the French dressing.
3. Rinse the aubergines, drain and dry well. Marinate in the French dressing for 2 hours. Drain well.
4. Preheat the grill to its highest setting.
5. Grill the aubergines for about 8 minutes on each side, or until soft and brown.
6. Spread one side of each aubergine slice with the parsley pesto and return to the grill for 1 minute.
7. Arrange on a warm plate and serve immediately.

LIGHT RED/ROSÉ

Onion Tart

SERVES 6
1 quantity of rich shortcrust pastry (see p. 172)
55g/2oz butter
1 tablespoon olive oil
675g/1½lb onions, sliced
2 eggs
2 egg yolks
150ml/5fl oz single cream
salt and freshly ground black pepper
freshly grated nutmeg

1. Preheat the oven to 200°C/400°F/gas mark 6.
2. Roll out the pastry and line a 20cm/8 inch loose-bottomed flan tin with it (see p. 183). Leave in the refrigerator for 20 minutes.
3. Melt the butter, add the oil and onions and cook very slowly until soft but not coloured. This may take up to 30 minutes. Leave to cool.
4. Bake the pastry case 'blind' (see p. 183), then lower the oven temperature to 180°C/350°F/gas mark 4.
5. Mix together the eggs, cream and onions. Season to taste. Pour into the pastry case and sprinkle with nutmeg. Bake until golden and just set, about 20 minutes.
6. Leave to cool for 10 minutes before removing from the tin.

BEAUJOLAIS/ALSACE WHITE

◆ ◆

Sage and Corn Pancakes with Field Mushrooms

SERVES 8
FOR THE BATTER:
140g/5oz plain flour
30g/1oz cornmeal or polenta
1 egg
2 tablespoons finely chopped sage leaves
290ml/10fl oz water, or half milk and half water
salt and freshly ground black pepper
1 tablespoon olive oil

FOR THE TOP:
30g/1oz butter
1 large onion, finely chopped

1 clove of garlic, crushed
1 teaspoon paprika pepper
675g/1½lb large flat, black field mushrooms, wiped and cut into 1cm/½ inch chunks
½ red pepper, seeded and cut into chunks
150ml/5fl oz red wine
4 sage leaves
2–3 tablespoons finely chopped parsley
salt and freshly ground black pepper

TO SERVE:
Greek yoghurt
110g/4oz shavings of Parmesan cheese
8 sprigs of sage

1. Make the batter: mix the batter ingredients in a blender. Alternatively, make according to instructions on p. 176.
2. Refrigerate for 30 minutes (this allows the starch cells to swell, and gives a lighter result).

3. Make the topping: melt the butter in a large frying pan and cook the onion and garlic over a low heat for about 10 minutes, or until soft and transparent. Increase the heat slightly, add the paprika and mushroom chunks and stir to combine thoroughly with the onion mixture. Add the red pepper chunks, pour in the wine and cook for a further 10 minutes until the mushrooms and peppers are cooked and the moisture has evaporated. Mix in the herbs and seasoning. Remove the pan from the heat and keep the mixture warm.

4. Cook the pancakes: heat a large, non-stick frying pan over a moderately high heat and lightly grease with oil. When hot, pour in 2 tablespoons of the batter to make two ×

7.5cm/3 inch circles. Cook for 2–3 minutes on each side. Remove and keep warm. Repeat with the remaining batter to make a total of eight pancakes, brushing the pan lightly with oil between batches.

5. To serve: place one pancake on each of eight plates, smear with 2 teaspoonfuls of Greek yoghurt, then add some of the topping followed by shavings of Parmesan. Garnish with a sprig of sage.

NOTE:
* To serve as a main course, make four larger pancakes and serve as above.

MEDIUM DRY RED

◆ ◆

Mushroom Pâté

SERVES 8
225g/8oz cottage cheese
55g/2oz butter
450g/1lb button mushrooms
55g/2oz fresh white breadcrumbs
4 teaspoons grated onion
170g/6oz butter, softened
pinch of freshly grated nutmeg to taste
2 teaspoons lemon juice
salt and freshly ground black pepper

TO GARNISH:
flat-leaf parsley or any suitable fresh herb

1. Put the cottage cheese into a sieve and leave to drain for 30 minutes.

2. Melt the butter in a sauté pan. Add the mushrooms and coat with the butter but do not cook any further (they should be almost raw). Add the breadcrumbs to absorb any excess moisture. Transfer to a food processor and process until the mixture resembles very coarse breadcrumbs.

3. Add the onion, softened butter, cottage cheese, nutmeg and lemon juice and mix until quite smooth. Taste and season well. Add more nutmeg if necessary.

4. Line a 1kg/2lb loaf tin with cling film and spoon in the mushroom mixture. Tap the tin to remove any air bubbles and smooth the top with the back of a spoon.

5. Refrigerate for at least 3 hours, but preferably overnight.

6. To serve: put an oblong dish on top of the loaf tin and invert both together. When the pâté has dropped out, remove the tin and the cling film. Serve chilled, garnished with fresh herbs.

NOTE:

* The pâté, once unmoulded, may weep a little after about an hour. This moisture can be removed with the help of paper towels.

MEDIUM DRY WHITE

♦ ♦

Melitzanosalata (Aubergine Salad)

SERVES 4

2 large aubergines, cut in half lengthways
salt
290ml/10fl oz extra virgin olive oil
2 small onions, coarsely chopped
2 cloves of garlic, crushed
juice of ½ lemon
2 large handfuls of chopped parsley
110g/4oz fresh white breadcrumbs
salt and freshly ground black pepper

TO SERVE:

warm pitta bread or crusty flat bread

1. Sprinkle the aubergine halves with salt and leave them on a rack, or in a colander, to disgorge their juices for 30 minutes.
2. Preheat the oven to 190°C/375°F/gas mark 5.
3. Rinse the aubergines under running cold water, pat dry with paper towels and place in a roasting tin. Brush the cut surfaces with some of the olive oil and place on the top shelf of the oven to roast for 30–40 minutes, or until completely soft. Remove from the oven and leave until cool enough to handle.
4. Heat 1 tablespoon olive oil in a sauté or frying pan. Add the onions and cook over a low heat for about 10 minutes, or until soft and transparent. Add the garlic* and cook for a further minute. Remove from the heat.
5. When the aubergines are cool enough to handle, scoop out the flesh with a metal spoon. Put the flesh into a clean J-cloth or muslin and squeeze to extract all the juices. Put the aubergine flesh into a food processor or blender. Add the onion, garlic, lemon juice, parsley and fresh breadcrumbs and mix until smooth.
6. With the motor still running, pour the remaining olive oil in a thin stream through the feeder, until well emulsified. Season to taste.
7. Transfer into a bowl, cover with cling film and chill in the refrigerator.
8. Serve with warmed pitta bread or crusty flat bread.

NOTE:

* For a more pronounced taste of garlic, cook just 1 garlic clove and add the other at stage 5.

MEDIUM-BODIED RED

Guacamole

This authentic Mexican recipe calls for three chillies. We found this too hot and think one is enough, but use according to taste.

SERVES 4

1–3 fresh green chillies
1 large clove of garlic, crushed
1 teaspoon salt
3 tablespoons coriander leaves
juice of 1 lime
2 ripe avocados
1 large tomato, quartered and seeded
1–2 spring onions, sliced finely on the diagonal (optional)

TO SERVE:
crudités or tortilla chips

1. Wearing rubber gloves, quarter the chillies, remove the seeds and roughly chop the flesh. Place in a food processor or blender with the garlic, salt and coriander and mix to a fine pulp. Scrape down the sides of the bowl or goblet with a spatula as often as necessary. Use a little lime juice to help the mixture move, if necessary.
2. Peel and stone the avocados; reserve the stones*. Mash the avocados in a mixing bowl with a fork but leave some 'lumps' as this provides texture. Spoon in enough of the chilli mixture to taste and combine well. Add lime juice to taste.
3. Cut each tomato quarter into four fine slivers. Stir into the avocado mixture with the spring onions, if using them.
4. Serve with crudités or tortilla chips.

NOTE:
* Guacamole cannot be made too far in advance. To help prevent discoloration keep the reserved stones in the mixture until it is served.

FULL-BODIED RED
NEW WORLD WHITE SAUVIGNON

◆ ◆

Broad Bean Pâté

It may seem unnecessary to skin broad beans, but their colour and flavour are transformed by this simple task. Unless the beans are very new and tiny, we would never consider serving them any other way. For this recipe it is essential to skin them.

SERVES 4

3 tablespoons extra virgin olive oil
1 large onion, coarsely chopped
2 cloves of garlic, crushed
450g/1lb broad beans, cooked and skinned
1 tablespoon coriander leaves
salt and freshly ground black pepper

TO SERVE:
1 French stick made into toasted or deep-fried croûtes (see pp. 52/3)

1. Heat the oil in a saucepan and cook the onion gently for 10 minutes, or until soft but not browned. Add the garlic and cook for another 5 minutes.
2. Put the broad beans into a food processor and mix to a purée. Add the

onion mixture and mix again. Scrape down the sides of the bowl with a spatula and add the fresh coriander. Mix again. Add more coriander if required and season well. Allow to cool.

3. Serve in a bowl, with toasted or deep-fried croûtes.

CRISP WHITE SAUVIGNON BLANC
EASTERN EUROPEAN WHITE

♦ ♦

Spiced Broad Bean and Yoghurt Timbales

SERVES 4
2½ tablespoons sunflower oil
110g/4oz large spring onions, finely chopped
2 cloves of garlic, crushed
1 tablespoon cumin seeds, freshly ground
225g/8oz of podded, fresh or frozen broad
  beans, cooked and skinned, plus 85g/3oz for
  garnish
200g/7oz Greek yoghurt
1 tablespoon grated fresh ginger
grated zest and juice of ½ lime
salt and freshly ground white pepper
6 large mint leaves, chopped
3 tablespoons water
15g/½oz gelatine (for agar agar see p. 180)

TO SERVE:
French dressing (see p. 114)
mint leaves

1. Oil six ramekins lightly. Cut six greaseproof paper discs and place one in the bottom of each ramekin. Oil lightly.
2. For the garnish: arrange a few broad beans decoratively on the bottom of the dishes: when turned out, this becomes the top.
3. Heat the oil in a sauté pan, and gently sweat the spring onions over a low heat until soft and transparent. Do not allow to brown. Add the garlic and cumin and continue cooking for 2 minutes. Remove from the heat and allow to cool.
4. Tip the spring onion mixture into a blender or food processor. Add the broad beans, the yoghurt, ginger and the lime zest and juice, and process to a lumpy green sauce. Season to taste. Transfer the mixture to a mixing bowl. Add the mint leaves.
5. Put the water in a small saucepan, sprinkle on the gelatine and leave to soak for 5 minutes. Gently heat the gelatine until melted and quite clear; do not allow to boil.
6. Pour the gelatine into the bean mixture, stirring quickly until it is well incorporated. Spoon into the ramekins, cover and leave in the refrigerator overnight.
7. To serve: unmould one ramekin on to each of four plates and remove the disc of greaseproof paper. Spoon over French dressing and garnish with mint leaves.

MEDIUM DRY WHITE

Asparagus Charlottes

This first course is a rather extravagant recipe so it would suit an important occasion. The amount of asparagus required depends on the thickness of the spears, so the quantity given is a rough guide; we have estimated 14–16 finger-thick spears per head. Cooking time also depends on the thickness.

SERVES 4

56–64 spears fat asparagus (approximately 2kg/4¼ lb)
15g/½ oz butter
2 shallots, finely sliced
juice of ½ lime
2 egg yolks
150ml/5fl oz milk
1 tablespoon crème fraîche
salt and freshly ground white pepper
15g/½ oz gelatine (for agar agar see p. 180)
olive oil for glossing

TO SERVE:

150ml/5fl oz crème fraîche
15g/½ oz cooked Puy lentils
sprigs of dill

1. Put the asparagus into a tall, narrow saucepan and fill with enough salted water to come half way up the stems. Cover and bring to a gentle boil. Cook for about 8 minutes, or until the tips are soft but firm.* Remove from the heat and put into a large bowl of very cold water to stop the cooking. Drain on paper towels. Boil the cooking water until reduced by half and reserve 110ml/4fl oz for later use.

2. Cut off the tops of the asparagus to give 3.5cm/1½ inch long tips, put on to a plate, cover with cling film and set aside.

3. Remove 3.5cm/1½ inches of stalk from the woody end and dispose of these. Put the tender parts of the stalks aside.

4. Heat the butter in a saucepan and cook the shallot over a low heat for about 10 minutes or until quite soft. Do not allow to brown. Add the asparagus stalks and lime juice, raise the heat and cook, stirring all the time, until the moisture has evaporated.

5. Put the mixture into a blender or food processor and mix to a smooth pulp. Leave in the goblet or bowl.

6. Beat the egg yolks in another bowl. Bring the milk to the boil in a small saucepan then stir into the eggs. Return the mixture to the saucepan and heat gently, stirring until the custard coats the back of a wooden spoon. This may take a bit of time. Do not let custard boil or it will curdle. Strain the custard into the asparagus purée, add the crème fraîche and mix together using the pulse button. Season to taste.

7. Put 3 tablespoons of the reserved cooking water into a small saucepan, sprinkle on the gelatine and leave to soak for 5 minutes. Then heat the gelatine gently without allowing it to boil, until quite clear. Pour on to the asparagus mixture through the feeder in the blender or food processor lid, and, using the pulse button, mix in thoroughly. Put into the refrigerator and leave until beginning to thicken.

8. Meanwhile, oil four 6.5cm/2½ inch pastry cutters lightly and put one on to each of four serving plates. Brush the asparagus tips with oil, brushing towards the tips, and line the cutters with the spears, standing them upright to form a tight circle.

9. Spoon the asparagus purée into the centre of the rings to within 1cm/½ inch of

the top, leaving the tips free. Cover carefully with cling film and put in the refrigerator.
10. To serve: carefully remove the pastry cutters from the charlottes. Mix the crème fraîche with a little of the reserved cooking water to make a pouring consistency. Stir in the lentils and season to taste. Spoon a little around the charlottes. Garnish with a sprig of dill.

NOTES:

* For alternative methods of cooking asparagus see p. 181.

** These can be made 24 hours in advance if kept covered in a refrigerator.

FULL-BODIED WHITE
LIGHT FRUITY RED

♦ ♦

Asparagus Filo Tartlets

SERVES 4

225g/8oz extra fine asparagus spears, trimmed
2 sheets of fresh or frozen filo pastry
55g/2oz unsalted butter, melted
leaves from a small bunch of chervil
freshly ground black pepper
olive oil for glazing

FOR THE FILLING:

30g/1oz unsalted butter
225g/8oz onion, chopped
2 tablespoons double cream
sliced asparagus stems (see method)
salt and freshly ground black pepper

1. Put the asparagus into a tall, narrow saucepan and fill with enough water to come half way up the stems. Cover and bring to a gentle boil. Cook for about 8 minutes, or until the tips are soft but still firm.* Remove the pan from the heat. Put the asparagus into a large bowl of very cold water to stop the cooking and drain on paper towels. Return the pan to the heat and boil the cooking water until reduced by half; reserve.
2. Preheat the oven to 170°C/325°F/gas mark 3.
3. Make the filo cases: keeping one sheet of filo covered with a clean tea towel, lay the remaining sheet flat and brush lightly with melted butter. Working quickly, dot half the sheet with the chervil leaves, spacing them about 2.5cm/1 inch apart and sprinkle with freshly ground black pepper. Fold the undecorated half on to the decorated half, excluding any air. Brush the top with butter. Fold in half again (excluding any air), thus making four layers. Cut into half and trim the folded edges. Brush both rectangles with butter. Repeat with the other sheet of filo.
4. Tuck, rather than press, each rectangle of filo into a 10cm/4 inch tartlet tin. Because a rectangle is being fitted into a round shape, the two longer sides will be less high than the others. Make sure they are deep enough to contain the filling (which will not be runny). Prick the bases.
5. Put the tartlet tins on to a baking sheet and bake on the middle shelf of the oven for 8–10 minutes or until pale brown. Remove and place on a cooling rack.
6. Meanwhile, cut off the asparagus tips into

even lengths approximately 3.5cm/1½ inches long, to fit the tartlet cases. Remove and dispose of the woody ends; thinly slice the remainder of the stems. Leave, again, to drain on paper towels.

7. Make the filling: gently heat the butter and any left over melted butter from the pastry, in a saucepan. Add the onion, cover and cook for about 10 minutes, or until soft and transparent. Do not allow to brown. Transfer to a food processor and mix to a smooth purée. Return to a clean saucepan, add the cream and reduce by half, stirring all the time. This will take 8–10 minutes. Remove from the heat and allow to cool completely. Add the sliced asparagus stems and season to taste.**

8. Half-fill the filo cases with the purée mixture and lay the asparagus tips in a tight line across the top.
9. Before serving brush the asparagus with a little oil to glaze.

NOTES:
* For alternative methods of cooking asparagus see p. 181.
** The filling should be completely cold before using; the colder the filling the longer the filo cases will remain crisp. However, the tartlets should be not be assembled more than 1½ hours before serving.

LIGHT CRISP WHITE
CHILLED BEAUJOLAIS

◆ ◆

Artichoke and Green Olive Rillettes

SERVES 4
4 globe artichokes
1 lemon, halved, or 2 tablespoons white wine
  vinegar
110g/4oz green olives, pitted and chopped

FOR THE DRESSING:
250g/9oz mascarpone cheese
3 tablespoons white wine vinegar
4 tablespoons olive oil
pinch of sugar
3–4 tablespoons hot water
salt and freshly ground black pepper

1. Fill a large saucepan with about 7.5cm/3 inches of salted water, add a lemon half or tablespoon vinegar, and bring to the boil. Reduce the heat so the water simmers.
2. Prepare the artichokes: remove any damaged outside leaves and trim the stalks, leaving them 2.5cm/1 inch long.
3. Put the artichokes into the simmering water and cook for 35–40 minutes or until just firm when pierced with a skewer. Remove from the heat and drain upside down.
4. When the artichokes are cool enough to handle, cut two in half vertically. Carefully remove the choke and the young purple leaves to create a cavity (reserve some of the largest purple leaves for garnish). Brush the outside leaves and all cut surfaces with oil. Set aside.
5. Remove and discard all the leaves of the remaining artichokes then, using a sharp knife, remove the hairy chokes, leaving

clean bases. Dice the bases and any usable, soft part of the stalks, and put it all into a bowl. Add the olives.

6. Make the dressing: mix the ingredients in a small bowl, adding enough hot water to give a coating consistency. Add enough dressing to the artichokes and green olives to bind them and pour the rest into a bowl.

7. Fill the cavities of the four artichoke halves with the artichoke and olive mixture. Cover and refrigerate.

8. To serve: return the artichoke halves to room temperature and place one half on each serving plate with a small bowl of dressing. Brush the reserved leaves with oil and use as a garnish.

NOTE:
* Once the filling has been eaten, some dressing is spooned into the cavity to accompany the remaining leaves and the artichoke base. Finger-bowls are essential.

FULL-BODIED WHITE
RETSINA

◆ ◆

Saffron Rice Balls with Dolcelatte and Peas

SERVES 4–6 (20–24 balls)
15g/½ oz butter
1 onion, finely chopped
225g/8oz arborio (risotto) rice
425ml/15fl oz water
salt
good pinch of saffron filaments
110g/4oz Parmesan cheese, freshly grated
2 tablespoons tomato ketchup
freshly ground black pepper
110g/4oz dolcelatte cheese
110g/4oz small frozen peas, cooked
225g/8oz dried white breadcrumbs
oil for frying

TO GARNISH:
salad leaves

1. Melt the butter in a large saucepan over a low heat and cook the onion for 10 minutes or until soft but not coloured. Stir in the rice. Turn up the heat, pour in 150ml/5fl oz of the water, and bring to the boil. Cook until the rice has absorbed all the water, stirring all the time.

2. Meanwhile, heat the rest of the water with the saffron in a second pan, to make a saffron tea. Let the tea simmer gently.

3. As the rice absorbs the water start adding the hot saffron tea a little at a time, allowing the liquid to become absorbed before adding any more; stir all the time. Continue for about 15 minutes or until the rice is cooked but firm to the bite. Add more boiling water, if necessary.

4. Remove the pan from the heat and stir in the Parmesan, tomato ketchup and pepper. Allow to cool.

5. With wet hands, shape the mixture into 20 balls.

6. Mix the dolcelatte and peas together in a bowl with a wooden spoon.

7. Make a hole in one rice ball with a finger and fill with a small amount of the pea and cheese mixture. Close the hole and re-form the ball. Repeat with the remaining rice balls and cheese mixture.

8. Put the breadcrumbs into a bowl, add the rice balls and coat them thoroughly with the breadcrumbs.

9. Heat 7.5 cm/3 inches of oil in a deep saucepan until a cube of stale bread sizzles immediately it is dropped in. Fry a few rice balls at a time for 3–4 minutes or until golden brown. Remove with a slotted spoon and drain on paper towels. Repeat until all the balls are cooked, then re-fry in batches for 1–2 minutes.

10. Serve warm with salad leaves to garnish.

CHARDONNAY
LIGHT-BODIED RED

◆ ◆

Deep-fried Croûton Balls

SERVES 4–6 (18–20 BALLS)

110g/4oz mixed nuts, e.g. almonds, hazelnuts,
*   walnuts, peanuts*
1 large onion, coarsely chopped
110g/4oz fresh white or brown breadcrumbs
1 tablespoon chopped mixed herbs e.g. parsley,
*   thyme, rosemary*
1 teaspoon tomato purée
110g/4oz Cheddar cheese, crumbled
2 eggs, lightly beaten
salt and freshly ground black pepper
about 15 slices of white medium-sliced bread,
*   crusts removed*
oil for frying

TO SERVE:
dipping sauce (see p. 126)

1. Put the nuts into a food processor and mix until coarsely chopped. Set aside.

2. Put the onion, breadcrumbs and herbs into the food processor bowl and process until the onion is finely chopped.

3. Add the tomato purée, cheese, half the egg, and the chopped nuts and mix briefly until combined. Season to taste and set aside.

4. Cut the bread into 5mm/¼ inch cubes and put into a large open bowl.

5. Using the hands, shape the nut mixture into 24 balls about the size of a ping-pong ball. Brush with the remaining beaten egg and roll in the bowl of bread cubes. Press to make the bread cubes stick. This may take a minute or two.

6. Heat about 7.5cm/3 inches of oil in a deep saucepan until a cube of stale bread sizzles immediately it is dropped in.

7. Put a few balls at a time into the hot oil and fry for 2–4 minutes or until pale brown. Remove from the oil with a slotted spoon and drain on plenty of paper towels. Repeat with the remaining balls.

8. Re-fry all the balls, in batches if necessary, for 1–2 minutes until golden brown. Remove from the oil and drain again in the same way.

9. Serve with dipping sauce.

'Scotch' Quail's Eggs

SERVES 6
24 quail's eggs
2 eggs, beaten
about 225g/8oz dried white breadcrumbs
oil for frying

FOR THE NUT MIXTURE:
110g/4oz fresh breadcrumbs
110g/4oz mixed nuts, finely chopped e.g.
  almonds, walnuts, hazelnuts, peanuts
1 tablespoon finely chopped mixed herbs, e.g.
  parsley, thyme, oregano
1 large onion, finely chopped
1 teaspoon tomato purée
110g/4oz mature Cheddar cheese, grated
1 egg, lightly beaten
salt and freshly ground black pepper

TO SERVE:
mixed salad leaves

1. Bring a saucepan of water to the boil, carefully put in the eggs, in batches if necessary, and boil for 3 minutes. Remove with a slotted spoon and put into a bowl of cold water to stop cooking. When cold, peel the eggs.

2. Put all the ingredients for the nut mixture into a bowl and mix with a wooden spoon. Season well. Divide into 24 portions.
3. Using wet hands, encase each quail's egg in a portion of nut mixture.
4. Heat 7.5cm/3 inches of oil in a deep saucepan until a cube of stale bread sizzles immediately it is dropped in. Alternatively heat a deep fat fryer.
5. Put the breadcrumbs into a small bowl. Brush the scotch eggs with beaten egg then drop them into the bowl of breadcrumbs, tossing to ensure they are well coated.
6. Fry in batches for 3–4 minutes or until pale brown. Remove from the oil with a slotted spoon and drain on plenty of paper towels. Repeat with the remaining eggs.
7. Then, starting with the first batch, re-fry all the eggs for 1–3 minutes until golden brown. Drain on plenty of paper towels. Sprinkle with salt.
8. Serve three or five on warm plates with a few mixed salad leaves.

NOTES:
* These eggs can also be served as canapés, hot or cold.
** 18 gull's eggs can also be used; boil them for 5 minutes.

Baked Squash with Spiced Yellow Split Peas

SERVES 4

4 small butternut squash, or 2 yellow-fleshed squash, the size of a Spanish onion, cut in half and seeded
sunflower oil
freshly ground black pepper

FOR THE FILLING:
200g/7oz yellow split peas, soaked overnight
30g/1oz red lentils
1 tablespoon sunflower oil
30g/1oz salted butter
1 onion, finely chopped
2 cloves of garlic, crushed
1 teaspoon ground cumin
seeds from 4 cardamom pods, ground
1 teaspoon black mustard seeds
1 teaspoon grated fresh ginger
2 teaspoons ground turmeric
2 tablespoons lemon juice
1 tablespoon tomato purée
1 tablespoon chopped coriander
2 tablespoons plain yoghurt

TO GARNISH:
plain yoghurt
coriander leaves

1. Preheat the oven to 190°C/375°F/gas mark 5.
2. Drain the split peas and rinse under running cold water. Bring a saucepan of water to the boil and add the split peas. Reduce the heat and simmer for 30–35 minutes or until they are cooked but still firm. Drain.
3. Meanwhile, bring a small saucepan of water to the boil, add the red lentils and cook for about 5–8 minutes, or until just cooked. Drain and add to the split peas.
4. If using butternut squash, cut a little off the base so they stand firm, and slice off the rounded end to make a 'cup' (keep the top for another recipe). If using round squash, cut each one in half. Scoop out the pips and some of the flesh with a metal spoon, brush the inside with oil and season with pepper.
5. Wrap each squash 'cup' in a greased, salted foil 'sack'. Place on a baking sheet and put on the middle shelf of the oven. Bake for 20 minutes, or until cooked but still firm. Remove from the oven. Lower the oven temperature to 130°C/250°F/gas mark 1. Open the foil sacks and pour away any juices. Leave the squash in the opened sacks on the baking sheets. Return to the oven to keep warm.
6. Meanwhile, make the filling: heat the oil and butter in a sauté pan, add the onion and cook over a low heat for 10 minutes or until soft and transparent. Add the garlic and spices and cook for 1 minute.
7. Add the split peas, lentils, lemon juice and tomato purée. Continue to cook over a low heat for about 5 minutes, or until the mixture is quite dry. Remove from the heat, allow to cool for a few minutes, then add the coriander and yoghurt to make a moist mixture.
8. Remove the squash from their foil sacks and pile spoonfuls of the split pea mixture into the middle of each squash.
9. Serve each half on a warmed plate, garnished with yoghurt and coriander leaves.

NEW WORLD WHITE

Roast Garlic

Roast garlic is sweet, delicious, and completely inoffensive. The head can be left whole or divided into individual cloves. Leave the skin on as it is a perfect natural 'container'. It protects the garlic flesh from the heat and creates a steamy atmosphere in which the cloves cook to a creamy texture. It is, therefore, unnecessary to cook garlic in a greaseproof paper parcel, although we have done so in the following recipe purely for presentation purposes.

To eat, hold the root end and press the flesh out by running a knife from root to tip.

Serve with crostini, mayonnaise, and a selection of black olives, roasted peppers, sliced beef tomatoes with rosemary or thyme, feta or goat's cheese in olive oil. And finger bowls!

PER PERSON:
1 head of garlic
1 sprig of rosemary or thyme
1 tablespoon olive oil plus extra for brushing

1. Preheat the oven to 180°C/350°F/gas mark 4. Cut a circle of greaseproof paper large enough to take a whole head of garlic.
2. Remove any loose outside skin from the garlic, trim the root and brush generously with olive oil. Put it in the middle of the greaseproof paper circle, pour over 1 tablespoon olive oil and add a sprig of rosemary or thyme. Bring up the sides into a Dick Whittington sack and seal well, using string if necessary. Place on a baking sheet and bake for 35–40 minutes until the garlic feels soft when pinched very gently.
3. Serve straight from the oven in the greaseproof sacks.

NOTE:
* Individual cloves take about 20–25 minutes.

♦ ♦

Water Chestnuts and Chinese Mushrooms with Deep-fried Lentils

Chinese mushrooms are available by mail order from Steamboat Oriental Foods (see p. 250). They are also sometimes sold in good health food shops.

SERVES 4
65g/2½ oz dried Chinese mushrooms, soaked in

hot water for 2 hours, or 110g/4oz fresh shiitake mushrooms, finely sliced
2 tablespoons seasame oil
2 tablespoons groundnut oil
2 shallots, sliced, or 6 large spring onions, sliced diagonally
2 cloves of garlic, sliced
3.5cm/1½ inch piece of fresh ginger, peeled and cut into matchsticks
1 × 227g/8oz can whole water chestnuts, drained and halved horizontally
1 × 227g/8oz can of bamboo shoots, drained
1 small radicchio or 4 large lollo rosso leaves, torn into strips
3 tablespoons dark soy sauce

1 tablespoon rice wine, dry sherry or white
wine vinegar
1 teaspoon clear honey
55g/2oz Chinese noodles, cooked
oil for frying
55g/2oz brown lentils, cooked

TO GARNISH:
sesame seeds

1. Drain the Chinese mushrooms, pat dry with paper towels and then pinch out and discard the small stalks; these can be gritty. Tear up the larger of the mushrooms to make them all an even size.
2. Heat the sesame and groundnut oils in a wok or large sauté pan. Add the shallots or spring onions and stir-fry for 1 minute. Add the garlic and ginger and stir-fry for a further minute.
3. Keeping the heat high, stir in the

Chinese mushrooms (or shiitake if using), the water chestnuts, bamboo shoots, and radicchio or lollo rosso leaves. Stir-fry for about 3 minutes. Add the soy sauce, rice wine, sherry or vinegar, and honey. Toss quickly. If required, add more sesame oil at this stage. Stir-fry for a further 5 minutes or until all the moisture has evaporated and the lettuce leaves are wilted. Stir in the noodles. Transfer to a dish and keep warm.
4. Pour 2.5cm/1 inch of oil into the rinsed wok or sauté pan (add a drop of sesame oil for flavour if liked), heat and fry the lentils quickly until crisp. Remove from the heat.
5. Arrange the stir-fried vegetables on four warm plates and scatter with the fried lentils and sesame seeds.

MEDIUM DRY SHERRY

◆ ◆

Lentil, Caper and Parmesan Patties

These lentil patties are served on fried croûtes with lemon wedges and a few salad leaves. For an elegant look, dice the carrot and pepper to the same size as the lentils.

SERVES 4
170g/6oz brown lentils
bouquet garni
2 large shallots, very finely chopped
30g/1oz capers, preferably dry-salted, coarsely
chopped
2 carrots, cooked and very finely diced
¼ red pepper, seeded and very finely diced

2 large sage leaves, finely chopped
20 coriander leaves, finely chopped
1 tablespoon finely chopped parsley
20g/¾oz Parmesan cheese, freshly grated
4 anchovy fillets, mashed (optional)
½ quantity mayonnaise (see p. 114)
freshly ground black pepper
4 slices of white bread
oil for frying

TO SERVE:
salad leaves
4 lemon wedges

1. Put the lentils into a sieve and rinse under running cold water. Place in a saucepan with the bouquet garni and cover with water.

Bring to the boil, reduce the heat and simmer for 30–35 minutes or until the lentils are soft but firm. Drain, remove and discard the bouquet garni, and put the lentils into a bowl.

2. Add the shallots, capers, carrots, pepper, herbs and Parmesan cheese and mix together.

3. Mix the mashed anchovy fillets, if using, and mayonnaise together in a small bowl. Season with freshly ground black pepper.

4. Add enough anchovy mayonnaise to the lentil mixture to bind. Season again if necessary. Chill until required.

5. Cut a 7.5cm/3 inch circle from each slice of bread using a pastry cutter. Heat the oil in a frying pan and fry the circles on both sides. Drain on paper towels.

6. To serve: place the croûtes on four serving plates, put a pastry cutter of smaller circumference on top of one croûte and pack with the lentil mixture. Carefully remove the cutter. Repeat with the remaining croûtes and lentil mixture. Arrange the salad leaves and garnish with a lemon wedge.

NOTE:
* For a healthier version, toast the croûtes in the oven until golden brown.

◆ ◆

Fresh Beetroot Ravioli

SERVES 8

FOR THE PASTA:
225g/8oz whole raw beetroot, unpeeled or
    250g/9oz vacu-pack cooked beetroot
450g/1lb plain flour
salt
1 egg
1 egg yolk

FOR THE FILLING:
170g/6oz ricotta cheese
110g/4oz mozzarella cheese, grated
55g/2oz Parmesan cheese, freshly grated
55g/2oz hard goats' cheese, grated
1 egg
½ small carrot, very finely diced
55g/2oz cooked spinach, finely chopped

1 tablespoon finely chopped chives
pinch of freshly grated nutmeg
salt and freshly ground black pepper

TO GARNISH:
1 tablespoon balsamic vinegar
1 small red onion, finely sliced
150ml/5fl oz olive oil
purple basil

1. Cook the raw beetroot in a large saucepan of salted water for 30–40 minutes, or until just soft. Drain, leave until cool enough to handle, then remove the skins. Cut the beetroot into chunks, put into a processor and mix until completely smooth.

2. Line a sieve with muslin and put it over a bowl. Tip in the puréed beetroot. Gather up the edges of the muslin and squeeze the purée until quite dry. Reserve the juice.

3. Put the purée into a food processor* with the flour, salt, egg and egg yolk and process

until the mixture resembles coarse, moist breadcrumbs and sticks together when pinched between two fingers. If too sticky, add more flour and mix again. If too dry, add 1 teaspoon beetroot juice.

4. Tip on to a work surface and bring together to make a stiff dough. Knead for 15 minutes.** Wrap in cling film and leave to relax in a cool place for 30 minutes.

5. Make the filling: mix all the ingredients in a bowl until well combined (the raw carrot provides texture but should be suitably fine). Season well as the flavours will be diluted during cooking. Refrigerate until ready to use.

6. Cut the ball of dough into four pieces and roll out one piece at a time until paper thin. Cut into strips 5cm/2 inches wide. Repeat until all the pasta is used. Keep covered.

7. To assemble the ravioli: brush a strip of pasta with water. Place small teaspoonfuls of the filling at 4cm/1½ inch intervals and cover with another strip of pasta. Press together, firming all round each mound of filling. Take care to exclude any air pockets. Cut between each ravioli with a 5.5cm/2¼ inch pastry cutter, or a knife. Set aside on a sheet of silicone paper.

8. Meanwhile, boil a large saucepan of salted water. Reduce the heat and cook the ravioli in simmering water for 3–4 minutes. Drain well. Rinse in warm water.

9. Warm the reserved beetroot juice in a sauté pan taking care not to boil it. Add the balsamic vinegar. Toss the ravioli in the juice to restore the colour. The longer the ravioli is left in the juice the darker the colour will be.

10. Serve either one large or three small ravioli per person, with fine rings of red onion, and drizzle with olive oil. Garnish with purple basil.

NOTES:

* If a food processor is not available, sift the flour and salt on to a wooden board. Make a well in the centre and add the egg and beetroot purée. Using the fingers of one hand, mix together the egg and purée and gradually draw in the flour. The mixture should be a stiff dough.

** If a pasta machine is available, the time required for kneading will be less. Cut the ball of pasta into four and work each strip through the machine until the dough is soft and elastic (at least twelve times). Then progress from number 1 to number 6 on the dial.

*** To make large ravioli, cut sixteen 7.5cm/3 inch discs. Place a small tablespoon of filling on each of the eight discs and cover with the remaining discs. Continue from stage 8, cooking the ravioli for 6–7 minutes.

MEDIUM SWEET RED

MAIN COURSES

Three Cheese Galette
Ricotta and Herb Filo Tart
Aubergine Flan
Roast Garlic Tart
Tarte Mediterranean
Egg and Spinach Pie
Toasted Cashew Nut Flat Pie
Potato Tart
Chicory Tatin
Aubergine and Garlic Soufflés in Filo Baskets
Braised Pumpkin and Lentil Strudel
Winter Vegetable Pudding
Vegetable Feuilletées with Tarragon Beurre Blanc
Parsley and Garlic Pizza
Leek and Tahini Crumble
Salsify Croustade
Fried Gnocchi
Gnocchi and Flat Mushrooms with Tomato and Mascarpone Sauce
Fresh Pasta Cannelloni
Tagliatelle of Pasta, Leeks and Yellow Oyster Mushrooms
Crisp Pasta Cake with Garlic Mayonnaise
Baked Polenta Layered with Ricotta Cheese and Tapenade
Black Olive Polenta with Grilled Vegetable and Wild Mushroom Salad
Spinach Roulade with Arborio Rice Filling
Mushroom and Coriander Risotto
Carrot, and Courgette and Pea Moulds
Harlequin Terrine
Grilled Yellow and Green Courgette Terrine
Stuffed Red Peppers with Soufflé Tops

Wild and Field Mushroom Timbales with Star Anise Sauce
Beetroot Bavarois
Chestnut Crown Roast
Roast Onions with Spiced Lentil Stuffing
Wild Mushroom Sausages
Aubergine Bocconcini
Artichokes Greek-style
Artichokes with Mushroom Duxelle and Warm Mushroom Sauce
Gem Squash with Avocado and Black Olives
Barley Galettes with Port Salut Cheese
Baked Fennel with Sun-dried Tomatoes and Goats' Cheese
Egg and Caper Florentine
Tagine of Aubergines, Dates and Almonds with Spiced Dumplings
Aubergine, Kohl rabi and Black Olive Ragout
Black Bean Chilli
Mustard and Molasses Bean Hotpot

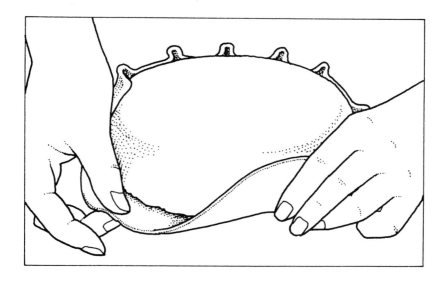

THREE CHEESE GALETTE

Three Cheese Galette

Semolina gives the pastry a crisp texture that makes a lovely contrast to the soft filling, especially when eaten cold. If preferred, the quantity can be reduced by 30g/1oz but don't omit it altogether.

SERVES 6

FOR THE PASTRY:

225g/8oz plain flour
85g/3oz semolina
1 teaspoon English mustard powder
170g/6oz butter
2 eggs
salt and freshly ground black pepper

FOR THE FILLING:

1 ripe Camembert, rind removed, and softened
110g/4oz mature Cheddar cheese, grated
110g/4oz cream cheese
110ml/4fl oz white wine or sherry
1 egg yolk
2 tablespoons semolina

TO FINISH:

beaten egg to glaze
1 teaspoon mustard seeds

1. Make the pastry: put all the ingredients in a food processor and mix to a soft dough.* It may be necessary to add 1 tablespoon water, but the pastry should not be too damp. Crumbly pastry is more difficult to handle but will produce a shorter, lighter result.
2. Remove the dough from the mixer bowl and knead it quickly into a ball on a lightly floured surface. Cut the ball in half.
3. Roll out one half thinly** and cut out a 25cm/10 inch diameter circle using a pan lid as a guide. Transfer to a baking sheet and leave to relax in a cool place for 30 minutes, but not in a refrigerator. Roll out the remaining half of pastry and cut out a 22.5cm/9 inch diameter circle. Leave to relax in a cool place also.
4. Make the filling: put the filling ingredients into a food processor and mix quickly to a soft, sticky, but not runny, consistency (the grittiness of the semolina will disappear during cooking). Add salt and pepper to taste. Alternatively, beat the ingredients together in a bowl.
5. Put the filling on to the middle of the larger circle of pastry, leaving a rim of 5cm/2 inches. Place the smaller circle over the filling and gently press the middle to flatten it. Brush round the rim with beaten egg. Also brush the rim of the bottom circle with beaten egg and very carefully ease it up and over on to the top circle, making sure it is well sealed (see illustration). Press any cracked edges together.
6. Make a diamond pattern on the pastry lid with a knife, taking care not to cut right through the pastry. Brush with beaten egg. Chill in the refrigerator for 30 minutes.
7. Preheat the oven to 200°C/400°F/gas mark 6.
8. Brush the galette again with beaten egg then sprinkle with mustard seeds.
9. Bake on the middle shelf of the oven for 15 minutes. Lower the temperature to 180°C/350°F/gas mark 4 and continue to bake for about 35 minutes until golden brown.
10. Leave to cool on a wire rack for 10 minutes before serving.

NOTES:

* If a food processor is not available, rub the butter into the dry ingredients, then blend to a dough with the eggs.

** The outer rims of both circles must be thin so that when they overlap the thickness of the pastry will be the same overall. This will then cook evenly.

*** The galette reheats very well.

CRISP DRY WHITE
MEDIUM-BODIED RED

♦ ♦

Ricotta and Herb Filo Tart

SERVES 8
6 sheets fresh or frozen filo pastry
55g/2oz butter, melted
3 sage leaves

FOR THE FILLING:
900g/2lb ricotta cheese
2 teaspoons tinned green peppercorns, drained
   and crushed
1 clove of garlic
3 eggs, beaten
4 tablespoons double cream
6 tablespoons chopped, mixed fresh herbs, e.g.
   chives, parsley, dill and sage
salt and freshly ground black pepper
55g/2oz butter, melted

TO SERVE:
crisp green salad

1. Preheat the oven to 180°C/350°F/gas mark 4. Put a baking sheet into the middle of the oven to heat.
2. Make the filling: put the ricotta cheese, peppercorns, garlic, eggs, cream and herbs into a bowl and beat together. Season to taste and set aside.
3. Put a 25cm/10 inch loose-bottomed cake tin on to another baking sheet and arrange a collar of crumpled foil around the tin to support the filo overhangs. Line the tin with the filo pastry, brushing each sheet with the melted butter and overlapping them 'daisy' fashion, around the tin.
4. Put on to the hot baking sheet already in the oven and cook for about 2–3 minutes to 'set' the pastry.
5. Remove the tart case (and its baking sheet) from the oven and fill it with the ricotta mixture. Arrange the 3 sage leaves on top and return it to the oven and bake for 35–40 minutes or until the filling is set and not wobbling. (If the pastry browns too quickly, cover it with foil.)
6. Remove the foil carefully. Leave the tart to cool in the tin.
7. To remove the tart from the tin, stand it on an upturned bowl so the outside ring drops off.
8. Transfer the tart on to a large plate, carefully, and serve at room temperature with a crisp green salad.

NOTES:
* Keep unused filo wrapped or covered with a clean, dry cloth.
** The inner sides of the pastry case will be paler than the overhanging pastry. If wished, the tart can be returned to a low oven after removing the ring, to dry out and crisp up. However, the sides will never be as brown as the frill.

LIGHT MEDIUM WHITE

Aubergine Flan

SERVES 6

1 aubergine, sliced

salt

double quantity lemon shortcrust pastry (see p. 186)

6 tablespoons olive oil

2 onions, finely sliced

3 cloves of garlic, crushed

6 large tomatoes, peeled and chopped

pinch of thyme

pinch of rosemary, chopped

pinch of cayenne pepper

4 eggs, beaten

150ml/5fl oz single cream

85g/3oz Cheddar cheese, grated

30g/1oz Parmesan cheese, freshly grated

12 black olives, pitted

salt and freshly ground black pepper

1. Put the aubergine slices in a colander, sprinkle with salt, toss and leave for 30 minutes to disgorge their juices.

2. Roll out the pastry and line a 27.5cm/11 inch loose-bottomed flan tin (see p. 183). Leave in the refrigerator for about 45 minutes to relax (this prevents shrinkage during cooking).

3. Preheat the oven to 200°C/400°F/gas mark 6.

4. Bake the pastry case 'blind' for 10–15 minutes (see p. 183). Remove from the oven. Lower the oven temperature to 180°C/350°F/gas mark 4. Remove the 'blind beans' and paper.

5. Rinse the aubergines well and pat dry. Fry in 2 tablespoons of the oil, until golden brown. Drain on paper towels.

6. Heat the remaining oil, add the onions, fry until lightly browned, add the garlic and fry for a further 30 seconds. Add the tomatoes, thyme, rosemary, cayenne, salt and pepper. Cook to a rich pulp. Allow to cool slightly.

7. Mix the eggs with the cream and cheeses then mix with the tomato pulp. Season to taste.

8. Spoon half the tomato mixture into the baked flan case, cover with the aubergine slices and then spoon in the remaining tomato mixture, adding the black olives at the same time.

9. Put on the middle shelf of the oven and bake for 40 minutes until the filling is set and lightly risen.

10. Put on a wire rack to cool.

MEDIUM-BODIED RED

◆ ◆

Roast Garlic Tart

The quantity of garlic used in this recipe sounds overpowering. However, do not be tempted to reduce it; roast garlic has a lovely mellow flavour.

SERVES 6

1 quantity of sun-dried tomato and polenta pastry (see p. 187)

3 heads of garlic, divided into cloves but skin left on

oil for brushing

290ml/10 fl oz double cream

290ml/10fl oz Greek yoghurt

4 egg yolks

1 egg

salt and freshly ground white pepper

2 red peppers, peeled, seeded and quartered (see p. 181)

1. Preheat the oven to 200°C/400°F/gas mark 6.

2. Line a deep 24.5cm/9½ inch loose-bottomed flan tin with the pastry (see p. 183). Chill for 30 minutes in a refrigerator.

3. Brush the garlic cloves with oil and put on a baking sheet. Place on the middle shelf of the oven for approximately 20 minutes or until soft. Remove from the oven and leave the cloves to cool on a plate.

4. Line the chilled tart case with greaseproof paper and bake 'blind' (see p. 183) for about 10 minutes. Remove from the oven. Lower the oven temperature to 180°C/325°F/gas mark 4. Take out the 'blind beans'. Return the tart case to the oven for a further 5 minutes or until the pastry has dried out but is not completely cooked. Leave to cool slightly.

5. Meanwhile make the filling: squeeze the garlic pulp from the cloves and mash in a large bowl. Add the cream, yoghurt and egg yolks and whole egg and whisk well. Alternatively, put into a food processor and mix together. Season to taste.

6. Line the bottom of the tart case with the peppers and pour over the garlic custard.

7. Place in the oven and bake for 35–40 minutes or until just set. Leave to cool in the tin.

8. When completely cold remove from the tin. Serve at room temperature.

MEDIUM-BODIED WHITE
NEW WORLD SAUVIGNON BLANC

♦ ♦

Tarte Mediterranean

SERVES 8
FOR THE PASTRY:
225g/8oz plain flour
1 teaspoon salt
150ml/5fl oz virgin olive oil
2 tablespoons chopped thyme
150ml/5fl oz warm water

FOR THE FILLING:
3 tablespoons olive oil
15g/½ oz unsalted butter
1.35kg/3lb red onions, finely sliced
2 large cloves of garlic, crushed
290ml/10fl oz milk or 290ml/10fl oz milk and double cream mixed
2 eggs, beaten

1 egg yolk
250g/9oz black olives, pitted
salt and freshly ground black pepper

TO FINISH:
2 large red peppers, grilled, peeled, seeded and cut into eighths (see p. 181)
2 large yellow peppers, grilled, peeled, seeded and cut into eighths (see p. 181)
1 red onion, finely sliced (optional)
olive oil

1. Make the pastry: sift the flour and salt into a bowl, add the oil, thyme and water and mix as quickly and lightly as possible to a smooth dough (alternatively, put all the ingredients into a food processor and blend until the mixture forms a ball).

2. Roll out the pastry and line a 25cm/10 inch loose-bottomed flan tin (see p. 183).

Chill in a refrigerator for 30 minutes.

3. Preheat the oven to 200°C/400°F/gas mark 6.

4. Make the filling: heat the oil and butter in a large frying pan. Fry the onions and garlic over a low heat until soft but not coloured. Remove from the heat.

5. Mix together the milk (and cream, if using), eggs and egg yolk in a large bowl. Stir in the onions and all but 30g/1oz of the black olives. Season to taste (remember the olives are salty). Set aside.

6. Line the pastry case with a double sheet of greaseproof paper. Put on to a baking sheet and bake 'blind' (see p. 183) for 10–15 minutes. Remove the 'blind beans' and return the pastry case to the oven for a further 5–10 minutes, or until the pastry has dried out but not completely cooked.

7. Lower the oven temperature to 170°C/325°F/gas mark 3.

8. Pour the onion and black olive mixture into the pastry case, and put on a baking sheet on the middle shelf of the oven. Bake for about 40 minutes until the filling is lightly set but not brown.

9. Meanwhile, cook the red onion, if using, in a little olive oil for about 5 minutes, until just limp.

10. Arrange the peppers in a fan on the top of the tart. Scatter with the remaining olives, and the red onion, if using. Brush with olive oil and return to the oven for 5 minutes to heat through. Serve immediately with a green salad.

ITALIAN WHITE
MEDIUM-BODIED RED

♦ ♦

Egg and Spinach Pie

SERVES 6
FOR THE PASTRY:
340g/12oz plain flour
salt
170g/6oz butter
110g/4oz Cheddar cheese, finely grated
1 tablespoon Dijon mustard
2 tablespoons very cold water

FOR THE FILLING:
30g/1oz butter
675g/1½ lb spinach, cooked, thoroughly
  drained and chopped (see p. 182)
salt and freshly ground black pepper

110g/4oz cream cheese
1 tablespoon mixed chopped herbs, e.g. parsley,
  thyme, oregano, sage
6 eggs
salt and freshly ground black pepper
1 egg, beaten to glaze

1. Make the pastry: sift the flour with the salt. Rub the butter into the flour until the mixture looks like coarse breadcrumbs. Stir in the cheese.

2. Add the mustard and water and mix to a firm dough, first with a knife and then with one hand. It may be necessary to add more water, but the pastry should not be too damp.

3. Roll out one third of the pastry thinly on a floured surface, and use to line a deep 22.5 cm/

9 inch loosed-bottomed flan tin (see p. 183) or spring-form cake tin (if using the latter, the pastry should come only two-thirds up the sides). Chill in the refrigerator for 30 minutes.

4. Preheat the oven to 200°C/400°F/gas mark 6.

5. Make the filling: melt the butter in a saucepan, add the spinach and season well. Remove from heat and set aside.

6. Mix the cream cheese with the herbs and spread over the pastry base. Make six hollows in the mixture and carefully break an egg into each. Sprinkle with salt and plenty of pepper.

7. Cover evenly with the spinach.

8. Roll out the remaining pastry and cut out a 22.5 cm/9 inch circle to make a lid for the pie. Brush the edge of the pastry shell with some of the beaten egg. Cover the pie with the lid. Seal the edges well. Trim off any excess pastry, re-roll and cut into narrow strips. Use these to decorate the lid with a lattice pattern.

9. Glaze generously with the remaining beaten egg.

10. Put the pie on a baking sheet on the middle shelf of the oven. Bake for 35–40 minutes or until golden brown.

11. Cool on a wire rack.

MEDIUM-DRY WHITE

◆ ◆

Toasted Cashew Nut Flat Pie

SERVES 4–6

110g/4oz long-grain rice
salt and freshly ground black pepper
double quantity of puff pastry (see p. 174) or
    450g/1lb frozen puff pastry
55g/2oz butter
1 onion, finely diced
225g/8oz cashew nuts, toasted
4 tablespoons chopped mixed herbs, e.g. parsley,
    marjoram and chives
55g/2oz dried apricots, roughly chopped
30g/1oz dried apple, roughly chopped
zest of ½ a lemon
150ml/5fl oz crème fraîche
1 egg, beaten

1. Preheat the oven to 200°C/400°F/gas mark 6.

2. Cook the rice in a large pan of boiling salted water for 10–12 minutes until tender. Drain in a colander or sieve and swish with plenty of hot water. Make a few holes through the rice with the handle of a wooden spoon to help the water and steam escape. Leave for 30 minutes.

3. Roll out a third of the pastry to a rectangle 15 × 20 cm/6 × 8 inches. Transfer to a baking sheet, prick lightly with a fork and chill for 10 minutes in a refrigerator.

4. Put on the middle shelf of the oven and bake for 15 minutes or until golden brown. Cool on a wire rack. Leave the oven on.

5. Melt the butter in a sauté pan over a moderate heat, and add the onion. Cook gently for 10 minutes or until soft and transparent.

6. Put the cooked rice into a bowl and mix in the toasted cashew nuts, onion, herbs,

dried fruit and lemon zest. Season to taste. Add the crème fraîche and two-thirds of the beaten egg.

7. Put the pastry base back on the baking sheet and pile on the rice mixture. Shape into a neat mound, making sure that the base is completely covered.

8. Roll out the remaining pastry to a 'blanket' large enough to cover the filling and tuck under the base.

9. Cut off the corners of the 'blanket' with a sharp knife. Lift the cooked base with a palette knife and carefully tuck the overlapping pastry blanket underneath, sealing it well all the way round with some of the beaten egg. Refrigerate for 10 minutes.

10. Make leaf shapes with the pastry offcuts and use to decorate the pie. Brush the pie and leaves with the remaining egg.

11. Put on the middle shelf of the oven and bake for 30 minutes or until the pastry is golden brown. Serve hot or cold.

MEDIUM DRY WHITE

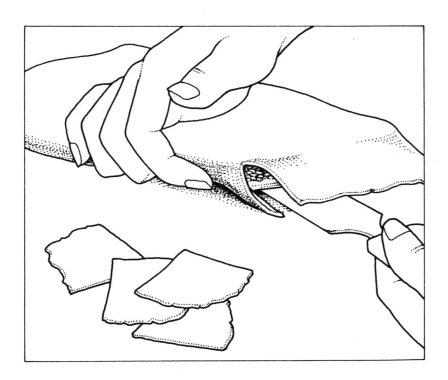

TOASTED CASHEW NUT FLAT PIE

Chicory Tatin

SERVES 6–8

FOR THE PASTRY:

170g/6oz plain flour

55g/2oz ground rice

salt and freshly ground black pepper

140g/5oz butter, chopped

grated zest of 1 orange

1 egg, beaten

FOR THE TOP:

6–8 heads of chicory

110g/4oz butter

1 tablespoon honey

1 tablespoon orange juice

½ teaspoon ground coriander

½ teaspoon ground cinnamon

1. Preheat the oven to 200°C/400°F/gas mark 6.

2. Make the pastry: sift the flour, ground rice and seasoning into a large bowl. Rub in the butter until the mixture looks like coarse breadcrumbs. Stir in the orange zest. Add the egg and bind the dough together. Alternatively, put all the pastry ingredients into a food processor and mix to bind. Chill in the refrigerator.

3. Make the top: trim the chicory and remove any bruised leaves. Cut in half lengthways.

4. Melt the butter in a 25cm/10 inch frying pan with a metal handle.* Add the honey and orange juice. Take off the heat and arrange the halved chicory heads, cut side down, to cover the bottom of the pan completely, fanning out from the middle.

5. Place the frying pan over a moderately high heat until the butter and honey start to caramelise. It may take 10–15 minutes but it is essential that the chicory starts to brown. Remove from the heat and scatter the spices evenly over the chicory.

6. Roll the pastry into a 5mm/¼ inch thick circle, to fit the top of the pan. Lay the pastry on top of the chicory and press down lightly.

7. Put the frying pan on the middle shelf of the oven. Bake for 25–30 minutes or until the pastry is golden brown.

8. Allow to cool slightly and then invert on to a plate. Serve warm.

NOTE:

* If a metal-handled frying pan is not available, cook the chicory in an ordinary frying pan and let the butter and honey become well caramelised. Remove from the heat and then transfer carefully to a shallow 25cm/10 inch ovenproof dish. Cover with the pastry and bake in the oven on a hot baking sheet and continue from stage 7.

GEWÜRTRAMINER
LIGHT-BODIED RED

Aubergine and Garlic Soufflés in Filo Baskets

SERVES 8

FOR THE SOUFFLÉS:
2 aubergines
oil for brushing
2 large cloves of garlic, unpeeled
2 tablespoons finely chopped parsley
30g/1oz butter
40g/1¼oz plain flour
290ml/10fl oz milk
85g/3oz mature Cheddar or Gruyère cheese, grated
4 eggs, separated
salt and freshly ground black pepper

FOR THE FILO BASKETS:
1 × 400g/14oz packet of fresh or frozen filo pastry
3 tablespoons olive oil
30g/1oz butter, melted

TO SERVE:
red ratatouille dressing (see p. 122)

1. Preheat the oven to 190°C/375°F/gas mark 5. Oil eight timbales lightly on the outside.
2. Brush the aubergines with a little oil, put them into a roasting tin and bake them for 40–60 minutes or until soft.
3. Brush the garlic with oil and put into the oven 20 minutes after the aubergines. When cooked, remove the aubergines and garlic from the oven and leave to cool.
4. Make the filo baskets: cut the filo pastry into twenty-four 17.5cm/7 inch squares. Mix the olive oil and melted butter and brush the sheets of filo on one side only.* Turn the timbales upside down and cover the outside of each one with three overlapping squares of filo pastry, 'daisy' fashion. Stand the timbales the right way up on a baking sheet and shape the pastry by carefully but firmly pressing it around the timbales. Arrange any overhanging filo (or snip it off with scissors) and brush with the oil and butter mixture. (See illustration.)
5. Put on the middle shelf of the oven and bake for about 7–8 minutes until the pastry is set and lightly browned. Remove from the oven, leave until cool enough to handle, then take the filo baskets off the moulds. Set aside.
6. Make the soufflés: peel the cooled aubergines and garlic cloves. Put the aubergine flesh into a clean cloth, squeeze to extract all the bitter juices, and put the aubergine into a food processor with the garlic and parsley. Mix until smooth. Set aside.
7. Melt the butter in a saucepan, stir in the flour and cook for 1 minute. Remove from the heat and gradually stir in the milk. Return to the heat and cook, stirring vigorously, for 2 minutes. The mixture will get very thick and leave the sides of the pan. Remove from the heat. Stir in the cheese and egg yolks then tip into a food processor.
8. Add the aubergine, garlic and parsley mixture and mix until smooth. Season well (the egg whites will dilute the flavour). Transfer the mixture to a large bowl.
9. Whisk the egg whites until stiff but not dry. Stir a spoonful into the aubergine mixture and then fold in the rest with a large metal spoon.

65

10. Put the baskets on to a baking sheet and spoon in the aubergine mixture. Return to the oven for 15–20 minutes or until the soufflés are set, well risen and evenly browned.

11. Serve immediately with red ratatouille dressing spooned around each basket.

NOTE:
* Keep unused pastry covered with a clean, dry cloth.

DRY LIGHT RED

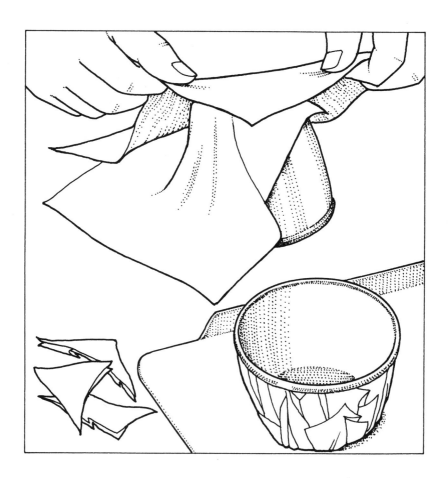

AUBERGINE & GARLIC SOUFFLÉS

Braised Pumpkin and Lentil Strudel

SERVES 4–6

1 tablespoon olive oil

4 shallots, sliced

1 large clove of garlic, crushed

675g/1½ lb pumpkin, peeled, seeded and cut into cubes

110g/4oz brown lentils, cooked

½ teaspoon sugar

salt and freshly ground black pepper

1 × 400g/14oz can of tomatoes

1 teaspoon fresh thyme

1 bay leaf

½ quantity strudel pastry (see p. 176) or 6 sheets of ready-made filo pastry

85g/3oz butter, melted

1 tablespoon very finely chopped parsley

1 egg, beaten

poppy seeds or sesame seeds, for sprinkling

1. Heat the oil in a large saucepan. Add the shallots and garlic and cook until soft and transparent.

2. Stir in the pumpkin and lentils. Season to taste with the sugar, salt and pepper.

3. Add the contents of the can of tomatoes, the thyme and bay leaf. Cook for 20 minutes or until the pumpkin is soft, but still holds its shape.* The mixture should be moist but not runny. Remove from the heat and leave to cool. Remove the bay leaf.

4. Preheat the oven to 200°C/400°F/gas mark 6. Grease a large baking sheet.

5. Make the strudel pastry, following the instructions on p.176. If using ready-made filo pastry, arrange overlapping sheets on the tea towel and brush with butter.

6. Place the filling in a line at one end of the pastry and scatter with parsley. Using the tea towel to help, roll up the pastry as for a Swiss roll, trying to maintain a fairly tight roll. Lift the cloth and gently tip the strudel on to the baking sheet. Brush with beaten egg and sprinkle with poppy or sesame seeds.

7. Put on to the middle shelf of the oven and bake for 30 minutes or until golden brown.

NOTES:

* Certain types of pumpkin vary in cooking time; it can take up to 1 hour to cook; add water, if necessary, to prevent it becoming too dry.

** The filling can be made in advance and frozen. Defrost before using.

MEDIUM DRY WHITE
LIGHT FRUITY RED

Potato Tart

This may sound rather uninteresting but it is delicious and a great favourite. If made into individual tarts, it makes a wonderful first course.

SERVES 6–8

1 quantity of rich shortcrust pastry (see p. 172)
290ml/10fl oz crème fraîche
freshly grated nutmeg

FOR THE POTATO FILLING:

6 large new or waxy potatoes, cut into 1cm/½
*   inch chunks*
2 tablespoons olive oil
salt

FOR THE TOMATO FILLING:

3 tablespoons olive oil
1 onion, finely chopped
8 tomatoes, peeled, seeded and chopped
1 tablespoon tomato purée
2 teaspoons thyme leaves
pinch of sugar
salt and freshly ground black pepper

FOR THE ONION FILLING:

85g/3oz unsalted butter
5 large onions, thinly sliced

1. Preheat the oven to 200°C/400°F/gas mark 6.
2. Roll out the pastry and use to line a loose-bottomed 22.5cm/9 inch cake tin (see p. 183). Refrigerate for 30 minutes and then bake 'blind' (see p. 183). Remove from the oven and leave to cool in the tin.
3. Make the potato filling: brush the potatoes with oil and sprinkle with salt. Put into a roasting tin and roast in the oven for about 40 minutes or until cooked and golden brown. Remove from the oven and allow to cool. Turn up the temperature to 230°C/450°F/gas mark 8.
4. Meanwhile, make the tomato filling: heat the oil in a saucepan, add the onion and cook gently for 10 minutes or until soft and transparent. Add the tomatoes, tomato purée, thyme, sugar and seasoning and cook until all the liquid has evaporated and the mixture is thick. This will take about 35 minutes.
5. Make the onion filling: melt the butter in a saucepan, add the onions and cook slowly for about 30 minutes or until soft and transparent. Allow to cool.
6. To assemble: spread the onions on the pastry base and cover with the tomato mixture. Arrange the potatoes on top. Cover with the crème fraîche and sprinkle with freshly grated nutmeg.
7. Put the cake tin on a baking sheet, put on the middle shelf of the oven and cook for 8–10 minutes or until lightly brown.
8. Remove the tart from the oven. Leave to cool for 10 minutes and then take out of the tin. Serve at room temperature.

MEDIUM-BODIED RED

Winter Vegetable Pudding

SERVES 4–6

1 quantity of suet pastry (see p. 175)
150–290ml/5–10fl oz vegetable stock (see p. 172)

FOR THE FILLING:
2 leeks, finely sliced
2 parsnips, finely diced
2 carrots, finely diced
1 turnip, finely diced
1 green pepper, seeded and finely diced
1 tablespoon finely chopped marjoram
1 tablespoon chopped thyme leaves
55g/2oz bulgar wheat
salt and freshly ground black pepper

1. Put a large, tightly-lidded saucepan of water on to boil. Grease a 1.1 litre/2 pint pudding basin.
2. Line the pudding basin with two-thirds of the pastry (see p. 175).
3. Make the filling: mix the vegetables with the herbs and bulgar wheat and season to taste.
4. Spoon the vegetables into the lined basin and three-quarters fill with vegetable stock.
5. Roll out the remaining third of the suet pastry to 5mm/¼ inch thick. Cut a circle large enough to cover the filling. Put in place, wet the edges of the lid and the lining and press them together securely.
6. Cover the pudding basin with a double thickness of greaseproof paper pleated down the middle to allow room for the pastry to expand, and repeat with a pleated piece of foil. Tie down with string.
7. Place the basin in the saucepan of boiling water, or in a steamer, for 5–6 hours (this will ensure a golden brown and dry pastry), taking care to top up with boiling water occasionally so the saucepan does not boil dry.
8. Remove the basin from the pan and take off the foil and greaseproof paper. The pudding can either be turned out on to a warm serving plate or served straight from the basin.

NOTES:
* This pudding is delicious served with braised red cabbage (see p. 194).
** If there is not enough time to cook the pudding all at once, steam it for at least 2 hours, leave it to cool and then refrigerate. It can be re-steamed for the balance of the cooking time.

DRY LIGHT RED

Vegetable Feuilletées with Tarragon Beurre Blanc

SERVES 4

1½ quantity of puff pastry (see p. 174) or 340g/
12oz frozen puff pastry
1 beaten egg, to glaze
tarragon beurre blanc (see p. 117)
450g/1lb fresh spinach, washed and cooked
any combination of the following:
   110g/4oz fine asparagus, cooked
   55g/2oz mangetout, cooked
   110g/4oz broad beans, cooked and skinned
   8 baby carrots, with a little green stalk left on,
     cooked
   8 button turnips, with a little green stalk left
     on, cooked
   8 broccoli sprigs, cooked
55g/2oz butter

1. Preheat the oven to 220°C/425°F/gas mark 7.
2. Roll the pastry to a large rectangle, about 5mm/¼ inch thick, and cut it into four 10cm/4 inch diamonds (i.e. each side should measure 10cm/4 inches). Place on a dampened baking sheet and brush with egg glaze. Trace a line with a sharp knife, about 1cm/½ inch from the edge of each diamond, without cutting all the way through the pastry (this will form the 'hat' for the pastry case). Make a design inside the diamond 'hat' with the back of a knife. Flour the blade of a knife and use this to 'knock up' the sides of the pastry case. Refrigerate for 15 minutes.
3. Put on the middle shelf of the oven and bake for 20 minutes, or until puffed up and golden brown. Outline and remove the 'hats' with the use of a sharp knife. Put the hats to one side. Scoop out, and discard, all the uncooked dough from inside the feuilletées. Return the cases to the oven to dry out for another 2 minutes.
4. Transfer the pastry cases to a wire rack. Reduce the oven temperature to 130°C/250°F/gas mark 1.
5. Meanwhile, make the tarragon beurre blanc and keep it warm in blood-warm water (any hotter and it will melt the butter and cause the sauce to curdle).
6. Assemble the feuilletées: toss the vegetables gently in the butter, keeping the spinach separate, to reheat them. Spread the spinach in the bottom of each pastry case. Divide the remaining vegetables between the cases, reserving one or two as a garnish. Return them to the oven to keep warm.
7. Just before serving, spoon a generous tablespoon of the sauce over the vegetables in each feuilletée and set the hat on top at an angle. Garnish with the reserved vegetables and serve the rest of the sauce separately in a warmed sauce boat.

MEDIUM-BODIED WHITE WITH
GOOD ACIDITY

Parsley and Garlic Pizza

SERVES 6–8

7g/¼oz fresh yeast or 1 teaspoon easy-blend
*   yeast*
425ml/15fl oz warm water
340g/12oz strong unbleached flour
1 teaspoon salt
4 tablespoons olive oil, plus extra for brushing
225g/8oz parsley, coarsely chopped
4 large or 8 small cloves of garlic, finely crushed
225ml/8fl oz double cream
salt and freshly ground black pepper

1. Cream the fresh yeast in a small bowl with 2 tablespoons of the water.
2. Sift the flour and salt into a mixing bowl (add the easy-blend yeast at this stage, if using) and make a well in the centre. Pour in the fresh yeast, the remaining water and the oil. Mix to a soft, but not wet, dough. Add more water if necessary.
3. Turn on to a floured surface and knead well for about 7 minutes, or until the dough is smooth. Place in a clean bowl and cover with cling film. Leave in a warm place for about 1 hour or until the dough has doubled in bulk.
4. Grease a large baking sheet, or a large roasting tin.
5. Knock back the dough and knead again for 5 minutes. Put on to the baking sheet, or into the roasting tin. Shape into an oblong 35 × 30cm/14 × 12 inches or to fit.
6. Crimp the edge to retain the filling. Brush the surface liberally with olive oil.
7. Combine the parsley, garlic and cream and seasoning. Spread thickly over the pizza base. Leave to rise again for 30 minutes.
8. Preheat the oven to 250°C/450°F/gas mark 8.
9. Bake the pizza near the bottom of the oven for 8–10 minutes and then lower the oven temperature to 200°C/400°F/gas mark 6 for a further 15 minutes or until the base is slightly risen and crisp but the topping is still moist.

ITALIAN MEDIUM-BODIED WHITE
VINO DA TAVOLA

◆ ◆ ◆ ◆ ◆ ◆ ◆ ◆ ◆ ◆ ◆ ◆ ◆ ◆ ◆ ◆ ◆ ◆ ◆ ◆

Leek and Tahini Crumble

SERVES 4–6

1 tablespoon olive oil
1kg/2lb leeks, sliced
1 large clove of garlic, crushed
1 bay leaf
salt and freshly ground black pepper

FOR THE SAUCE:

45g/1½oz butter
45g/1½oz plain flour
570ml/1 pint milk
1 tablespoon tahini (creamed sesame seeds)
1 tablespoon finely chopped parsley
salt and freshly ground black pepper

FOR THE CRUMBLE:

225g/8oz wholemeal flour
salt
110g/4oz butter
2 tablespoons rolled oats (optional)
1 tablespoon sesame seeds

1. Heat the oil in a large saucepan over a low heat. Add the leeks and garlic and cook gently for 10 minutes or until soft. Stir occasionally. Transfer to an ovenproof dish.
2. Make the sauce: melt the butter in a small saucepan over a low heat, stir in the flour with a wooden spoon and cook for 1 minute. Remove the pan from the heat, slowly pour in the milk, mixing well.
3. Return the pan to the heat, stir continuously until boiling, then simmer for 2–3 minutes. Remove from the heat and cool for 1 minute. Add the tahini and parsley and mix well. Season to taste.
4. Pour the sauce evenly over the leeks and leave to cool.
5. Preheat the oven to 200°C/400°F/gas mark 6.
6. Make the crumble: sift the flour and salt into a bowl. Rub in the butter until the mixture resembles coarse breadcrumbs. Mix in the oats, if using. Spoon the crumble evenly over the cold leek mixture and sprinkle with sesame seeds.
7. Place the dish on a baking sheet, place on the middle shelf of the oven and bake for 20–30 minutes or until nutty brown.
8. Serve immediately.

MEDIUM-BODIED WHITE

◆ ◆

Salsify Croustade

Salsify and scorzonera are classified as different vegetables but they taste, and are treated, the same. The only practical difference is that salsify is peeled before cooking and scorzonera is peeled afterwards. In fact both can be peeled before cooking, but the flavour of the latter, boiled in its skin, tastes better.

SERVES 4–6

FOR THE BASE:

170g/6oz fresh breadcrumbs, white or brown
55g/2oz butter, melted
55g/2oz Cheddar cheese, grated
1 tablespoon mixed chopped parsley and thyme
1 clove of garlic, crushed
1 teaspoon yellow mustard seeds

FOR THE FILLING:

2 leeks, finely sliced
1 tablespoon olive oil
salt and freshly ground black pepper
1 quantity mornay sauce (see p. 116)
1kg/2lb salsify, peeled, cut into 7.5cm/3inch lengths and boiled
4 tomatoes, peeled, seeded and cut into slivers
55g/2oz Cheddar cheese, grated
2 teaspoons fresh breadcrumbs, white or brown

1. Preheat the oven to 220°C/425°F/gas mark 7.
2. Make the base: put all the ingredients for the base into a bowl and mix well. Make sure that the breadcrumbs are coated with the melted butter and grated cheese. Put the mixture into a 25cm/10 inch loose-bottomed flan tin. Press the mixture evenly over the base and up the sides of the tin.

3. Bake the case on the top shelf of the oven for 10–15 minutes or until it is set and evenly browned. Lower the oven temperature to 200°C/400°F/gas mark 6.

4. Make the filling: put the leeks into a saucepan with the olive oil, add seasoning and cover. Cook over a low heat until the leeks are soft, stirring regularly to prevent them from burning.

5. Mix the leeks with the mornay sauce, season to taste and spread over the base of the croustade.

6. Arrange the salsify in a fan shape on top, and scatter over the tomatoes. Mix the grated cheese and breadcrumbs together and sprinkle over the tomatoes.

7. Return the croustade to the oven for 15–20 minutes until golden brown and hot through to the middle.

8. Remove the croustade from the flan tin and serve immediately.

MEDIUM-BODIED WHITE

◆ ◆

Fried Gnocchi

SERVES 6
570ml/1 pint milk
1 onion, sliced
1 clove
1 bay leaf
6 parsley stalks
110g/4oz semolina
200g/7oz mature Cheddar cheese, grated
2 tablespoons freshly grated Parmesan cheese
1 tablespoon chopped parsley
salt and freshly ground black pepper
pinch of English mustard powder
pinch of cayenne pepper
1 egg, beaten
110g/4oz dried white breadcrumbs
oil for deep-frying

TO SERVE:
tomato sauce (see pp. 117 and 118)

1. Gently heat the milk with the onion, clove, bay leaf and parsley stalks in a small saucepan. Bring to the boil, remove from the heat, cover and leave to infuse for 10 minutes. Strain the milk and discard the flavourings.

2. Return the milk to the pan, and bring to the boil. Sprinkle on the semolina, stirring steadily, and cook, still stirring, for about 1 minute or until the mixture is thick. Draw the pan off the heat and add the cheeses, chopped parsley, seasoning, mustard and cayenne pepper. The mixture should be well seasoned; adjust accordingly. Spread this mixture into a neat 1 cm/½ inch thick circle on a wet plate, cover and leave to chill for 30 minutes or overnight.

3. When the gnocchi paste is set, cut into eight equal wedges. Chill again.

4. Heat the oil in a deep sauté pan until a cube of stale bread sizzles immediately it is added. Dip the gnocchi into the beaten egg then coat with breadcrumbs.

5. Deep-fry for about 2 minutes, or until golden brown.* Drain well on paper towels. Sprinkle with salt and serve with the tomato sauce.

NOTE:
* The gnocchi can be grilled on both sides under a pre-heated grill if preferred.

LIGHT ITALIAN RED

Gnocchi and Flat Mushrooms with Tomato and Mascarpone Sauce

This delicious recipe was given to us by Valeria Sisti, who was a student and then a teacher at the school.

SERVES 4

FOR THE GNOCCHI:

570ml/1 pint milk
1 onion, sliced
1 clove
1 bay leaf
6 parsley stalks
170g/6oz semolina
110g/4oz Parmesan or pecorino cheese, grated
55g/2oz butter
2 egg yolks
salt and freshly ground white pepper

FOR THE SAUCE:

30g/1oz butter or 2 tablespoons olive oil
1 onion, sliced
1 × 200g/7oz can of chopped tomatoes
1 teaspoon tomato purée
1 tablespoon Tabasco sauce
1 tablespoon chopped oregano
1 tablespoon chopped thyme
110g/4oz mascarpone cheese
salt and freshly ground black pepper

FOR THE MUSHROOM FILLING:

30g/1oz butter
225g/8oz flat mushrooms, sliced
melted butter for brushing

1. Make the gnocchi: heat the milk gently in a small saucepan with the onion, cloves, bay leaf and parsley stalks. Bring to boiling point, remove from the heat, cover and leave to infuse for 10 minutes. Strain and discard the flavourings.

2. Return the flavoured milk to a clean saucepan and sprinkle on the semolina, stirring steadily, and cook for about 1 minute or until the mixture is thick. Remove the pan from the heat and stir in 85g/3oz of the Parmesan or pecorino cheese, the butter and egg yolks. Season well.

3. Line a roasting tin with greaseproof paper. Spread the mixture evenly in a 1cm/½ inch layer in the roasting tin using a wet spatula. Leave to cool for 1 hour or overnight, in a refrigerator.

4. Make the sauce: heat the butter, or oil if using, in flameproof dish, add the onion and cook over a low heat for 10 minutes, or until soft and transparent.

5. Add the canned tomatoes, tomato purée, and Tabasco sauce and cook for 15 minutes. Remove from the heat. Add the herbs, stir in the mascarpone cheese and season to taste. Set aside.

6. Heat the butter in a sauté pan, add the mushrooms and cook gently until the liquid has evaporated. This may take up to 20 minutes. Set aside.

7. Preheat the oven to 200°C/400°F/gas mark 6.

8. Cut the gnocchi into circles with a 5cm/2 inch pastry cutter. Gather up the remaining gnocchi, press back into the tin again, flatten with a wet spatula, then stamp out more circles, repeating until there are enough circles to fill a medium ovenproof dish.

9. To assemble: spread the tomato and mascarpone mixture in the bottom of the dish. Cover with a layer of mushrooms and

then top with overlapping circles of gnocchi. Brush with melted butter and sprinkle with the remaining Parmesan or pecorino cheese.

10. Put on the middle shelf of the oven and bake for 20 minutes or until crisp and brown on top. Serve immediately.

MEDIUM ITALIAN RED

♦ ♦

Fresh Pasta Cannelloni

SERVES 4

½ quantity of fresh pasta (see p. 177)
olive oil for brushing

FOR THE SAUCE:

2 tablespoons olive oil
110g/4oz shallots, finely chopped
1kg/2lb tomatoes, peeled, seeded and diced
1 teaspoon tomato purée
pinch of sugar
2 tablespoons dry white vermouth
salt and freshly ground black pepper

FOR THE FILLING:

1kg/2lb spinach, cooked, drained and chopped
   (See p.182)
250g/9oz mascarpone cheese
30g/1oz Parmesan cheese, freshly grated
freshly grated nutmeg
salt and freshly ground black pepper
225g/8oz French beans, cooked
1 tablespoon shredded basil
4 tomatoes, peeled, quartered and seeded
2 tablespoons olive oil

TO GARNISH:

thyme leaves
extra virgin olive oil
the reserved French beans (see method)
2 tomatoes, peeled, seeded and diced finely

1. Make the pasta and leave it to relax in a cool place for 30 minutes.

2. Make the sauce: heat the oil in a medium-sized saucepan. Add the shallots and cook gently for 10 minutes or until soft and transparent. Add the remaining sauce ingredients and leave to simmer for a further 10 minutes.

3. Make the filling: put the spinach, mascarpone and Parmesan cheeses into a bowl and mix together. Season to taste with the nutmeg, salt and freshly ground black pepper.

4. Preheat the oven to 190°C/375°F/gas mark 5.

5. Roll out the pasta thinly and cut into eight 12 × 13.5cm/4 × 5½ inch strips. Bring a large saucepan of salted water to the boil, add the pasta and cook, in batches, for 3 minutes. Drain and put into a bowl of cold water until ready to use.

6. To assemble: drain the pasta thoroughly and pat dry with paper towels. Brush both sides with olive oil.

7. Lay the strips out on a flat surface. Divide the spinach mixture between them, keeping it to one end. Cover with the French beans (reserving a few for garnish) and two quarters of tomato, the basil and plenty of seasoning. Roll up the pasta (now cannelloni), brush with oil, and trim the ends if necessary.

8. Put the finished cannelloni into an ovenproof dish, seam side down. Spoon over two-thirds of the tomato sauce. Cover with a

lid or wet greaseproof paper and bake on the middle shelf of the oven for 20–30 minutes or until completely reheated.

9. Gently reheat the remaining tomato sauce.

10. To serve: put two cannelloni on to each of four plates and spoon around the tomato sauce. Sprinkle with thyme leaves, drizzle with olive oil and garnish with the reserved French beans and diced tomato. Serve immediately.

MEDIUM LIGHT ITALIAN RED

♦ ♦

Tagliatelle of Pasta, Leeks and Yellow Oyster Mushrooms

SERVES 4

½ quantity of fresh pasta (see p. 177)
1 large leek, white and pale green part only
2 tablespoons olive oil
salt and freshly ground black pepper
110g–140g/4–5oz yellow oyster mushrooms, sliced if large
1 × 400g/14oz can of artichoke hearts, rinsed, drained and quartered (optional)

TO SERVE:
sage velouté sauce (see p. 116)

1. Roll out the pasta thinly and cut into tagliatelle (see p. 178). Leave to dry.

2. Cut the leek into half lengthways, then cut into narrow strips lengthways, about the same thickness as the tagliatelle. Wash thoroughly and drain.

3. Heat half the oil in a large saucepan, add the leek, season, and sauté for 3–4 minutes, stirring occasionally, until beginning to soften. Add the mushrooms. Cover with a lid and cook until the mushrooms are barely soft. Add the artichokes, if used. Cover and leave to heat through.

4. Fill a large saucepan with plenty of salted water, bring to the boil and add the pasta with the remaining oil. Cook for 3–4 minutes or until cooked but firm to the bite. Drain and refresh under running warm water. Drain again.

5. Heat the sage velouté sauce.

6. Put the pasta on to a warm serving dish. Spoon over the vegetables. Serve with the sage velouté sauce.

NOTE:
* The tagliatelle can be twisted into 'nests' with a fork and served topped with the vegetables. Spoon over the sauce.

CRISP DRY WHITE
LIGHT MEDIUM-BODIED RED

Crisp Pasta Cake with Garlic Mayonnaise

SERVES 4

6 tablespoons olive oil
2 large onions, finely chopped
3 cloves of garlic, crushed
1 × 400g/14oz can of tomatoes
1 tablespoon coarsely chopped parsley
570ml/1 pint vegetable stock (see p. 172)
285g/10oz angel hair pasta

FOR THE GARLIC MAYONNAISE:

1 egg yolk
1 large clove of garlic, crushed
salt and freshly ground black pepper
150ml/5fl oz olive oil
1 teaspoon lemon juice

1. Heat 4 tablespoons of the oil in a large saucepan. Add the onions and garlic and cook over a gentle heat for about 10 minutes or until soft but not browned.

2. Add the canned tomatoes and parsley and cook for a few minutes. Pour in the stock and simmer for 20 minutes. Remove from the heat.

3. Preheat the oven to 200°C/400°F/gas mark 6.

4. Break the pasta into 5cm/2 inch lengths. Heat the remaining oil in a large flameproof casserole and cook the pasta carefully until pale brown (the pasta will brown further in the oven). It may be necessary to do this in batches.

5. Pour over the tomato mixture to coat the pasta. The liquid should all but cover the pasta. Bring to the boil, then turn down the heat and simmer for about 5 minutes.

6. Put the casserole on the middle shelf of the oven and bake for about 20–25 minutes until the liquid has reduced by half. The pasta should be crisp and brown on top and soft underneath.

7. Make the garlic mayonnaise: put the egg yolk and garlic in a bowl with a pinch of salt and beat well with a wooden spoon, or a hand whisk.

8. Add the oil, literally drop by drop, beating all the time, until half the oil has been added.

9. Beat in the lemon juice.

10. Continue pouring in the remaining oil, rather more confidently, still beating. A little water can be added if the mixture is too thick. Add freshly ground pepper to taste. Transfer to a serving bowl.

11. Serve the pasta in the casserole accompanied by the bowl of garlic mayonnaise.

NOTE:

* Serve this crisp but moist pasta cake with a platter of grilled Mediterranean vegetables, or by itself with a leafy salad.

RIOJA

Baked Polenta Layered with Ricotta Cheese and Tapenade

SERVES 6

FOR THE POLENTA LAYER:

860ml/1½ pints vegetable stock (see p. 172)

225g/8oz coarse instant polenta

3–4 tablespoons water

110g/4oz Parmesan cheese, freshly grated

2 tablespoons tomato purée (optional)

salt and freshly ground white pepper

FOR THE RICOTTA LAYER:

285g/10oz ricotta cheese

3 tablespoons chopped herbs, e.g. chives, thyme,
    sage, rosemary, basil

225g/8oz Parmesan cheese, freshly grated

1 egg, beaten

salt and freshly ground black pepper

FOR THE TAPENADE:

140g/5oz black olives, pitted

1 large clove of garlic, crushed

1 tablespoon capers, preferably dry-packed,
    rinsed

2 anchovy fillets (optional)

150ml/5fl oz olive oil

freshly ground black pepper

TO SERVE:

parsley pesto (see p. 119) or fresh tomato sauce
    (see p. 117)

1. Make the polenta layer: bring the vegetable stock to the boil in a large saucepan. Slake the polenta with the water (this will help prevent it from going into lumps when added to the boiling liquid) and add to the stock. Stir until thickened. Reduce the heat and cook for a further 5–10 minutes. Add the cheese, and tomato purée, if using. Season to taste, adding only a little salt (the Parmesan cheese and tapenade are both salty).

2. Grease a 860ml/1½ pint soufflé dish or 17.5cm/7 inch deep cake tin. Pour in the polenta and smooth the top with a wet spatula. Leave to set until quite cold, or overnight.

3. Meanwhile, make the ricotta layer: put the ricotta into a bowl, add the herbs, Parmesan cheese and egg, and combine well. Season generously.

4. Make the tapenade: place the ingredients in a food processor and, using the pulse button, mix to a coarse purée.

5. Preheat the oven to 190°C/375°F/gas mark 5.

6. To assemble: turn out the polenta. Grease the soufflé dish or cake tin again and place a disc of greaseproof paper in the bottom. Cut the polenta 'cake' into three layers, and place one layer in the base of the dish or cake tin.

7. Divide the tapenade in half and spread the layer of polenta with one half.

8. Divide the ricotta mixture in half and spoon one portion over the tapenade.

9. Place the second disc of polenta on top and press flat.

10. Repeat with a layer of tapenade and then with a layer of ricotta, ending with the last disc of polenta.

11. Put the dish on a baking sheet, put on the middle shelf of the oven and bake for about 30 minutes or until the polenta is crisp and brown.

12. Leave to cool for 15 minutes. Put a plate on top of the soufflé dish or cake tin and invert both together. Shake gently and carefully and remove the dish or tin, and the greaseproof paper, if necessary.

13. Serve immediately with parsley pesto or fresh tomato sauce.

NOTES:

* To make the tapenade without a food processor or blender, chop the olives, garlic, capers and anchovies, if using, then pound together in a mortar using a pestle. Slowly pour in the oil, pounding constantly. Season with black pepper.

** The top, after the dish has been turned out, can be browned under a preheated grill. Brush with oil before grilling.

*** This recipe can be made 24 hours in advance and kept in a refrigerator. Return to room temperature before reheating at 180°C/350°F/ gas mark 4 for 30 minutes.

ITALIAN MEDIUM RED
NEW WORLD SAUVIGNON BLANC

◆ ◆

Black Olive Polenta with Grilled Vegetable and Wild Mushroom Salad

This recipe can be used with any combination of Mediterranean vegetables, but the wild mushrooms, sun-dried tomatoes and artichoke hearts are essential.

SERVES 4

FOR THE BLACK OLIVE POLENTA:
1 litre/1 ¾ pints vegetable stock (see p. 172)
200g/7oz coarse instant polenta
3-4 tablespoons water
85g/3oz Parmesan cheese, freshly grated
110g/4oz black olive paste
110g/4oz pitted black olives, coarsely chopped
2 tablespoons olive oil
salt and freshly ground black pepper

FOR THE GRILLED VEGETABLE AND WILD MUSHROOM SALAD:
4 tablespoons olive oil
1 clove of garlic
1 aubergine
110g/4oz shiitake mushrooms, sliced
110g/4oz oyster mushrooms, sliced
110g/4oz sun-dried tomatoes in oil
1 small red pepper, grilled, peeled, seeded and sliced (see p. 181)
1 small yellow pepper, grilled, peeled, seeded and sliced (see p. 181)
1 fresh red chilli, grilled, seeded and finely sliced
110g/4oz pitted black olives, left whole
225g/8oz canned artichoke hearts, rinsed, drained and halved
2 tablespoons balsamic vinegar

TO GARNISH:
basil leaves

1. Make the polenta: bring the vegetable stock to the boil in a large saucepan. Slake the polenta with the water (this will help prevent it from going into lumps when

added to the boiling liquid) and add to the stock, stirring all the time. Reduce the heat and cook for 5–10 minutes or until the mixture leaves the sides of the pan.

2. Add the cheese, black olive paste, olives and olive oil. Season to taste. Cover with a layer of damp greaseproof paper to prevent a skin forming, and set aside.

3. Make the salad: heat the oil in a small saucepan and add the garlic. Cover, remove from the heat and leave to infuse for 30 minutes. Strain and set aside.

4. Preheat the grill to its highest setting.

5. Cut the aubergine, lengthways, into long 1cm/½ inch wide strips and lightly salt them. Leave for 30 minutes to disgorge their juices. Rinse the strips and dry thoroughly with paper towels. Brush generously with the garlic olive oil and grill on both sides for about 8 minutes, or until charred and soft.

6. Toss the mushrooms with the sun-dried tomatoes and their oil in a sauté pan over a high heat for 3 minutes. Remove to a large bowl.

7. Mix in the grilled peppers, chilli, aubergines, olives and artichoke hearts. Toss gently with the balsamic vinegar.

8. Reheat the polenta over a low heat and then spread it on a warmed serving dish, making a well in the centre. Pile the warm salad into the centre of the polenta and garnish with basil leaves.

NOTE:
* Crumbled feta cheese can be sprinkled over the finished dish just before serving.

FULL-BODIED WHITE
MEDIUM-BODIED RED

◆ ◆

Spinach Roulade with Arborio Rice Filling

SERVES 4
FOR THE ROULADE:
4 eggs, separated
15g/½ oz butter, softened
450g/1lb fresh spinach, cooked and chopped (see
  p.182), or 170g/6oz frozen leaf spinach
salt and freshly ground black pepper
freshly grated nutmeg to taste

FOR THE FILLING:
1 tablespoon olive oil

1 small onion, finely chopped
1 large clove of garlic, crushed
85g/3oz arborio (risotto) rice
1 bay leaf
salt and freshly ground black pepper
290–425ml/10–15fl oz vegetable stock (see
  p. 172)
55g/2oz mature Cheddar cheese or Parmesan
  cheese, freshly grated
1 tablespoon Greek yoghurt or fromage frais

1. Make a roulade case (see p. 183).

2. Make the filling: heat the oil in a saucepan and gently cook the onion and garlic for 10 minutes or until soft and transparent. Stir in the rice, bay leaf and seasoning and cook very slowly for 4 minutes.

3. Meanwhile, heat the vegetable stock in another saucepan and leave to simmer gently.

4. Start adding the hot stock to the rice mixture, a little at a time, stirring constantly. Allow the stock to become absorbed between each addition. Keep adding the stock until the rice is cooked but still 'al dente' and the stock is absorbed. This may take about 10 minutes. Set aside.

5. Preheat the oven to 190°C/375°F/gas mark 5.

6. Make the roulade: gradually beat the egg yolks and butter into the spinach and season with the salt, pepper and nutmeg.

7. Whisk the egg whites until stiff but not dry. Stir 2 tablespoons into the spinach then lightly fold in the remainder using a large metal spoon. Pour into the roulade case and spread into an even layer with a spatula.

8. Put the roulade on the middle shelf of the oven and bake for 10–12 minutes, or until it feels firm to the touch.

9. Remove from the oven, cover with a clean tea towel and leave to cool.

10. Remove the bay leaf from the risotto, stir in the cheese and yoghurt or fromage frais and mix thoroughly. Season to taste.

11. Place a piece of greaseproof paper on a flat surface, turn the roulade on to the paper and remove the lining paper. Spread the filling on the roulade and roll it up like a Swiss roll, removing the paper as you go. Trim and neaten the ends of the roulade with a serrated knife.

12. Serve warm or cold.

LIGHT ITALIAN WHITE
ITALIAN RED

◆ ◆

Mushroom and Coriander Risotto

SERVES 4

15g/½ oz dried porcini or cep mushrooms, soaked in 150ml/5fl oz hot water for 15–20 minutes

450g/1lb flat black field mushrooms, wiped and coarsely chopped

15g/½ oz coriander, large stalks removed

2 tablespoons olive oil

1 onion, finely chopped

1 clove of garlic, crushed

400g/14oz arborio (risotto) rice

710–860ml/1¼–1½ pints vegetable stock (see p. 172)

170g/6oz mature Cheddar cheese, finely grated

salt and freshly ground black pepper

TO GARNISH:

shavings of Parmesan cheese

coriander leaves

1. Remove the porcini mushrooms from the water with a slotted spoon. Strain the water through a J-cloth or muslin, and reserve.

2. Put the flat mushrooms, porcini mushrooms and coriander in a food processor and mix until smooth. Alternatively chop them very finely.

3. Heat the oil in a large saucepan and cook the onion and garlic over a moderate heat until soft and transparent.

4. Add the rice, stir to coat in the oil and cook for 1 minute. Add the mushroom and coriander purée with the mushroom water. Cook until the liquid is absorbed.

5. Meanwhile, heat the vegetable stock in another saucepan and leave it to simmer gently.

6. Gradually add the vegetable stock to the rice, stirring continuously. As the liquid is absorbed by the rice, add a little more and continue in this way until the rice is cooked. It will take about 15–20 minutes. The consistency of the rice should be sticky but loose.

7. Stir in the cheese and season to taste.

8. Serve immediately, garnished with shavings of Parmesan cheese and coriander leaves.

FULL-BODIED RED

◆ ◆

Carrot, and Courgette and Pea Moulds

SERVES 4

FOR THE MOULDS:

1 leek, white part only, very finely chopped
425ml/15fl oz double cream or
    150ml/5fl oz milk and 290ml/10fl oz double
    cream
285g/10oz carrot, coarsely grated
1 teaspoon sugar (optional)
salt
1 tablespoon finely chopped herbs, e.g. sage,
    parsley
200g/7 oz courgettes, coarsely grated
110g/4oz frozen peas
1 tablespoon finely chopped mint
3 large eggs
1 egg yolk

FOR THE VEGETABLE BEURRE BLANC:

1 tablespoon white part only of leek, finely
    chopped

150ml/5fl oz reserved vegetable liquor (see
    method)
110ml/4fl oz dry white wine
2 tablespoons double cream
85g/3oz unsalted butter, chilled
salt and freshly ground white pepper
squeeze of lemon

TO GARNISH:

5cm/2 inch piece of carrot, finely julienned,
    cooked
5cm/2 inch piece of courgette, finely julienned,
    cooked
a few peas

1. Preheat the oven to 190°C/375°F/gas mark 5.

2. Grease eight dariole moulds or ramekin dishes. Line the bottoms with discs of greaseproof paper and grease again.

3. Put the leek and cream, and milk, if using, into a medium saucepan and cook together over a low heat for about 10 minutes or until the leek is soft. Leave to cool.

4. Cook the carrot in just enough salted water to cover, for 3–4 minutes or until soft

but firm to the bite. (Use the sugar only if the carrots lack flavour.) Strain and reserve the water. Add the chopped herbs to the carrots and set aside.

5. Cook the courgettes and peas together in the same way as the carrots, reserving enough of the cooking water to make the carrot liquor up to 150ml/5fl oz. Add the mint to the vegetables and set aside.

6. Beat the eggs and egg yolk thoroughly in a bowl and mix with the leek mixture. Add half the mixture to the carrot and half to the courgettes and peas.

7. Fill four dariole moulds or ramekins with the carrot mixture and four dariole moulds or ramekins with the courgette and pea mixture.

8. Place the moulds in a baking tin and surround with hot water to come half-way up the sides of the moulds. Put on the middle shelf of the oven and bake for 25–30 minutes or until set. Remove from the oven and leave to cool for a few minutes.

9. Meanwhile, make the vegetable beurre blanc: put the wine, leek and reserved vegetable liquor into a small heavy saucepan and boil until reduced to 2 tablespoons. Strain and return to the pan.

10. Add the cream and boil again until reduced to 2 tablespoons.

11. Keep the sauce hot but do not allow to boil. Using a wire whisk and plenty of continuous whisking, gradually add the butter, piece by piece. This should take about 5 minutes and the sauce should become creamy and pale and be the consistency of single cream. Add salt, freshly ground white pepper and lemon juice to taste.

12. To serve: unmould one carrot, and one courgette and pea mould onto each of four warm plates. Pour over some of the beurre blanc and garnish with the vegetables. Serve immediately.

MEDIUM DRY WHITE
LIGHT NEW WORLD RED

◆ ◆

Harlequin Terrine

This terrine can be served as part of a buffet, as the main course for a light lunch, or as a first course.

SERVES 4–6
2 small aubergines, thinly sliced lengthways
salt
150ml/5fl oz French dressing (see p. 114)
1 quantity of pesto (see p. 119)
2 large green peppers, grilled, peeled, seeded and quartered (see p. 181)
2 large red peppers, grilled, peeled, seeded and quartered (see p. 181)
2 large yellow peppers, grilled, peeled, seeded and quartered (see p. 181)

FOR THE FILLING:
55g/2oz fine fresh white breadcrumbs
4 tablespoons olive oil
225g/8oz feta cheese, crumbled
20 capers, preferably dry-packed, roughly chopped
20 black olives, pitted and halved
10 leaves of basil, coarsely chopped

20 *walnuts, chopped*
5 *tablespoons Greek yoghurt*
red pepper trimmings, diced (see method)
20 *French beans, topped and tailed and cooked*

1. Lightly grease a 450g/1lb loaf tin and line with cling film, leaving an overhang all round.
2. Put the aubergine slices in a colander and toss with salt. Leave for 30 minutes to disgorge their juices. Rinse well and pat dry with paper towels.
3. Soak the aubergine slices in the French dressing in a large flat dish for 2 hours, turning them now and again.
4. Preheat the grill to its highest setting.
5. Drain the aubergine slices and dry with paper towels. Grill for about 8 minutes a side until cooked and browned. Spread one side of each slice with 1 tablespoon of pesto sauce and set aside.
6. Make the filling: fry the breadcrumbs in the oil until golden brown. Allow to cool.
7. Put the cheese, capers, black olives, basil and walnuts into a large bowl and mix well. Add the fried breadcrumbs and the yoghurt and mix to a stiff consistency.
8. To assemble: trim the top and bottom of the pepper quarters (chop the trimmings and add them to the filling) and use them to line the bottom and sides of the loaf tin, skinned side out, slightly overlapping each slice and allowing an overhang if possible.
9. Line with the aubergine slices, pesto side next to the peppers, lying them lengthways along the bottom and sides, and again leaving an overhang if possible. (This is not essential.)
10. Using a spoon, add a layer of the filling, cover with a few French beans laid lengthways, then add another layer of the filling and repeat with the rest of the mixture. Press down firmly. Cover with any overhanging aubergines and then the overhanging peppers, using extra slices of each as necessary.
11. Cover with cling film. Cut a piece of strong cardboard to fit on top of the loaf tin and weight evenly. Stand the terrine on a plate and refrigerate overnight.
12. To serve: put a serving plate on top of the tin and invert both together. Shake gently and carefully remove the tin. Remove the cling film.

MEDIUM DRY WHITE
CHILLED BEAUJOLAIS

Grilled Yellow and Green Courgette Terrine

SERVES 6

5 green courgettes
5 yellow courgettes
170g/6oz Parmesan cheese or mature Cheddar
  cheese, freshly grated
110g/4oz fresh white breadcrumbs
salt and freshly ground black pepper

TO SERVE:
½ quantity of mayonnaise (see p. 114)
150ml/5fl oz Greek yoghurt

1. Cut the courgettes lengthways into 5mm/¼ inch thick slices.
2. Oil a ridge-bottomed grill pan lightly and heat over a moderate heat. When very hot, put on as many courgette slices as will fit. Cook both sides of each slice for 5–8 minutes until the char lines are distinct and the courgettes are cooked through. Remove with a fish slice and set aside. Repeat with the remaining slices. Oil the grill pan lightly between each batch.
3. Preheat the oven to 180°C/350°F/gas mark 4.
4. Line the bottom and sides of a 450g/1lb loaf tin with alternating slices of yellow and green courgette. Trim the courgettes to the top edge of the tin.
5. Mix the grated cheese and breadcrumbs in a small bowl and season well. Sprinkle the bottom of the lined tin with two tablespoons of the mixture. Cover with a layer of courgettes and then with a layer of the cheese mixture and repeat, finishing with a layer of courgette.
6. Put the loaf tin on a baking sheet on the middle shelf of the oven and bake for about 20 minutes.
7. Leave to cool in the tin.
8. Meanwhile, cut two pieces of stiff cardboard to fit the top of the tin. Cover the cold terrine with cling film and place the cardboard then weights on top. Stand the terrine on a plate and leave overnight in a refrigerator.
9. To serve: remove the weights, cardboard and cling film and carefully run a rounded knife down and around the sides of the tin. Put a rectangular serving dish over the tin and invert both together. Slide the terrine into place and remove the tin.
10. Mix the mayonnaise and yoghurt in a small bowl and serve with the terrine.

NOTE:
* Use a very sharp knife to slice the terrine.

CRISP DRY WHITE
MEDIUM-BODIED RED

Stuffed Red Peppers with Soufflé Tops

SERVES 4
4 large red peppers

FOR THE STUFFING:
1 tablespoon olive oil
1 onion, finely chopped
2 carrots, finely chopped
55g/2oz red lentils
55g/2oz brown lentils
1 × 400g/14oz can of tomatoes
1½ teaspoons tomato purée
2–3 tablespoons mango chutney
1 bay leaf
salt and freshly ground black pepper
Tabasco sauce and sugar to taste

FOR THE TOP:
110g/4oz fromage frais
55g/2oz Cheddar cheese, grated
1 egg
salt and freshly ground black pepper

1. Cut the tops off the peppers, remove and discard the stalks and finely dice the flesh; reserve. Remove and discard the core and seeds from the pepper 'cups'.

2. Bring a saucepan of water to the boil, add the peppers, and boil for 5 minutes. Drain and refresh under running cold water. Leave to drain upside down.

3. Make the stuffing: heat the oil in a large saucepan. Add the onion, carrot and reserved diced red pepper and cook for 10 minutes or until the onion is soft and transparent. Add the remaining ingredients, bring to the boil, reduce the heat and simmer for 15–20 minutes until the lentils are cooked. Boil away any excess liquid. Remove the bay leaf. Add seasoning, Tabasco sauce and sugar to taste.

4. Preheat the oven to 200°C/400°F/gas mark 6.

5. Put the peppers in an ovenproof dish and three-quarters fill them with the lentil stuffing.

6. Make the top: mix together the ingredients, reserving a little of the cheese, and spoon on to the lentil mixture. Sprinkle with the reserved cheese.

7. Place on the middle shelf of the oven and bake for 20 minutes or until the topping has puffed up and is golden brown. Serve immediately.

LIGHT RED
MEDIUM DRY WHITE

◆ ◆

Wild and Field Mushroom Timbales with Star Anise Sauce

These timbales, which are a good substitute for the meat in a 'meat and two veg' dish, are rich and satisfying. The juice from the mushrooms is reduced with star anise and produces a deep, brown sauce.

SERVES 4

55g/2oz butter

1 onion, finely chopped

3 cloves of garlic, crushed

30g/1oz dried ceps, soaked in 290ml/10fl oz hot water for 15–20 minutes

100g–110g/3½oz–4oz shiitake mushrooms, finely sliced

110g–125g/4oz–4½oz oyster mushrooms, finely sliced

225g/8oz field mushrooms, finely sliced

110g/4oz brown cap mushrooms, finely sliced

15g/½oz plain chocolate

2 egg whites

about 1 tablespoon balsamic vinegar

salt and freshly ground black pepper

2 whole star anise

2 tablespoons water

1. Heat the butter in a large saucepan, add the onion, cover and cook for about 10 minutes or until transparent and soft. Remove the lid, turn up the heat, add the garlic and fry until the onion is golden brown.

2. Meanwhile, remove the soaked ceps from their water with a slotted spoon, line a sieve with a J-cloth and strain the water into a bowl to remove any grit. Reserve the liquid.

3. Add all the mushrooms to the onion mixture together with the strained cep water and the chocolate. Mix well with a wooden spoon. Cover and cook for about 15 minutes over a moderate heat. Put the cooked mushrooms into a sieve over a saucepan and leave to drain for about 1 hour. Press with the back of a wooden spoon to help extract the moisture.

4. Preheat the oven to 180°C/350°F/gas mark 4. Lightly grease four timbales.

5. Put the egg whites into a food processor and mix briefly. Add about half of the mushrooms and mix to a coarse purée.

6. Put the remaining mushrooms into a bowl, add the puréed mushrooms and mix. Season to taste with balsamic vinegar, salt and pepper. Spoon the mixture into the timbales, level the top with a knife and cover with some lightly greased foil.

7. Put the timbales in a roasting pan and surround with hot water to come half-way up the sides of the timbales. Put on to the middle shelf of the oven and cook for 20 minutes. Turn off the oven but leave the timbales in the oven to keep warm until ready to serve.

8. Put the 2 star anise and water into the saucepan with the mushroom juices and bring to the boil. If wished, add a little balsamic vinegar. Boil rapidly until reduced to a thin syrup. Season to taste.

9. To serve: invert the timbales onto four warm serving plates and spoon over the juices.

NOTE:

* The sauce can be thickened with cornflour.

FULL-BODIED RED
NEW WORLD CHARDONNAY

Beetroot Bavarois

We have chosen to use fresh beetroot for this recipe as it has a natural sweetness, but the bavarois is nearly as good made with vacu-packed vinegared beetroot, which is available in supermarkets. Serve with mayonnaise (see p. 114) and a red-leafed salad.

SERVES 8

1 tablespoon sunflower oil
1 large onion, thinly sliced
1 large clove of garlic, crushed
grated zest of 1 orange
450g/1lb fresh beetroot, cooked and peeled
4 large egg yolks
290ml/10fl oz milk
3 tablespoons water
30g/1oz gelatine (for agar agar see p. 180)
200g/7oz Greek yoghurt
salt and freshly ground black pepper

1. Lightly oil a charlotte mould or a 1.1 litre/2 pint ring mould.
2. Heat the oil in a sauté pan and cook the onion and garlic gently for about 10 minutes or until soft but not brown. Allow to cool.
3. Put the beetroot and onion mix into a food processor and mix to a smooth purée. Push through a sieve, stir in the orange zest and set aside.
4. Beat the egg yolks in a bowl. Put the milk into a saucepan and heat until just below boiling. Pour on to the egg yolks, stirring all the time. Return the mixture to the clean saucepan and heat gently, stirring, for 8–10 minutes, until the custard coats the back of a wooden spoon; do not allow to boil. Strain into the beetroot purée.
5. Put the water into a small saucepan, sprinkle on the gelatine and leave to soak for 5 minutes. Heat gently until the gelatine has melted and is quite clear. Do not allow to boil.
6. Pour the gelatine into the purée, stirring all the time. Allow to cool and begin to thicken.
7. Stir in the yoghurt and season to taste. Pour into the prepared mould. Refrigerate overnight or until set.
8. To serve: dip the mould quickly into very hot water and turn out on to a serving plate.

MEDIUM SWEET RED
PINOT NOIR

Chestnut Crown Roast

This recipe makes a perfect meatless main course for Christmas. It is made in a large brioche tin and topped with whole chestnuts braised in red wine, and looks impressive. Serve with crisp roast potatoes, traditional vegetables and cranberry sauce.

SERVES 8–10

FOR THE NUT LAYER:

225g/8oz mixed nuts, coarsely ground
110g/4oz fresh white breadcrumbs
2 tablespoons sunflower oil
2 onions, finely chopped
55g/2oz button mushrooms, coarsely chopped
3 tomatoes, peeled and coarsely chopped
2 tablespoons tomato pureé
½ teaspoon freshly grated nutmeg
2 cloves, freshly ground
1 small egg, beaten
salt and freshly ground black pepper

FOR THE SPINACH LAYER:

30g/1oz butter
2 cloves of garlic, crushed
1kg/2lb fresh spinach, washed, cooked and
   drained (see p.182), or 450g/1lb frozen leaf
   spinach, thawed and drained
salt and freshly ground black pepper

FOR THE CHESTNUT LAYER:

1 tablespoon sunflower oil
1 large onion, finely chopped
2 sticks of celery, finely chopped
225g/8oz unsweetened chestnut pureé
110g/4oz braised chestnuts (see p. 194) or 110g/
   4oz vacu-packed chestnuts
85g/3oz pitted prunes, taken from the braised

chestnuts (optional)
1 tablespoon fresh white breadcrumbs

TO SERVE:
braised chestnuts (see p. 194)
watercress (optional)

1. Make the nut layer: put the nuts, in batches, into a food processor and, using the pulse button, process until the mixture resembles very coarse breadcrumbs. Tip into a large bowl and stir in the breadcrumbs.
2. Heat the oil in a frying pan and cook the onion for about 10 minutes or until soft and transparent. Add the mushrooms and tomatoes and cook for 5 minutes or until the moisture has evaporated. Remove from the heat, cool a little and then tip into the nut mixture and mix.
3. Add the tomato pureé, nutmeg and cloves to the nut mixture and combine thoroughly. Stir in the egg to make a moist, but not wet, mixture. Add a little water if necessary. Season to taste. Leave aside.
4. Make the spinach layer: melt the butter in a saucepan and add the garlic. Cook over a low heat for 1 minute, then add the spinach. Stir to coat the spinach with butter. Season to taste. Put aside.
5. Make the chestnut layer: heat the oil in a large saucepan, add the onion and celery and cook for 10 minutes or until soft, but not brown. Add the chestnut purée and cook until it has softened. Remove from the heat and tip into a bowl. Add the rest of the ingredients and mix well, keeping the chestnuts whole. Set aside.
6. Preheat the oven to 180°C/350°F/gas mark 4.
7. Assemble the roast: lightly oil a large, non-stick, fluted brioche tin.* Line the

bottom with a circle of greaseproof paper, cut to fit, and oil again lightly.

8. Divide the nut mixture into four portions, and the spinach into two portions. Layer the mixtures into the brioche tin, starting with the nut mixture. Then add a layer of spinach, a layer of nut mixture, the chestnut mixture, the nut mixture, the remaining spinach and end with a layer of nut mixture. Press down each layer with a spatula, making sure that the edges are neat. Cover with lightly oiled greaseproof paper.

9. Put the tin on to a baking sheet and put on the middle shelf of the oven. Bake for 35–40 minutes. Remove from the oven and turn up the heat to 220°C/425°F/gas mark 7.

10. Allow the roast to cool on a wire rack for 10 minutes. Line a baking sheet with greaseproof paper and invert the tin on to it. Remove the tin and the greaseproof disc and return the roast to the oven for a further 10 minutes or until browned.

11. Transfer to a serving dish. Top with braised chestnuts and spoon over some of their sauce. Garnish with a small bunch of watercress, if using. Serve immediately.

NOTES:
* If a non-stick brioche mould is not available, line an ordinary brioche tin with cling film and layer up as instructed. Leave in the refrigerator overnight. Before cooking, turn the loaf out of the mould on to a greased baking sheet (it will hold its shape). Peel off the cling film carefully and proceed from stage 9, omitting stage 10. Brush with melted butter before putting the roast into the oven.

** This roast can be made well in advance and kept in a refrigerator for several days, or frozen. To reheat a frozen roast, allow it to thaw, then put in a moderate oven for 30 minutes or until hot through to the centre.

FULL-BODIED MEDIUM DRY RED
FULL-BODIED WHITE BURGUNDY

♦ ♦

Roast Onions with Spiced Lentil Stuffing

SERVES 6
6 large Spanish onions

FOR THE FILLING:
1 tablespoon oil
170g/6oz of the onion cores (see method), finely chopped
2 cloves of garlic, crushed

1 teaspoon ground cinnamon
3 whole cloves, ground
¼ whole nutmeg, grated
1 × 400g/14oz can of tomatoes
3–4 tablespoons tomato purée
110g/4oz brown lentils, cooked
55g/2oz toasted almonds, chopped
55g/2oz raisins
2 heaped tablespoons chopped marjoram
grated zest of 1 lemon
salt and freshly ground black pepper

TO GARNISH:
plenty of marjoram, finely chopped

1. Preheat the oven to 180°C/350°F/gas mark 4.

2. Prepare the onions: trim the hairy root of the onions, but do not cut away any more of the root as this holds the onions together. Keeping the knife parallel to the root, cut the tops off the onions and remove the outer skin. Leaving three layers of each onion intact, scrape away the insides with a teaspoon. Reserve the 'cores' for the filling.

3. Blanch the onions in boiling water for 3–4 minutes. Drain and pat dry.

4. Make the filling: heat the oil in a sauté pan. Add the reserved onion flesh with the garlic and cook slowly over a low heat until soft. Add the cinnamon, cloves and nutmeg. Cook for a further minute.

5. Add the rest of the ingredients and cook until the mixture is dry. Taste and add more seasoning or spices as necessary.

6. Fill the onions with the lentil mixture, packing them well. Place together closely in a roasting tin or a baking dish. Add enough water to come a quarter of the way up the onions and then cover with foil.

7. Bake on the middle shelf of the oven for 1½–2 hours until the onion flesh is soft. 15 minutes before the end of the cooking time increase the oven temperature to 200°C/400°F/gas mark 6, brush the onions with oil and allow them to caramelise, uncovered.

8. Serve the onions in their own juices and garnished generously with chopped marjoram.

FULL-BODIED RED

◆ ◆

Wild Mushroom Sausages

Most good butchers will supply edible non-gut sausage casing although they may want to sell more than is required for this recipe! If a sausage-making machine is available the job will be easier, but we have found that a piping bag works nearly as well.

SERVES 4 (MAKES ABOUT 16 SAUSAGES)
45g/1½ oz butter
1 large onion, very finely chopped
2 large cloves of garlic, crushed
30g/1oz dried ceps, soaked in 290ml/10fl oz hot water for 30 minutes
110g/4oz shiitake mushrooms, sliced
110g/4oz oyster mushrooms, sliced
225g/8oz field mushrooms, sliced
225g/8oz brown cap mushrooms, sliced
1 tablespoon chopped thyme leaves
1 tablespoon finely chopped oregano
1 tablespoon tomato purée
2 tablespoons dark soy sauce
2 tablespoons sherry vinegar, plus 1 teaspoon (optional)
2 eggs
85g/3oz fine white fresh breadcrumbs
freshly ground black pepper
about 1.8m/6 feet of sausage casing
seasoned flour
oil for frying

TO SERVE:
mashed potato

1. Heat the butter in a large saucepan, add the onion, cover and cook for about 10 minutes or until transparent and soft. Remove the lid, turn up the heat, add the garlic and fry until both are golden brown.

2. Meanwhile, remove the soaked ceps from their water with a slotted spoon. Drain and chop. Line a sieve with a J-cloth or muslin and strain the water to remove any grit. Reserve the liquid.

3. Add all the mushrooms to the onion mixture, together with the strained cep water, herbs, tomato purée, soy sauce and sherry vinegar. Mix with a wooden spoon. Cover and cook for about 5 minutes over a moderate heat. Put the mushrooms into a sieve and drain over a bowl for about 1 hour. Press with the back of a wooden spoon to extract the maximum amount of liquid. Reserve the juices.

5. Put the eggs into a food processor and mix briefly. Add the mushroom mixture and mix to a coarse purée. Transfer to a bowl, mix in the breadcrumbs and season well with black pepper (add salt only if necessary).

6. Make the sausages: put a 1cm/½ inch plain nozzle into a piping bag and fill with the mushroom mixture. Insert the nozzle into the sausage skin and hold it there with one hand while squeezing the mixture through the piping bag with the other. Do not fill the skins too tightly or they will burst during cooking. Tie into 10cm/4 inch sausages. Refrigerate for 1–2 hours.

7. Heat the oil in a shallow sauté or frying pan over a moderate heat. Toss the sausages in the seasoned flour and fry gently for 10 minutes or until browned. Do not cook over too high a heat as this will make the sausages burst.

8. Meanwhile, pour the reserved mushroom liquid into a small saucepan and reduce, by boiling rapidly, to a syrupy consistency. Add a teaspoon of sherry vinegar if preferred.

9. Serve the sausages with mashed potato and the mushroom 'gravy'.

MEDIUM-BODIED RED

◆ ◆

Aubergine Bocconcini

SERVES 6
4 large aubergines
salt
olive oil for brushing

FOR THE FILLING:
450g/1lb ricotta cheese

2 egg yolks
110g/4oz pine nuts, toasted
110g/4oz Parmesan cheese, freshly grated
30g/1oz butter, melted
handful of mixed herbs, e.g. parsley, thyme,
    rosemary, or chives, finely chopped
freshly grated nutmeg
salt and freshly ground black pepper

TO SERVE:
Easy tomato sauce (see p. 118)

1. Wipe the aubergines and cut each one lengthwise into 5mm/¼ inch thick slices. Put into a colander, toss with salt and leave for 30 minutes to disgorge their juices. Rinse well and pat dry.

2. Preheat the grill to its highest setting.

3. Brush the aubergine slices with olive oil and grill for 8 minutes on each side, or until cooked and brown. Set aside.

4. Make the filling: put all the ingredients into a bowl and mix together using a wooden spoon. Season to taste with nutmeg, salt and pepper.

5. Place a slice of grilled aubergine on a board and put 2 tablespoons of the filling at one end. Roll up the aubergine. Repeat until all the aubergine slices and filling have been used. Put on a large plate and refrigerate for 30 minutes.

6. Preheat the oven to 190°C/375°F/gas mark 5.

7. Butter an ovenproof dish large enough to take the aubergine rolls, and arrange them standing upright, side by side.*

8. Cover with foil and bake for 25 minutes. Remove the foil and bake for a further 5 minutes. Serve hot and hand the tomato sauce separately.

NOTE:

* If the aubergine bocconcini do not fill the dish, place in a ring around the edge and fill the middle with the easy tomato sauce, boiled until thickened.

ITALIAN MEDIUM-BODIED RED
OAKED CHARDONNAY

◆ ◆

Artichokes Greek-style

This is very a simple, but delicious, traditional Greek dish. Buy small, young artichokes. Older artichokes are unsuitable for this recipe. Serve with plenty of crusty bread and some feta cheese.

SERVES 4

4 young, small globe artichokes with stalks
1 tablespoon lemon juice
150ml/5fl oz good quality olive oil
8 very small onions
3 large carrots, scrubbed but not peeled
8 small potatoes, scrubbed but not peeled
4 small bulbs of fennel, trimmed and cut in half

8 spring onions, trimmed
1 lemon
2 tablespoons coarsely chopped parsley
salt and freshly ground black pepper

1. Prepare the artichokes: trim the stalks leaving them 2.5cm/1 inch long. Remove the thick skin from the stalks with a potato peeler. Break off any damaged leaves. Cut 2.5cm/1 inch off the leaves, prise the artichokes open and expose the chokes. Scrape out the chokes using a rounded teaspoon. This is not easy, and care should be taken to remove all the hairs without damaging the hearts. Put the artichokes into a bowl of water acidulated with the lemon juice.

2. Heat the oil in a large, heavy-bottomed, flameproof casserole, add the onions and

cook over a low heat for 10 minutes. Do not allow to colour. Add the artichokes, standing them on their heads.

3. Cut each carrot into four large chunks and add to the casserole with the remaining ingredients and just enough water to cover the vegetables. (The artichoke stalks will cook in the steam.) Cover and simmer for about 40 minutes or until most of the water has evaporated. The vegetables should be cooked through and glistening with oil.

4. Remove the casserole from the heat, cover with a clean tea towel (to absorb any steam), and replace the lid. Leave for 10 minutes.

5. Serve straight from the casserole, disturbing the vegetables as little as possible.

NOTE:

* The potatoes and onions should be the size of the prepared artichokes, and the other vegetables should be cut as near that size as possible to ensure even cooking.

FULL-BODIED WHITE
FULL-BODIED RED
RETSINA

◆ ◆

Artichokes with Mushroom Duxelle and Warm Mustard Sauce

SERVES 4

4 globe artichokes, damaged outside leaves
    removed
1 tablespoon lemon juice
1 tablespoon oil
salt

FOR THE DUXELLE:

1 tablespoon olive oil
1 small onion, finely chopped
1 clove of garlic, crushed
110g/4oz chestnut mushrooms, or button
    mushrooms, finely chopped
150ml/5fl oz vegetable stock (see p.172)
1 bay leaf
salt and freshly ground black pepper

FOR THE SAUCE:

1 egg yolk
1 teaspoon Dijon mustard (with truffle*,
    optional)
150ml/5fl oz sunflower oil, warmed
salt and freshly ground white pepper
1 tablespoon Greek yoghurt

1. Prepare the artichokes: mark around the stalk of each artichoke with a sharp knife, as near to the base as possible. Twist and pull off the stalk. Trim the base of the artichokes so they sit flat.

2. Trim off the tips of the tough, outer leaves with a pair of scissors. Wash the artichokes thoroughly.

3. Bring a large saucepan of water to the boil. Add the lemon juice, oil and salt. Add the artichokes, cover and cook for 45 minutes or until an outside leaf pulls away easily. Remove the artichokes from the saucepan and drain upside down.

4. Meanwhile, make the duxelle: heat the oil

in a small saucepan, add the onion and garlic, and cook over a low heat until soft and transparent. Add the mushrooms, stock and bay leaf, and bring to the boil. Reduce the heat and simmer until all the liquid has evaporated. Season to taste. Remove the bay leaf.

5. Prise open the middle leaves of the artichokes and remove the central cluster of purple leaves. Scrape out the fibrous choke with a teaspoon and discard. Take care not to damage the heart underneath the choke. Keep the artichokes warm.

6. Make the sauce: put the egg yolk, mustard, 1 teaspoon of the oil and a pinch of salt into a small bowl and beat well with a wooden spoon.

7. Half-fill a roasting tin with water and put over a gentle heat. Stand the bowl in the water and cook, beating the mixture with a wooden spoon, until the sauce has thickened to the consistency of single cream. Do not allow the surrounding water to boil.

8. Add the remaining oil, drop by drop to begin with, beating all the time. The mixture should be very thick by the time half the oil is added.

9. Beat in a little water to loosen the mixture. Continue to add the oil more quickly now. If the mixture becomes difficult to beat add a few more drops of water. Once all the oil is added, season to taste and stir in the Greek yoghurt.

10. To serve: put one artichoke on to each of four plates. Divide the duxelle between the hollowed out artichokes and pour in a little of the warm sauce. Hand the rest of the sauce separately in a warm dish.

NOTE:
* *Moutarde aromatisée à la truffe* can be bought at good delicatessens.

NEW WORLD FULL-BODIED RED

♦ ♦

Gem Squash with Avocado and Black Olives

SERVES 4

4 gem squash, trimmed
2 large, ripe avocados
20 black olives, pitted
4 tablespoons extra virgin olive oil
1 teaspoon French mustard
1 tablespoon white wine vinegar
anchovy essence, to taste (optional)
salt and freshly ground black pepper

1. Bring a large saucepan of salted water to the boil. Prick the squash several times and boil for 20–30 minutes, or until the stalk end gives a little. Transfer the squash to a bowl of very cold water to prevent further cooking.

2. Meanwhile, peel the avocados, remove the stones, cut into 1cm/½ inch cubes and put into a bowl. Add the black olives, olive oil, mustard, vinegar and anchovy essence, if used, and seasoning to taste.

3. Drain the squash and pat dry with paper towels. Cut each squash in half with a serrated knife. Carefully remove the seeds with a metal spoon. Fill the cavities of the squash with the avocado and black olive mixture.

4. Put two halves on to each of four plates and serve immediately.

MEDIUM-BODIED RED

Barley Galettes with Port Salut Cheese

SERVES 4

2 tablespoons olive oil

1 onion, finely diced

140g/5oz pearl barley

30g/1oz dried mushrooms, soaked in 150ml/
    5fl oz hot water for 15–20 minutes

425ml/15fl oz vegetable stock (see p. 172)

salt and freshly ground black pepper

3 tablespoons finely chopped herbs, e.g. parsley
    and oregano

110g/4oz Port Salut cheese, coarsely grated

1 egg, beaten

TO SERVE:

robust mushroom sauce (see p. 121)

1. Heat the olive oil in a saucepan and cook the onion gently until soft and transparent. Do not allow it to go brown.

2. Add the pearl barley, stir and remove from the heat.

3. Remove the dried mushrooms with a slotted spoon and slice them thinly. Strain the liquid through a J-cloth or muslin. Add the mushrooms, mushroom liquid and vegetable stock to the barley mixture. Return to the heat and bring to the boil. Half cover with a lid and simmer gently, stirring occasionally, for 10–15 minutes or until the barley is soft. It may be necessary either to add extra liquid or to increase the heat and boil off any excess liquid. Season to taste and allow to cool.

4. Preheat the oven to 200°C/400°F/gas mark 6.

5. Add the herbs, cheese and beaten egg to the barley mixture and mix thoroughly. Adjust the seasoning if necessary.

6. Divide the mixture into four. Lightly grease a baking sheet. Put a 9cm/3½ inch pastry cutter on the baking sheet, half fill it with some of the barley mixture, pressing down firmly with a teaspoon. Fill up the 'mould' with more of the mixture and press down again. Remove the cutter and make three more galettes.

7. Put the galettes on the middle shelf of the oven and bake for 15–20 minutes or until firm to the touch.

8. Serve immediately with the robust mushroom sauce.

NOTE:

* The galettes can be frozen once cooked; they reheat well. Open-freeze, then pack in a freezer-proof container. Heat from frozen for 15–20 minutes in a moderate oven.

MEDIUM- TO FULL-BODIED WHITE

WILD AND FIELD MUSHROOM TIMBALES WITH STAR ANISE SAUCE

CHICORY TATIN

HARLEQUIN TERRINE

Tagine of Aubergines, Dates and Almonds with Spiced Dumplings

Vegetable Feuilletées with Tarragon Beurre Blanc

CHESTNUT CROWN ROAST

Parsley and Garlic Pizza

WILD MUSHROOM SAUSAGES

Baked Fennel with Sun-dried Tomatoes and Goats' Cheese

SERVES 4

4 even-sized bulbs of fennel
30g/1oz butter
1½ teaspoons chopped parsley
juice of 1 lemon
1 tablespoon olive oil
4 tablespoons water
1 onion, finely diced
6 whole sun-dried tomatoes, soaked in boiling
    water for 10 minutes*
30g/1oz pine nuts
140g/5oz goats' cheese log e.g. Roubillac
salt and freshly ground black pepper

1. Preheat the oven to 180°C/350°F/gas mark 4.
2. Discard any damaged outside leaves from the fennel and cut the bulb neatly in half. Carefully remove some of the dense core.
3. Put the fennel halves into an ovenproof dish, cut side uppermost. Melt the butter in a saucepan, add the parsley and lemon juice. Pour over the fennel, add the water and cover tightly with a lid or foil. Bake for about 1 hour or until cooked.
4. Heat the oil in a small saucepan, and cook the onion over a gentle heat until soft and transparent. Slice the sun-dried tomatoes finely and mix with the pine nuts, goats' cheese and onion.
5. Increase the oven temperature to 200°C/400°F/gas mark 6.
6. Take the fennel out of the oven, remove the foil and pile the cheese mixture on top. Return to the oven for 15–20 minutes.
7. Serve immediately.

NOTE:
* There is no need to soak sun-dried tomatoes that have been packed in oil.

FULL-BODIED WHITE

♦ ♦

Egg and Caper Florentine

SERVES 4

15g/½oz butter
1kg/2lb fresh spinach, cooked and chopped (see
    p. 182)
salt and freshly ground black pepper
freshly ground nutmeg
290ml/10fl oz fresh tomato sauce (see p. 117)
2 tablespoons capers, preferably dry-packed,
    rinsed and roughly chopped
8 eggs, poached or hard-boiled
290ml/10fl oz mornay sauce (see p. 116)
1 tablespoon Cheddar cheese, grated
1 tablespoon dried white breadcrumbs

1. Preheat the oven to 180°C/350°F/gas mark 4.
2. Melt the butter in a sauté pan, add the spinach, mix and heat thoroughly. Season to taste with the salt, pepper and nutmeg. Spread the spinach in the bottom of a medium-sized ovenproof dish. Pour over the tomato sauce.
3. Sprinkle with the capers.

4. Place the eggs on top of the capers. (If using hard-boiled eggs, cut them in half lengthways and lay them cut side down.)
5. Heat the mornay sauce and pour evenly over the eggs. Sprinkle with the cheese and breadcrumbs.
6. Bake for 15 minutes, or until bubbling and hot. Grill to brown the top, if necessary.

MEDIUM DRY WHITE

♦ ♦

Tagine of Aubergines, Dates and Almonds with Spiced Dumplings

If a tagine (an earthenware cooking pot with a conical lid) is not available, this recipe can just as easily be cooked in a standard casserole.

SERVES 4

4 large aubergines, cut into large chunks
salt
5 tablespoons groundnut oil
2 large onions, cut into chunks
4 wide strips of lemon zest
2 large cloves of garlic, crushed
2 tablespoons ground turmeric
1 tablespoon ground cinnamon
1 × 800g/28oz can of tomatoes
2 tablespoons chopped coriander
juice of ½ lemon
110g/4oz cooked chick peas or 55g/2oz raw
  chick peas, soaked and cooked
200g/7oz fresh dates, stoned and cut into
  quarters lengthways
55g/2oz blanched almonds, toasted
salt and freshly ground black pepper

FOR THE DUMPLINGS:
110g/4oz self-raising flour
1 tablespoon ground mixed spice
1 tablespoon cayenne pepper
pinch of chilli powder
salt and freshly ground black pepper
30g/1oz hard butter, grated
about 5 tablespoons water

1. Put the aubergine chunks into a colander, sprinkle with salt and toss. Leave to disgorge their juices for 30 minutes. Rinse well and drain.
2. Heat the oil in a flame-proof tagine or earthenware casserole, or a large, thick-bottomed pan, add the onions and lemon zest and cook over a low heat for 10 minutes or until the onions are soft and transparent. Add the garlic, turmeric and cinnamon. Turn up the heat a little and fry until the onions and spices begin to brown.
3. Stir in the aubergine chunks, and fry until brown. Lower the heat, add the whole of the contents of the can of tomatoes, the coriander and lemon juice, and simmer for 20 minutes, stirring now and again to prevent sticking.
4. Meanwhile make the dumplings: put all the ingredients into a bowl and mix well. Stir in enough water to make a soft dough. Turn the dough onto a floured surface,

divide into eight, and shape into balls using floured hands.

5. Add the chick peas, dates and almonds to the aubergine mixture; it should not be too dry. Add some water if necessary. Season to taste.

6. Put the dumplings on top and spoon over some of the juices. Cover and cook for 15–20 minutes until the dumplings have doubled in size.

7. Serve straight from the casserole.

NOTE:
* If the tagine or casserole is more than two-thirds full, cover it loosely with foil when cooking the dumplings so they will have room to rise.

FULL-BODIED RED

◆ ◆

Aubergine, Kohl rabi and Black Olive Ragout

SERVES 4
2 large aubergines, diced
salt
1 tablespoon olive oil
2 red onions, finely chopped
1 large clove of garlic, crushed
2 medium purple kohl rabi, peeled and diced
1 quantity of fresh tomato sauce (see p. 117)

20 black olives, pitted
salt and fresly ground black pepper

1. Put the aubergines in a colander and sprinkle with salt. Toss and leave for 30 minutes to disgorge their juices. Rinse the aubergines and dry thoroughly with paper towels.

2. Heat the oil in a large saucepan, add the onions and garlic and cook over a gentle heat until soft but not browned.

3. Add the kohl rabi, aubergine and tomato sauce. Cover and simmer gently for about 20 minutes, or until the vegetables are tender. Add the olives and season to taste.

ITALIAN RED

◆ ◆

Black Bean Chilli

SERVES 4
225g/8oz black beans, soaked overnight
2 tablespoons corn oil
1 large onion, coarsely chopped
4 cloves of garlic, crushed
1 tablespoon freshly ground cumin

½ teaspoon chilli powder
½ teaspoon cayenne pepper
2 green peppers, quartered, seeded and chopped
2 fresh green chillies, halved, seeded and finely chopped
1 × 800g/28oz can of tomatoes
1 tablespoon tomato purée
1 tablespoon molasses

2 tablespoons chopped coriander leaves
grated zest and juice of 1 lime
salt and freshly ground black pepper

TO SERVE:
boiled rice or tortillas

1. Drain and rinse the beans under running water. Put into a saucepan and cover with water (do not add salt as this toughens the skins, thereby reducing the beans' ability to absorb water). Bring to the boil, and continue boiling for 10 minutes before reducing the heat to a simmer. Cook gently for 1 hour. Skim the water with a slotted spoon if necessary. Drain the beans.
2. Heat the oil in a large saucepan, add the onion and fry over a high heat until brown. Add the garlic, cumin, chilli powder and cayenne pepper and fry for 1 minute.
3. Add the peppers, chilli, can of tomatoes, tomato purée, molasses and beans, mix well with a wooden spoon, scraping up the sediment from the bottom of the saucepan. Simmer very gently for about 40 minutes or until the beans have absorbed most of the liquid and the chilli is thick. Stir occasionally to prevent sticking.
4. Add the coriander, lime zest and juice and season to taste.
5. Serve with boiled rice or tortillas.

CHILEAN CABERNET SAUVIGNON
RIOJA

♦ ♦

Mustard and Molasses Bean Hotpot

This hotpot is even better if made the day before because the flavours will have time to develop.

SERVES 4
110g/4oz salt
4 Spanish onions, peeled and left whole
85g/3oz black-eyed beans, soaked overnight
110g/4oz butter beans, soaked overnight
85g/3oz black kidney beans, soaked overnight
85g/3oz red kidney beans, soaked overnight
2 tablespoons oil
1 × 800g/28oz can of chopped tomatoes
2 tablespoons English mustard powder
3 tablespoons molasses or black treacle
salt and freshly ground black pepper
1 tablespoon chopped oregano

TO SERVE:
bread or tortillas or boiled rice

1. Make a brine solution in a large bowl by mixing the salt with enough water to cover the onions. Add the onions and soak overnight.
2. Drain the beans and onions and rinse under running cold water.
3. Put all the beans into a large saucepan, cover with cold water and bring to the boil (do not salt the water as this toughens the skins, thereby reducing the beans' ability to absorb water). Boil for 10 minutes,* removing the scum with a slotted spoon. Reduce the heat and simmer very gently for

a further 25 minutes until the beans are nearly soft but not cooked. Remove from the heat and drain.

4. Heat the oil gently in a flameproof casserole large enough to hold the onions tightly. Add the onions and turn to coat them with oil. Add the beans to cover the onions.

5. Drain the tomatoes in a sieve over a small bowl. Add the tomatoes to the casserole, spreading them evenly over the beans. Add the mustard and molasses or black treacle to the strained tomato juice, mix and pour over the casserole. Season with salt and pepper and add the oregano.

6. Cover and simmer over a low heat for about 2 hours or until the onions are cooked. The bean sauce should be reduced and thick. If the sauce is too thin, boil until reduced to the desired consistency. Season to taste.

6. Serve with plenty of bread to mop up the juices, or with tortillas or rice.

NOTES:
* Red kidney beans must be boiled for at least 10 minutes before reducing the water to a simmer. This will destroy the toxins present in the skin.
* If the hotpot is made a day in advance, reheat it gently over a low heat or in a preheated moderate oven for 20–25 minutes until the onions are hot right through.

CHILEAN CABERNET SAUVIGNON
ANY NEW WORLD RED

SALADS

Mung Bean and Toasted Pumpkin Seed Salad
Puy Lentils with Feta Cheese
Chick Pea, Couscous and Toasted Seaweed Salad
Wide-rolled Pasta, Rocket and Courgette Salad
Wild Rice and Roast Brazil Nut Salad
Wild Rice and Mini Patty Pan Squash Salad
Potato, Chilli and Coconut Salad
Sun-dried and Plum Tomato Salad
Warm Bitter Salad
Green Cauliflower, Sun-dried Tomato and Walnut Salad
Oriental Cucumber Salad
Arranged All Red Salad
Flat-leaf Parsley Salad

Mung Bean and Toasted Pumpkin Seed Salad

SERVES 4

*170g/6oz mung beans, soaked for 2 hours and
    drained*

720ml/1¼ pints vegetable stock (see p. 172)

225g/8oz brown rice

2 tablespoons pumpkin seeds

6–8 spring onions, sliced

*3 tablespoons fresh herbs, e.g. parsley, mint,
    basil, thyme, finely chopped*

FOR THE DRESSING:

2 tablespoons white wine vinegar

2 tablespoons medium dry sherry

1 tablespoon light soy sauce

1 clove of garlic, very finely crushed

4 tablespoons sesame oil

*2.5cm/1 inch piece fresh ginger, peeled and
    grated (optional)*

1. Put the mung beans in a medium-sized saucepan and cover with cold water. Do not add salt (this toughens the outer skin so the beans absorb the water less quickly). Bring to the boil, lower the heat and simmer gently for 35–40 minutes until tender. If necessary, add more water. Drain and refresh under running cold water. Drain again and put to one side.
2. Pour the vegetable stock into a large saucepan and bring to the boil. Add the rice, reduce the heat, cover and simmer for 35–40 minutes, or until just cooked. Drain, and spread out on a tray to cool. Fork through to separate the grains.
3. Heat a sauté pan over a medium high heat without any oil. When it is very hot add the pumpkin seeds and cook until they begin to pop and just turn brown. Shake the pan so they brown evenly. Remove from the heat and turn out on to a cold plate to prevent further cooking. Leave until cold.
4. Make the dressing: put the ingredients into a jar and shake well to mix.
5. Put the beans, rice, spring onions, herbs and dressing into a bowl and mix together.
6. Stir in the pumpkin seeds just before serving.

◆ ◆

Puy Lentils with Feta Cheese

It is not necessary to soak lentils. However, it does cut down on the cooking time, so, if required, soak them for 1 hour.

SERVES 4

225g/8oz Puy lentils

1 yellow pepper

1 red pepper

grated zest of 1 lemon

55g/2oz feta cheese, crumbled finely

1 quantity of French dressing (see p. 114)

1. Rinse the lentils under running cold water. Put them into a saucepan, cover with water and bring them to the boil. Reduce the heat and cook slowly for about

30 minutes or until 'al dente' (firm to the bite). Remove from the heat, drain and rinse under running cold water. Drain in a sieve.

2. Cut the peppers into four and remove the stalks, seeds and pithy white parts. Cut the quarters into narrow strips and the strips into dice the same size as the lentils.

3. Mix the ingredients together in a large bowl and toss in the French dressing.

♦ ♦

Chick Pea, Couscous and Toasted Seaweed Salad

SERVES 4

140g/5oz chick peas*, soaked overnight

140g/5oz couscous

7g/¼oz dried seaweed, cut into 5mm/¼ inch strips

FOR THE MARINADE:

2.5cm/1 inch piece fresh ginger, peeled and grated

2 tablespoons white wine vinegar

2 tablespoons dry sherry

1 tablespoon light soy sauce

1 clove of garlic, crushed

4 tablespoons sesame oil

1 teaspoon clear honey

1. Drain the chick peas. Cook them in boiling water for 25–30 minutes or until cooked but firm to the bite. Remove from the heat, drain and then rinse under running cold water to stop the cooking. Drain in a colander.

2. Put the couscous into a large bowl and add just enough cold water to cover. Leave to soak for 5 minutes. Drain, if necessary, and squeeze dry.

3. Make the marinade: mix the ingredients in the same large bowl. Return the couscous to the bowl and leave to soak up the marinade for about 1 hour, forking through occasionally to break up any lumps.

4. Add the chick peas and leave for another hour. All the marinade should be absorbed.

5. Meanwhile, preheat the grill. Flash the seaweed under the grill for about 1 minute or until just brown.

6. Stir the seaweed into the salad just before serving.

NOTE:

* A 400g/14oz can of chick peas can be used instead; drain them before using.

Wide-rolled Pasta, Rocket and Courgette Salad

SERVES 4–6

¼ *quantity of fresh pasta (see p. 177)*
225g/8oz rocket
1 bunch of flat leaf parsley
1 quantity of French dressing (see p. 114)
6 small, thin yellow courgettes
oil for frying
seasoned flour
a few thyme leaves
freshly ground black pepper

TO GARNISH (OPTIONAL):
3 cloves of roast garlic per head (see p. 51)

1. Cut the ball of pasta into four pieces. Using the hands, roll the pasta into four pencil-thin sausage shapes. Pinch off 2.5cm/1 inch lengths. Using a pasta machine from setting 1 through to setting 6, flatten the lengths into rough rectangular shapes. If no pasta machine is available, use a rolling pin and roll out as thinly as possible to make rectangles approximately 5cm/2 inches long. The more irregular the edges, the more interesting the pasta shape. Leave to one side on silicone paper.*

2. Bring a large saucepan of salted water to the boil and drop in the pasta, piece by piece, gently stirring to prevent sticking. Reduce the heat to a rolling boil and cook for 3–5 minutes or until firm to the bite. Remove the pasta with a slotted spoon, rinse, then leave in a bowl of very cold water.

WIDE-ROLLED PASTA

3. Wash and spin-dry the rocket and sprigs of parsley.

4. Cut the courgettes into 2.5cm/1 inch high 'drums'. Pour 5cm/2 inches oil into a deep saucepan or wok and heat over a moderately high heat. Toss the courgettes in the seasoned flour and fry for 5–8 minutes or until golden brown. Remove with a slotted spoon and drain on paper towels.

5. Reheat the pasta in boiling water for 1 minute, drain and toss in half of the French dressing while still warm. It will absorb a lot of French dressing. Toss the rocket, parsley and courgettes in a bowl with the remaining French dressing.

6. To assemble: gently toss the pasta and the rest of the salad together and arrange on four serving plates. Do not allow the ingredients to lie flat, but twist the pasta and separate out the leaves to make an attractive arrangement. Scatter with thyme leaves and coarsely ground black pepper.

7. Garnish with the roast garlic cloves if using.

8. Serve immediately.

NOTE:
* Greaseproof paper, even if oiled, is not a suitable alternative to silicone paper.

◆ ◆

Wild Rice and Roast Brazil Nut Salad

Wild rice is not really rice at all, but the seed of an aquatic grass. Some cooks say that to bring out its fullest flavour it needs to be cooked until the grains have burst open. We feel that this spoils the look, and that it should be cooked, over a low heat, until soft and only a few grains have burst. It is a matter of choice.

SERVES 4
200g/7oz Brazil nuts
salt
140g/5oz wild rice, soaked and drained*
1 bulb of fennel
1 small red onion, finely diced

2 tablespoons currants, soaked in the juice of 1 orange
1 Granny Smith apple, skin on, cored and diced

FOR THE DRESSING:
2 teaspoons white wine vinegar
2 teaspoons lemon juice
5 tablespoons olive oil
pinch of sugar
grated zest of 1 orange
1 tablespoon finely chopped parsley
1 tablespoon finely chopped chervil
½ teaspoon fennel seeds

1. Preheat the oven to 190°C/375°F/gas mark 5.

2. Put the Brazil nuts on to a baking sheet and place on the middle shelf of the oven for 10 minutes, or until evenly brown. Remove, allow to cool a little and then chop into large pieces.

3. Boil some salted water in a saucepan, tip in the rice, reduce the heat and cook gently

for 8–10 minutes or until soft and some of the grains have burst open. Drain and put into a large bowl.

4. Make the dressing: whisk the dressing ingredients in a bowl or in a blender. Pour over the rice whilst the rice is still warm.

5. Trim the shoots of the fennel and remove any damaged leaves. Cut into small dice, put into a saucepan and pour on enough boiling water to cover. Leave to stand for 5 minutes.

Drain and add to the rice. Mix in the red onion.

6. Before serving, add the currants, apple and Brazil nuts and toss well.

NOTE:

* By soaking rice for a minimum of 2 hours, preferably overnight, the cooking time is greatly reduced.

♦ ♦

Wild Rice and Mini Patty Pan Squash Salad

This salad can be served either warm as a vegetable dish, or cold as a salad.

SERVES 4

225g/8oz wild rice, rinsed and soaked overnight (see above)

2 tablespoons olive oil

2 tablespoons light soy sauce

2 teaspoons lemon juice

12 mini yellow patty pan squash, wiped

1 teaspoon chopped rosemary

freshly ground black pepper

TO GARNISH:

sprigs of rosemary, flowering if possible

1. Bring a large saucepan of salted water to the boil. Drain the rice and add to the pan, reduce the heat and cook gently for 8–10 minutes or until soft and some of the grains have burst open. Drain well in a sieve, then tip into a large bowl.

2. Mix the oil, soy sauce and lemon juice to taste and pour over the rice while it is still warm.

3. Bring another large saucepan of salted water to the boil, add the squash and cook for 5–8 minutes or until soft but firm. Put into a bowl of cold water to stop further cooking. Drain on paper towels.

4. Mix the rice and squash, stir in the rosemary and season with pepper to taste. Garnish with rosemary sprigs.

NOTE:

* If time does not allow the rice to be soaked, cook it gently for about 20–25 minutes.

Potato, Chilli and Coconut Salad

SERVES 6

675g/1½ lb small new potatoes, scraped
salt
290ml/10fl oz coconut milk
2–3 bay leaves
1 lime leaf (optional)
1 cinnamon stick, broken into three
1 small green chilli

1. Boil the potatoes in salted water for 10–15 minutes, or until just cooked. Drain.
2. Return the potatoes to a clean saucepan and add the coconut milk, bay leaves, lime leaf (if using), cinnamon sticks and salt. Bring to the boil and simmer for about 20 minutes until the milk has been absorbed by the potatoes.
3. Cut open the chilli under running water, or wearing rubber gloves. Discard the seeds and the stem, and chop the flesh very finely.
4. Add the chilli to the potatoes, transfer to a serving dish and allow to cool.

◆ ◆

Sun-dried and Plum Tomato Salad

SERVES 4

4 plum tomatoes, peeled and seeded
8 whole sun-dried tomatoes packed in oil, drained
1 small red pepper, grilled, peeled, seeded and quartered (see p. 181)
20 capers, preferably dry-packed

FOR THE DRESSING:
3 tablespoons olive oil

freshly ground black pepper
pinch of sugar

TO SERVE:
oakleaf lettuce, torn into small pieces

1. Cut both types of tomato and the peppers into strips, making them as similar in size as possible. Put them into a bowl and add the capers.
2. Make the dressing: mix the ingredients in a screw-top jar and shake well.
3. Pour the dressing over the salad ingredients and leave for about 1 hour to allow the flavours to develop.
4. Serve with the oakleaf lettuce.

Warm Bitter Salad

SERVES 4

2 heads white chicory
2 radicchio
2 tablespoons extra virgin olive oil
450g/1lb small young spinach leaves, thin stalks
  left on
salt and freshly ground black pepper
340g/12oz crotins (small hard goats' cheese)

1. Discard any damaged leaves from the chicory and radicchio. Separate out the rest, and leave them whole.
2. Heat 1 tablespoon of the oil in a sauté pan, add the chicory leaves, a few at a time, and cook until just beginning to soften. Remove from the pan and keep warm.
3. Heat the remaining oil in the pan and add the radicchio leaves, again, a few at a time. Cook until they begin to wilt but there are still some red streaks left in the leaves. Remove and keep warm.
4. Put the spinach into the pan, only adding more oil if necessary, and stir-fry until the leaves have wilted and the spinach is bright green. Season to taste.
5. Arrange the chicory in a fan on to four plates. Partially cover with three or four radicchio leaves, then place a layer of the spinach in the centre.
6. Crumble over the goats' cheese and serve immediately.

♦ ♦

Green Cauliflower, Sun-dried Tomato and Walnut Salad

SERVES 4

FOR THE SALAD:

1 green cauliflower, washed, broken into very
  small florets and lightly cooked
8 large halves of sun-dried tomatoes packed in
  oil, drained and sliced
1 red pepper, grilled, peeled (see p. 181) and cut
  into fine slivers
1 green pepper, grilled, peeled (see p. 181) and
  cut into fine slivers
55g/2oz green walnuts*, broken into pieces
1 small shallot, very finely sliced

FOR THE DRESSING:

2 tablespoons walnut oil
1 tablespoon olive oil
2 tablespoons white wine vinegar
salt and freshly ground black pepper
1 tablespoon toasted black mustard seeds**

1. Put all the salad ingredients into a bowl.
2. Make the dressing: mix the ingredients, except the mustard seeds, in a screw-top jar, add to the salad and toss until coated.
3. Sprinkle with mustard seeds just before serving.

NOTES:

* Green walnuts are fresh or 'wet'.
** To toast or dry-roast seeds and spices, whole or ground, heat a thick-bottomed sauté pan over a moderately high heat. When the pan is very hot, add the seeds or spices and cook until they start to darken and whole ones jump about. Remove from the heat, tip the seeds or spices on to a plate and spread them out to cool them down.

Oriental Cucumber Salad

SERVES 4–6

2 cucumbers, peeled, seeded and cut into 1cm/
    ½ inch wide slices
55g/2oz beansprouts, picked over

FOR THE DRESSING:

2 teaspoons grated fresh ginger
2 tablespoons white wine vinegar
2 tablespoons groundnut oil
1 tablespoon sesame oil
1 teaspoon horseradish cream
1 tablespoon light soy sauce
1 teaspoon light soft brown sugar
1 tablespoon finely chopped coriander leaves

1. Make the dressing: put the ingredients into a bowl and mix well.
2. Put the cucumber pieces into a bowl and pour over the dressing. Just before serving toss in the beansprouts.

◆ ◆

Arranged All Red Salad

Some of the ingredients in this salad are cooked and will need to be prepared in advance. Though the quantities given are for a light main course salad, it serves six as an elegant first course (buy one extra head of red chicory). We do not think it is necessary to degorge the aubergines if they are young.

SERVES 4

1 mini red cabbage, or 1 large red cabbage,
    outside leaves removed to reduce its size
5 tablespoons olive oil, plus extra for brushing
juice of 1 small lemon
2 small aubergines
2 heads of red chicory
4 small beetroot, cooked and diced
110g/4oz red radishes, cut into thin matchsticks

FOR THE DRESSING:

150ml/5fl oz soured cream or Greek yoghurt
½ quantity mayonnaise (see p. 114)
salt and freshly ground white pepper

1. Remove any damaged outside leaves from the cabbage, trim the stalk and cut the cabbage into four quarters. Cut each quarter into four wedges, taking care that each piece is held together by the stalk.
2. Put the cabbage into a wide-bottomed sauté pan with two tablespoons of the olive oil, the lemon juice and enough salted water to just cover. Bring to the boil, then reduce the heat, cover and simmer for 10–15 minutes. Remove the lid and continue cooking until the water has almost evaporated and the cabbage is soft and glistening with oil. Remove from the heat and leave to cool in the pan. (If the cabbage is cooked before the water has evaporated, remove it to a plate with a slotted spoon, and boil the liquid until reduced to 2 tablespoons. Pour over the cooling cabbage.)
3. Meanwhile, cut four 2.5cm/1 inch thick slices of skin from the aubergines, leaving a rectangle of flesh for another recipe (see aubergine salad p. 41).
4. Heat the remaining oil in a sauté pan and

add the aubergine slices, cut side down, cover and fry gently for about 10–15 minutes or until soft and very brown but not burnt. Do not turn the aubergines over. Remove from the pan, and when cool enough to handle, cut crossways into 1cm/½ inch strips with a sharp knife.

5. Make the dressing: mix the soured cream or yoghurt and the mayonnaise in a bowl. Season to taste.

6. Assemble the salad: brush the red chicory leaves with oil and arrange on four plates in a fan, root end towards the middle. Repeat the pattern with a few pieces of red cabbage. Mix the beetroot with the dressing and spoon a heap on to the middle of the salad. Scatter over the radish matchsticks and the aubergine strips.

7. Serve immediately.

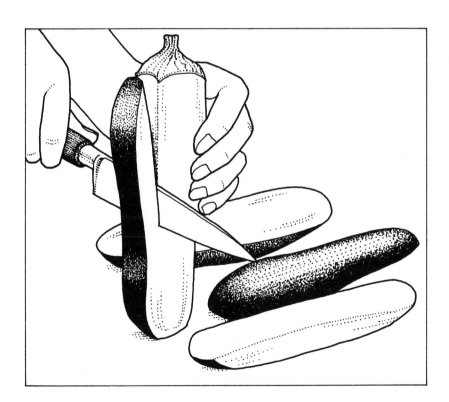

ARRANGED ALL RED SALAD

Flat-leaf Parsley Salad

This sensational salad was demonstrated to us by Carla Tomasi who came to the school to help promote non-intensively farmed salmon. The salmon was declared delicious by those who tasted it, but the salad eclipsed the fish in our opinion!

SERVES 4

6 tablespoons basil-infused olive oil*
6–8 large cloves of garlic, sliced
2 large bunches flat-leaf parsley
225g/8oz sun-dried tomatoes packed in oil, drained and chopped
110g/4oz capers, preferably dry-packed, rinsed **
fine strips of zest from 1 lemon

1. Heat 2 tablespoons of the basil olive oil in a sauté pan and gently fry the garlic until pale golden brown. Remove the garlic from the pan with a slotted spoon, drain on paper towels and leave to cool. Reserve the oil.

2. Pick off the leafy sprigs from the parsley stalks and rinse under cold water. Spin dry and put into a salad bowl.

3. Mix the sun-dried tomatoes, capers and lemon zest in a bowl with enough basil-infused oil to cover the mixture.

4. Just before serving, combine the parsley leaves and the sun-dried tomato mixture thoroughly and scatter with the crisp slices of garlic.

5. Serve immediately.

NOTES:

* To infuse oil with basil, put two sprigs of basil in a bottle of virgin olive oil and leave for at least a week. Use within two months unless kept in a refrigerator, where it will keep indefinitely (see p. 236).

** Capers dry-packed in sea salt, rather than vinegar or brine, are infinitely superior in flavour and should be used in this recipe. They are easily obtained in good delicatessens or from Taylor and Lake of Oxford (see p. 250 for mail order addresses).

SAUCES

French Dressing
Tomato Vinaigrette
Mayonnaise
Roast Garlic Mayonnaise
Béchamel Sauce
Mornay Sauce
Sage Velouté Sauce
Tarragon Beurre Blanc
Fresh Tomato Sauce
Easy Tomato Sauce
Roast Tomato Sauce
Pesto
Herb Pesto
Parsley Pesto
Watercress Sauce
Plum and Red Onion Confit
Robust Mushroom Sauce
Avocado, Tomato and Chilli Salsa
Red Ratatouille Dressing
Red and Green Pepper Salsa
Yellow Pepper Sauce
Red and Yellow Pepper Relish
Minted Yoghurt
Peanut and Coriander Sauce
Chilli, Lime Leaf and Coconut Sauce
Lime and Szechuan Peppercorn Sauce
Dipping Sauce
Black Bean Sauce

French Dressing

MAKES ABOUT 110ml/4fl oz
6 *tablespoons olive oil*
2 *tablespoons wine vinegar*
salt and freshly ground black pepper

1. Put all the ingredients into a screw-top jar. Before using shake until well emulsified.

NOTES:
* This dressing can be flavoured with crushed garlic, mustard, a pinch of sugar, chopped fresh herbs etc. as desired.
** If kept in the refrigerator, the dressing will form an emulsion more easily when whisked or shaken, and has a slightly thicker consistency.

◆ ◆

Tomato Vinaigrette

SERVES 4
1 *tomato, chopped*
4 *tablespoons oil*
1 *tablespoon water*
1 *tablespoon tarragon vinegar*

small pinch of English mustard powder
small pinch of sugar

1. Mix all the ingredients in a blender until well emulsified.
2. Push the dressing through a sieve. If the dressing looks as though it might separate add a little very cold water.

◆ ◆

Mayonnaise

MAKES ABOUT 290ml/10fl oz
2 *egg yolks*
salt and freshly ground black pepper
1 *teaspoon Dijon mustard*
290ml/10fl oz olive oil, or 150ml/5fl oz each
   olive oil and salad oil
squeeze of lemon juice
1 *tablespoon wine vinegar*

1. Put the yolks into a bowl with a pinch of salt and the mustard and beat well with a wooden spoon.

2. Add the oil, literally drop by drop, beating all the time. The mixture should be very thick by the time half the oil is added.
3. Beat in the lemon juice.
4. Resume pouring in the oil, going rather more confidently now, but alternating the dribbles of oil with small quantities of vinegar.
5. Add salt and pepper to taste.

NOTE:
* If the mixture curdles, another egg yolk should be beaten in a separate bowl, and the curdled mixture beaten drop by drop into it.

Roast Garlic Mayonnaise

This is delicious, especially when eaten with fresh corn-on-the-cob.

MAKES ABOUT 290ml/10fl oz
2 heads of garlic, roasted (see p. 51)
2 egg yolks
2 anchovy fillets, mashed (optional)
2–3 teaspoons lemon juice
290ml/10fl oz virgin olive oil
salt and freshly ground white pepper

1. Squeeze the garlic from the cloves into a bowl and mash with a fork.
2. Add the egg yolks, the anchovy, if using, and 1 teaspoon of the lemon juice, and beat hard.
3. Add the olive oil, drop by drop, beating well all the time, until half the oil has been added. Beat in another 1 teaspoon lemon juice.
4. Continue trickling in the rest of the oil, going rather more confidently now. The mixture should have a loose, dropping consistency by the end. Season to taste. Add more lemon juice if required.

NOTE:
* Chopped black olives, parsley, capers, gherkins or fresh herbs make interesting additions.

♦ ♦

Béchamel Sauce

MAKES ABOUT 290ml/10fl oz
290ml/10fl oz creamy milk
slice of onion
blade of mace
few fresh parsley stalks
4 peppercorns
1 bay leaf
30g/1oz butter
20g/¾oz plain flour
salt and freshly ground white pepper

1. Put the milk with the onion, mace, parsley, peppercorns and bay leaf into a saucepan and bring slowly to simmering point.
2. Lower the heat and allow the flavours to infuse for about 8–10 minutes.
3. Melt 20g/¾oz of butter in a thick saucepan, stir in the flour and stir over heat for 1 minute.
4. Remove from the heat. Slowly strain in the infused milk, mixing well.
5. Return the pan to the heat and stir or whisk continuously until boiling. Add the remaining butter and beat very well (this will help to make the sauce shiny).
6. Simmer, stirring well, for 3 minutes.
7. Season to taste.

NOTE:
* To make a professionally shiny béchamel sauce pass through a tammy strainer before use or mix in a blender.

Mornay Sauce (Cheese Sauce)

MAKES ABOUT 290ml/10fl oz

20g/¾ oz butter
20g/¾ oz plain flour
pinch of dry English mustard
pinch of cayenne pepper
290ml/10fl oz milk
55g/2oz Gruyère or mature Cheddar cheese,
  grated
15g/½ oz Parmesan cheese, freshly grated
salt and freshly ground black pepper

1. Melt the butter in a saucepan and stir in the flour, mustard and cayenne pepper. Cook, stirring, for 1 minute.
2. Remove from the heat and stir in the milk.
3. Return the pan to the heat and stir until boiling. Simmer, stirring, for 2 minutes.
4. Add the cheeses and mix well, but do not allow to boil.
5. Season with salt and pepper to taste.

◆ ◆

Sage Velouté Sauce

MAKES ABOUT 290ml/10 fl oz

15g/½ oz fresh sage leaves
15g/½ oz butter
15g/½ oz plain flour
290ml/10fl oz vegetable stock (see p. 172)
4 tablespoons Noilly Prat or dry white vermouth
salt and freshly ground black pepper
1 tablespoon fromage frais

1. Put the sage into a small saucepan of boiling water. Bring the water back to the boil. Remove from the heat, drain and refresh the sage under running cold water. Drain and pat dry with paper towels. Chop finely.

2. Melt the butter in a small saucepan, add the flour and mix to a smooth paste. Cook for 1 minute.
3. Slowly pour in the vegetable stock and Noilly Prat, stirring all the time. Add most of the chopped sage and season to taste. Bring to the boil, stirring, then simmer gently for 10–15 minutes, stirring occasionally.
4. Pour into a blender or food processor, mix until smooth then return to a clean saucepan over a low heat. Whisk in the fromage frais and remaining sage, and heat gently; do not allow to boil. Adjust the seasoning and use immediately.

NOTE:
* Fromage frais will curdle if added to a very hot liquid or allowed to boil.

Tarragon Beurre Blanc

MAKES ABOUT 290ml/10fl oz
225g/8oz unsalted butter, chilled
1 tablespoon chopped shallot
3 tablespoons tarragon vinegar
3 tablespoons water
1 tablespoon chopped tarragon
squeeze of lemon
salt and freshly ground white pepper

1. Cut the butter into three lengthways and then into six crossways to make eighteen small cubes. Put into a bowl and place in refrigerator until required.
2. Put the shallot, vinegar and water into a small thick-bottomed saucepan. Boil until about 2 tablespoons remain. Strain through a plastic or nylon sieve and return the liquid to the saucepan.
3. Lower the heat and gradually add the butter, cube by cube, whisking vigorously and continuously with a small wire sauce whisk, until the sauce has become thick and creamy, but pourable; do not allow to boil. This should take about 5 minutes.
4. Add the tarragon and lemon juice, and season to taste.

NOTE:
* This sauce is difficult to keep warm without curdling. However, it is possible with care: stand the container or sauceboat in a larger container with some blood-warm water in it – if the water is any hotter the sauce will curdle. Stir the beurre blanc now and again until ready to serve.

♦ ♦

Fresh Tomato Sauce

MAKES ABOUT 290ml/10fl oz
3 tablespoons oil
1 large onion, finely chopped
10 tomatoes, peeled, seeded and chopped
salt and freshly ground black pepper
pinch of sugar
150ml/5fl oz vegetable stock (see p. 117)
1 teaspoon thyme leaves

1. Heat the oil then cook the onion for 3 minutes. Add the tomatoes, salt, pepper and sugar and cook, stirring for a further 25 minutes.
2. Add the stock and cook for 5 minutes.
3. Pour into a blender or food processor and mix until smooth and push through a sieve.
4. Return the sauce to the pan. If it is too thin, reduce, by boiling rapidly, to the desired consistency. Take care: it will spit and has a tendency to catch.
5. Add the thyme. Taste and adjust the seasoning if necessary.

Easy Tomato Sauce

MAKES ABOUT 570ml/1 pint
1 × 400g/14oz can of plum tomatoes
1 small onion, chopped
1 small carrot, chopped
1 stick of celery, chopped
½ clove of garlic, crushed
1 bay leaf
parsley stalks
salt and freshly ground black pepper
juice of ½ lemon

dash of Worcestershire sauce (optional)
1 teaspoon sugar
1 teaspoon chopped basil or thyme

1. Put all the ingredients in a thick-bottomed pan, cover and simmer over medium heat for 30 minutes.
2. Pour into a blender or food processor and mix until smooth and push through a sieve.
3. Return the sauce to the pan. If the sauce is too thin, reduce by boiling rapidly. Check the seasoning, adding more salt or sugar if necessary.

◆ ◆

Roast Tomato Sauce

MAKES ABOUT 290ml/10fl oz
3 tablespoons olive oil
4 firm beef tomatoes
1 red pepper, quartered and deseeded
3 cloves of garlic, peeled but left whole
15g/½oz whole hazelnuts
15g/½oz whole blanched almonds
salt and freshly ground black pepper
vegetable stock (see p. 172)

1. Preheat the oven to 180°F/350°F/gas mark 4.
2. Brush a little of the olive oil over the tomatoes, pepper and garlic. Put them on to a baking sheet, protecting the garlic cloves by tucking them under the tomatoes, and

bake for 10 minutes.
3. Add the nuts to the baking sheet and cook for a further 15–20 minutes until the nuts are brown, the tomato skins have broken and the pepper and garlic cloves are soft. Turn the nuts occasionally so they brown evenly.
4. Remove the baking sheet from the oven and allow everything to cool slightly. Remove the skin from the tomatoes and peppers. Put the hazelnuts in a clean tea towel and rub off the skins.
5. Put all the ingredients into a blender or food processor and mix until smooth. Sieve the mixture into a bowl to make a smoother sauce.
6. Add the remaining olive oil and season to taste. If the sauce is too thick, add some vegetable stock.
7. Serve the sauce hot or cold.

Pesto Sauce

2 cloves of garlic
2 large cups basil leaves
55g/2oz pine nuts
55g/2oz Parmesan cheese, freshly grated
150ml/5fl oz olive oil
salt

1. Put the garlic and basil into a blender and mix to a paste.
2. Add the nuts and cheese, then, with the motor running, slowly pour in the oil through the feed hole in the lid. Season to taste.
3. Keep in a covered jar in a cool place.

NOTES:
* Pesto is sometimes made with walnuts instead of pine nuts, and the nuts may be pounded with the other ingredients to give a smooth paste.
** If the sauce is in danger of curdling, add 1 tablespoon warm water and mix again.
*** Pesto sauce can be kept in the refrigerator for 2–3 weeks.

◆ ◆

Herb Pesto

Use any combination of herbs in this pesto, but do not miss out the parsley as it gives the sauce a bright green colour.

2 cloves of garlic, crushed
2 large cups mixed herbs, e.g. thyme, sage,
    rosemary, mint, chives, parsley
55g/2oz pistachio nuts
55g/2oz Parmesan cheese, freshly grated
150ml/5fl oz olive oil
salt

1. Put the garlic and herbs into a blender and mix to a paste.
2. Mix in the nuts and the cheese. With the motor running, slowly pour in the olive oil through the feed hole in the lid. Season to taste.
3. Keep in a covered jar in a cool place.

NOTES:
* If the pesto is in danger of curdling, add 1 tablespoon warm water, and mix again.
** Pesto can be kept in the refrigerator for 2–3 weeks.

◆ ◆

Parsley Pesto

2 cloves of garlic
1 large handful parsley, coarsley choppped
30g/1oz blanched almonds
150ml/5fl oz good quality olive oil
55g/2oz Cheddar cheese, finely grated

1. Put the garlic and parsley into a blender and mix to a paste.
2. Mix in the nuts, then, with the motor still running, slowly pour in the olive oil through the feed hole in the lid.

3. Quickly mix in the cheese.

4. Keep in a covered jar, in a cool place.

NOTES:

* If the pesto is in danger of curdling, add 1 tablespoon warm water and mix again.

** The pesto can be kept in the refrigerator for 2–3 weeks.

♦ ♦

Watercress Sauce

This is a wonderfully quick and simple bright green sauce. Serve it hot or cold with green vegetables, mousses, pasta, or even as a soup, thinned with its own cooking water and extra stock.

110g/4oz watercress, end of the stalks trimmed
150ml/5fl oz single cream
salt and freshly ground black pepper

1. Bring a medium saucepan of water to the boil. Add the watercress and return to the boil. Strain through a sieve and refresh under running cold water to prevent further cooking. Squeeze out any excess moisture.

2. Put into a blender with the single cream and mix until smooth and pale green. Season to taste.

NOTE:

* If reheating the sauce, do not allow it to boil as the single cream will curdle.

♦ ♦

Plum and Red Onion Confit

Use this confit wherever a chutney or pickle is called for. Szechuan peppercorns are available in the spice sections of many supermarkets. (See p. 250 for mail order suppliers.)

30g/1oz butter
450g/1lb red onions, sliced
450g/1lb red plums, halved and stoned
290ml/10fl oz water
salt
1 tablespoon red wine vinegar

1 tablespoon dark soft brown sugar
1 tablespoon Szechuan peppercorns, dry-roasted and ground

1. Heat the butter in a thick-bottomed saucepan. Add the onions and cook over a low heat for 10 minutes, or until soft and transparent.

2. Add the plums, water, salt, vinegar, sugar and peppercorns and continue cooking, without the lid, until the liquid has evaporated and the fruit has begun to disintegrate. If necessary, remove the plums and onions and reduce the liquid to a thick syrup. Replace the fruit and serve either warm or cold.

Robust Mushroom Sauce

This sauce is an ideal accompaniment for the poached ricotta and feta dumplings (see p. 34). It can also be used as a sauce for pasta.

SERVES 4

6 tablespoons extra virgin olive oil
340g/12oz flat black field mushrooms*, very finely chopped
1–2 tablespoons lemon juice
5 tablespoons dry white vermouth
water or vegetable stock (see p. 172), if necessary

1. Heat the oil in a sauté pan, add the mushrooms and lemon juice and cook gently until all the moisture is driven off.
2. Add the vermouth and cook for about 3 minutes or until well reduced. If necessary, add a little water or vegetable stock, scraping down the sides of the pan to collect the brown sediments, to make a thick pouring sauce.

NOTE:
* A selection of wild mushrooms can be substituted for the field mushrooms.

◆ ◆

Avocado, Tomato and Chilli Salsa

This salsa can be served as an accompaniment to an avocado mousse; a garnish for a cold tomato soufflé or salad; a filling for a baked potato.

SERVES 4

1 avocado, peeled and finely diced
1 small shallot, finely diced
juice and grated zest of 1 lime
2 ripe tomatoes, peeled, seeded and diced
2 small red chillies, seeded and very finely diced
20 large coriander leaves, finely chopped
8 chives, finely chopped
1 tablespoon light soy sauce
1 tablespoon medium dry sherry
2 tablespoons groundnut oil
1 teaspoon sesame oil
1 teaspoon sugar
freshly ground black pepper

1. Put the ingredients into a bowl and mix carefully.
2. Use as required.

Red Ratatouille Dressing

½ red onion, very finely diced
½ red pepper, grilled, skinned, seeded and very
    finely diced (see p. 181)
150ml/5fl oz olive oil
½ teaspoon Dijon mustard

1–2 tablespoons balsamic vinegar
salt and freshly ground black pepper

1. Put the red onion and red pepper into a
bowl.
2. Mix together the mustard, balsamic
vinegar, salt and pepper in a small bowl and
add to the onions. Leave for at least 30
minutes, preferably overnight.

◆ ◆

Red and Green Pepper Salsa

This salsa can be served with harlequin
terrine (see p. 83); and omelettes; used as a
warm sauce for braised or grilled vegetables;
or used to stuff tomatoes or halved peppers.
Top with cheese, and grill.

SERVES 4
3 tablespoons olive oil
2 small shallots, very finely diced
2 cloves of garlic, crushed
2 red peppers, quartered, seeded and very finely
    diced

2 green peppers, quartered, seeded and very
    finely diced
150ml/5fl oz white wine
sugar
salt and freshly ground black pepper

1. Heat the oil in a saucepan, add the
shallots and cook for 5 minutes or until soft
and transparent but not brown. Add the
garlic and cook for a further minute.
2. Add the peppers and wine and cook for
about 5 minutes or until the liquid has
reduced by half. Season with sugar, salt and
pepper.
3. Serve either warm or cold.

Yellow Pepper Sauce

SERVES 4

1 tablespoon olive oil
1 onion, finely chopped
2 yellow tomatoes, peeled, seeded and chopped
2 yellow peppers, grilled, peeled, seeded and
    chopped (see p. 181)
1 clove of garlic, crushed
1 bouquet garni
6 tablespoons water
salt and freshly ground white pepper

1. Heat the oil in a medium saucepan, add the onion and cook gently for 10 minutes or until soft and transparent.
2. Add the remaining ingredients, cover and continue cooking over a low heat for 20 minutes. Discard the bouquet garni.
3. Purée in a blender or food processor. Discard the bouquet garni. Push through a sieve. If the sauce is too thick, add a little more water. Serve hot or cold.

◆ ◆

Red and Yellow Pepper Relish

The colours in this relish are important, so if possible, use the microwave oven method for peeling the peppers. However, if a microwave oven is not available, then use the grilling method. The relish will be as delicious but will look slightly browned.

MAKES ABOUT 225g/8oz

2 red peppers, peeled and seeded (see p. 181)
2 yellow peppers, peeled and seeded (see p. 181)
2 tablespoons olive oil
1 red onion, quartered and sliced
2 teaspoons tomato purée
110ml/4fl oz water
2 tablespoons raspberry or cider vinegar
salt and freshly ground white pepper

1. Slice the quartered peppers very finely.
2. Heat the oil in a sauté pan, add the onion and cook for 10 minutes or until soft and transparent. Add the peppers, tomato purée and water. Lower the heat and cook until the peppers are very soft and the liquid has evaporated. This will take about 15 minutes.
3. Add the vinegar and bring to the boil. Cook until very little liquid remains. Season to taste.

NOTE:
* The relish can be kept in a glass jar with an acid-proof lid, in the refrigerator for 3–4 weeks.

Minted Yoghurt

The mint leaves can be chopped and mixed into the yoghurt with the other ingredients by hand, but it is quicker, and the flecked result prettier, if the ingredients are put into a food processor and mixed until blended. Serve with spiced food.

225g/8oz plain yoghurt
14 large mint leaves

1 teaspoon white wine vinegar
1 teaspoon caster sugar
½ teaspoon chilli powder (optional)
2 teaspoons water (optional)
salt and freshly ground white pepper

1. If making this sauce by hand, put all the ingredients, except the mint leaves, into a bowl.
2. Chop the mint leaves finely and stir into the yoghurt mixture.

◆ ◆

Peanut and Coriander Sauce

This sauce is delicious served hot with deep-fried aubergines or stir-fried vegetables. It is also good as a cold dressing for dark salad leaves, such as oakleaf or lollo rosso, where the colours are not affected by the darkness of the sauce.

55ml/2fl oz light soy sauce
55ml/2fl oz red wine vinegar

55g/2oz fresh ginger, peeled and chopped
2 teaspoons red chilli sauce
3 tablespoons crunchy peanut butter
3 tablespoons black bean sauce
1 tablespoon caster sugar
5 tablespoons chopped coriander
85ml/3fl oz groundnut oil
2 tablespoons sesame oil

1. Beat all the ingredients in a bowl, or mix in a food processor or blender, until well emulsified.

◆ ◆

Chilli, Lime Leaf and Coconut Sauce

This sauce is not for those who like mild flavours. The coconut milk balances the hot chilli; the quantities of each are, therefore, a

matter of personal preference. Use for stir-fried vegetables and fragrant yellow coconut rice (see p. 191).

2 tiny fresh red chillies, seeded (optional)
2 large fresh red chillies, seeded
10cm/4 inches galangal*, peeled and chopped
3.5cm/1½ inches fresh ginger, peeled and chopped

3.5cm/1½ inches fresh turmeric, peeled and
   chopped, or 1 teaspoon ground turmeric
3 shallots, chopped
2 large cloves of garlic, crushed
1 stalk of lemon grass, tender part only, chopped
2 lime leaves, or grated zest and juice of 1 lime
15g/½oz coriander seeds, finely ground
1 whole nutmeg, grated (not a mistake!)
15g/½oz sugar
salt and freshly ground black pepper
2 tablespoons groundnut oil
200ml/7fl oz can of coconut milk

1. Put all the ingredients except the
groundnut oil and coconut milk into a
blender and mix to a moist paste.** Add a
little water to help the blades go round, if
necessary.

2. Heat the groundnut oil in a sauté pan
and gently cook the spice paste for a few
minutes, stirring all the time. Add the
coconut milk and simmer for about 5
minutes.
3. Use as required.

NOTES:
* Galangal is a hard, fleshy root with a flavour
similar to ginger which it resembles. Stocked in
most good supermarkets, and available in Thai
shops in both fresh and dried form.
** The ingredients for this sauce have to be
mixed in a liquidiser rather than a food
processor, which will not grind the ingredients
finely enough.

◆ ◆

Lime and Szechuan Peppercorn Dressing

This dressing is particularly good when
served with a cold rice or cold pasta salad.

juice of 6 limes
110ml/4fl oz groundnut oil
salt and freshly ground black pepper

1 tablespoon sugar
1 tablespoon dry-roasted Szechuan peppercorns,
   ground
4 small cloves of garlic, crushed
1 tablespoon each parsley, basil and coriander

1. Put the ingredients into a blender and
mix until smooth. Season well to make a
strong dressing.

NOTE:
* This dressing will lose its colour, but not its
flavour, if kept for more than a few hours.

Dipping Sauce

This sauce goes well with deep-fried croûton balls (see p. 48) and deep-fried finger food.

SERVES 4

1 tablespoon sesame oil
2 tablespoons soy sauce
1 tablespoon clear honey
3–4 tablespoons syrup from a jar of preserved ginger
1 tablespoon red wine vinegar
4 spring onions, finely chopped

1. Mix all the ingredients together, except the spring onions.

2. Put the sauce into a bowl, add the spring onions and serve.

NOTE:
* Any dish which is served with this sauce can be garnished with spring onion bows.

SPRING ONION BOWS
Choose large cylindrical spring onions that do not have especially bulbous roots. Cut off a large part of the green tops and the roots. With a small, sharp knife cut vertical lines halfway through the onions at both ends. Leave in icy water for 2 hours – by which time they will have opened out.

♦ ♦

Black Bean Sauce

SERVES 4

3 tablespoons fermented black beans
1 tablespoon sunflower oil
2 spring onions, chopped
1 clove of garlic, sliced
2.5 cm/1 inch piece of fresh ginger, peeled and sliced
2 tablespoons soy sauce
2 tablespoons dry sherry
1 teaspoon sugar
290ml/10fl oz water
2 teaspoons sesame oil

1. Rinse the beans twice.
2. Heat the oil in a saucepan, add the spring onions, garlic and ginger and cook for 1 minute.
3. Add the soy sauce, sherry, beans, sugar and water. Bring slowly to the boil, then simmer for 15 minutes to allow the flavours to infuse.
4. Stir in the sesame oil.

PUDDINGS

Prune and Macadamia Caramel Tart
Date and Almond Lattice Flan
Apple, Apricot and Plum Filo Galettes
Duke of Cambridge Tart
Nearly Normandy Apple Flan
Sweet Pasta Pie
Sweet Beet and Orange Tart
Deep-fried Choux Pea Ring
Chocolate and Chestnut Fudge Roulade
Banana and Lime Cheesecake
Prune and Brandy Mousse
Creamed Cheeses with Fresh Figs and Honey
Mascarpone al Caffe
Sweet Ricotta Fritters
Caramelised Gnocchi with Apricot Sauce
Baked Sauternes Creams
Damson Roulade
Poached Tamarillos with Coconut Tapioca Timbales
Fresh Redcurrants, Brown Breadcrumbs and Crème Fraîche
Apples and Blackberries in Cassis Syrup
Star Fruit and Kumquats Poached with Star Anise
Poached Fresh Figs with Mascarpone Mousse
Poached Pears with Ginger and Chinese Five Spice
Exotic Fresh Fruit Platter
Elderflower and Champagne Jellies
Black Velvet Ice Cream
Ratafia and Crème Fraîche Ice Cream
Honey and Greek Yoghurt Ice Cream

Prune and Macadamia Caramel Tart

SERVES 8–10

1 quantity of pâte sucrée (see p. 173)
675g/1½ lb pitted prunes, soaked over-night in
  brandy to cover, drained
3 tablespoons apricot jam

FOR THE FILLING:

225g/8oz blanched almonds
225g/8oz uncooked marzipan (see p. 179)
55g/2oz butter
2 tablespoons plain flour
2 eggs
55ml/2fl oz brandy from the prunes

FOR THE TOP:

285g/10oz granulated sugar
85ml/3fl oz water
85g/3oz butter
150ml/5fl oz double cream
340g/12oz raw, unsalted macadamia nuts

TO SERVE:
fromage frais

1. Roll out the pastry and use it to line a
27.5cm/11 inch loose-bottomed flan tin (see
p. 183). Chill in the refrigerator for 30 minutes
(this prevents shrinkage during cooking).
2. Preheat the oven to 200°C/400°F/gas
mark 6.
3. Line the pastry case with greaseproof paper
and fill with rice, dried beans or ceramic balls.
Bake 'blind' (see p. 183) for about 10–15
minutes. Take the tart out of the oven and
lower the temperature to 190°C/375°F/gas
mark 5. Remove the 'blind beans'. Return the
pastry case to the oven for a further 5–10
minutes or until the case is dried out but not

completely cooked. Cool on a wire rack.
Lower the oven temperature to 180°C/
340°F/gas mark 4.
4. Using the back of a spoon, spread the
base of the pastry case with apricot jam.
5. Cut the prunes in half and spread an even
layer over the bottom of the pastry case (it
should be completely covered). The quantity
required will vary according to the size of the
prunes.
6. Make the filling: put the almonds in a
food processor* and, using the pulse button,
process until they resemble coarse
breadcrumbs. Add the marzipan, butter,
flour, eggs and brandy and blend until the
mixture is well combined.
7. Spread the filling over the prunes with
the back of a spoon and bake on the middle
shelf of the oven for 15 minutes or until the
filling is just set. Remove from the oven and
cool on a wire rack.
8. Make the top: put the sugar, water and
butter in a heavy saucepan and heat gently
until the sugar has melted. Then boil the
mixture, undisturbed, until it is a deep
caramel colour for 15–20 minutes. Remove
from the heat and gradually stir in the cream
until the mixture is thick and smooth. It
should be the consistency of clear honey.
Chop the macadamia nuts if preferred, or
leave whole, and stir into the caramel.
9. Spoon the still warm caramel over the top
of the tart and leave to set.
10. Remove the tart from the flan ring and
serve, slightly warm, with fromage frais.

NOTE:

* If a food processor is not available, chop the
almonds finely. Beat the marzipan and butter
together, then mix in the remaining filling
ingredients, including the almonds.

Date and Almond Lattice Flan

SERVES 8

FOR THE PASTRY:

225g/8oz plain flour
pinch of salt
140g/5oz butter
1 egg yolk
2 teaspoons brandy
1–2 tablespoons water

FOR THE FILLING:

250g/9oz pitted dates
150ml/5fl oz orange juice
150g/5oz whole blanched almonds
110g/4oz caster sugar
1 egg white
2 teaspoons brandy
caster sugar for sprinkling

1. Sift the flour and salt into a bowl. Rub in the butter until the mixture resembles coarse breadcrumbs.

2. Mix the egg yolk, brandy and half the water together. Using a knife, stir this into the flour and butter mixture and mix to a dough. Add a little more water if necessary.

3. Roll out the pastry on a lightly floured surface until 5mm/¼ inch thick and use to line a 25cm/10 inch loose-bottomed flan tin (see p. 183). Keep the pastry trimmings for the lattice decoration. Chill in a refrigerator for 30 minutes (this prevents shrinkage during cooking).

4. Make the filling: put the dates and orange juice into a saucepan and heat gently, stirring occasionally, until thick and smooth. Leave to cool.

5. Preheat the oven to 190°C/375°F/gas mark 5. Place a baking sheet on the middle shelf of the oven, to heat.

6. Put the almonds and sugar in a food processor and mix until smooth. Add the egg white and brandy and mix again until well combined.

7. Spread the almond mixture over the pastry case. Cover with the date mixture. Cut the pastry trimmings into thin strips and use them to make a lattice on the top of the flan. Stick the ends down with a little water. Brush the lattice with water and sprinkle with caster sugar.

8. Put the flan tin on to the hot baking sheet and bake on the middle shelf of the oven for 20–25 minutes or until the pastry is golden brown.

9. Remove the flan from the tin, leave to cool slightly and serve warm.

Apple, Apricot and Plum Filo Galettes

This recipe is best made with ripe plums. If they are not fully ripe they should be pre-cooked with a little sugar syrup and then thoroughly drained.

MAKES 4 INDIVIDUAL GALETTES

4 sheets of filo pastry

55g/2oz butter, melted

2 tablespoons ground almonds

2 tablespoons Demerara sugar, plus extra for sprinkling

8 dried apricots

1 Granny Smith apple

2 small red plums

1 tablespoon flaked almonds (optional)

TO SERVE:

fromage frais or Greek yoghurt

1. Preheat the oven to 180°C/350°F/gas mark 4. Lightly grease a baking sheet.
2. Working quickly, brush one sheet of filo pastry with melted butter and fold it in half (keep the remaining sheets of filo covered with a clean cloth until ready to use). Crumple the sheet of filo to form a 11.5cm/4½ inch circle, creating tucks and folds in the pastry like a circle of crumpled fabric.
3. Mix together the ground almonds and the Demerara sugar and sprinkle over the pastry. This will help soak up any juices from the fruit.
4. Core, quarter and slice the apple, stone and slice the plums.
5. Using plenty of fruit, tuck pieces of each type into the hollows and folds of the pastry.

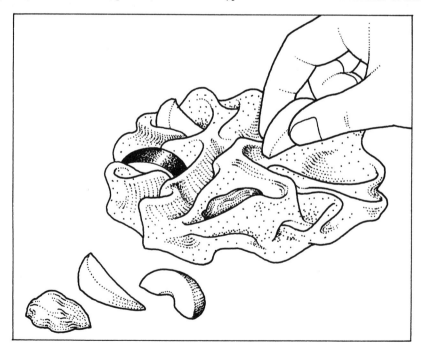

APPLE, APRICOT, & PLUM FILO SALETTE

6. Sprinkle the galette with Demerara sugar and scatter over a few flaked almonds, if using.

7. Repeat with the other three sheets of filo.

8. Put the galettes on the baking sheet, place on the middle shelf of the oven and bake for about 20 minutes or until the apple is cooked and the pastry is golden brown.

9. Allow to cool slightly, before serving with fromage frais or Greek yoghurt.

◆ ◆

Duke of Cambridge Tart

There are probably many versions of this tart. This one is very simple, but its success depends on the quality of the candied peel. Buy it unchopped, either loose or in packets, but buy the best available.

SERVES 6

1 quantity of rich shortcrust pastry (see p. 172)
110g/4oz butter
55g/2oz light brown cane sugar
2 large egg yolks
225g/8oz good quality candied peel, diced

TO SERVE:

crème anglaise (see p. 172) or Greek yoghurt

1. Line a 24cm/9½ inch loose-bottomed flan tin with the pastry (see p. 183) and chill in a refrigerator for 30 minutes.

2. Preheat the oven to 200°C/400°F/gas mark 6.

3. Melt the butter and sugar in a small saucepan over a low heat. Remove from the heat, allow to cool and then beat in the yolks. Set aside.

4. Bake the pastry case 'blind' (see p. 183) for 10–15 minutes. Take out of the oven and lower the oven temperature to 180°C/350°F/gas mark 4. Remove the 'blind beans'. Return the pastry case to the oven for a further 5 minutes or until dried out but not completely cooked.

5. Scatter the candied peel over the pastry and then pour on the yolk and butter mixture. Level the top with a fork.

6. Place the flan tin on a baking sheet, put on the middle shelf of the oven and bake for about 30 minutes or until the filling is golden brown and set.

7. Serve with crème anglaise or Greek yoghurt.

Nearly Normandy Apple Flan

We made this recipe one day for our staff lunch using left-overs from the fridge. It was so good that we decided to share it. Not for weight watchers!

SERVES 8–10

1 quantity of walnut pastry (see p. 179)
3 large dessert apples

FOR THE FILLING:

375g/12oz uncooked marzipan (see p. 179)
100g/3½oz unsalted butter, softened
1 egg
2 teaspoons Calvados or Kirsch
juice of 1 lemon
2 tablespoons plain flour
½ quantity of Eccles cake filling (see p. 198)

TO FINISH:

110g/4oz apricot jam, sieved and kept warm

1. Line a 30m/12 inch loose-bottomed flan tin with the walnut pastry (see p. 183). Chill in a refrigerator for 30 minutes.
2. Make the filling: break up the marzipan and put into a food processor with the butter, egg, Calvados or Kirsch, lemon juice and flour. Mix together. If necessary, add some water to help the blades go round.
3. Preheat the oven to 200°C/400°F/gas mark 6, and put a baking sheet on the middle shelf to heat.
4. Spread the Eccles cake filling in the pastry case then cover with the marzipan mixture.
5. Peel the apples, halve them and scoop out the cores. Cut each half crosswise into very thin slices. Holding the slices together, depress them to make the slices slope and fan out. Slide a palette knife under the fanned apple halves and place five round the edge of the marzipan mixture. Put the remaining half in the middle. Gently press the apples down until they touch the base.

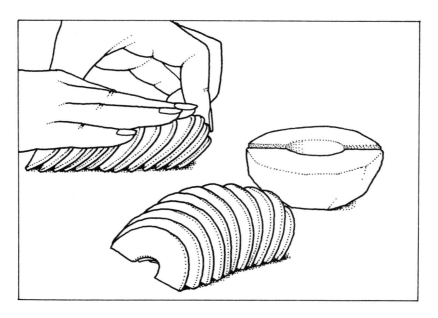

NEARLY NORMANDY APPLE FLAN

6. Place the flan tin on the hot baking sheet on the middle shelf of the oven for 15–20 minutes or until browned. Lower the oven temperature to 180°C/350°F/gas mark 4 and continue cooking for 30–35 minutes or until the apples are soft and the marzipan mixture is set.

7. Put the flan on a wire rack and leave to cool in the tin.

8. Shortly before serving, brush the tart with the warm apricot jam. Serve at room temperature with Greek yoghurt or fromage frais.

NOTE:

* This flan freezes well. Reheat thoroughly in a medium oven but serve at room temperature. Glaze with warm apricot jam before serving.

♦ ♦

Sweet Pasta Pie

Pasta pie is a traditional Italian recipe and comes in many forms. This is our version. Make it several days in advance as the flavours improve with keeping. It can also be served as a 'cake' for special occasions.

SERVES 6–8
1 quantity of pâte sucrée (see p. 173)

FOR THE FILLING:
110g/4oz blanched almonds
110g/4oz whole hazelnuts
55g/2oz pine nuts
110g/4oz mixed candied peel
140g/5oz granulated sugar
1 teaspoon cocoa powder
grated zest of 1 orange
grated zest of 1 lemon
140g/5oz unsalted butter
½ quantity fresh pasta*, cut into fine tagliatelle
   (see pp. 177 and 178)
5 tablespoons rum
5 tablespoons Cointreau
2 tablespoons Amaretto

1. Line a deep 25 cm/10 inch loose-bottomed cake tin with the pastry, bringing the pastry 6.5 cm/2½ inches up the sides (see p. 183). Tidy the pastry edge and refrigerate for about 30 minutes.

2. Preheat the oven to 190°C/375°F/gas mark 5. Place a baking sheet on the middle shelf of the oven to heat.

3. Put the nuts, mixed peel and sugar in a food processor and process to a coarse mixture.** Do not overgrind. Add the cocoa powder and orange and lemon zests. Mix in quickly using the pulse button. Divide the mixture into three equal portions.

4. Spread one-third of the pasta over the bottom of the pastry case. Sprinkle one third of the nut mixture evenly over the pasta. Dot with one third of the butter. Repeat twice more, finishing with butter.

5. Put the cake tin on the hot baking sheet, bake for 15 minutes, then loosely cover the pie with greaseproof paper to protect the pastry. Bake for a further 20–25 minutes.

6. Remove from the oven and sprinkle the rum, Cointreau and Amaretto over the pie whilst still hot. Transfer the cake tin to a

wire rack and leave the pie to cool in the tin. 7. When the pie is cold remove it from the cake tin. Add another tablespoon of any of the spirits and liqueurs if wished. This will help to keep the 'pie' moist. Store in an airtight container.

NOTES:
* Good quality fresh pasta is also available in most supermarkets and would be suitable for this recipe. Buy fine tagliatelle.
** If a food processor is not available, finely chop the nuts and peel, then mix with the sugar, cocoa powder and orange and lemon zests.

◆ ◆

Sweet Beet and Orange Tart

The idea for making a sweet tart using beetroot came from the Italian *crostada di bietola* which uses the related vegetable, chard.

SERVES 8–10
FOR THE PASTRY:
225g/8oz plain flour
55g/2oz caster sugar
pinch of salt
85g/3oz butter
2 egg yolks
2 tablespoons milk

FOR THE FILLING
225g/8oz beetroot, cooked and peeled
2 cloves, finely ground
4 tablespoons sugar
juice of 1 lemon
juice of 1 large orange
1 tablespoon crème de cassis

FOR THE CRÈME PÂTISSIÈRE:
425ml/15fl oz milk

zest of 1 lemon, cut into thin strips
zest of 1 large orange, cut into thin strips
1 cinnamon stick
seeds from ½ vanilla pod
2 egg yolks
55g/2oz caster sugar
20g/¾oz plain flour
20g/¾oz cornflour

2 tablespoons pine nuts
icing sugar for dusting

TO SERVE:
crème anglaise (see p. 179) or crème fraîche

1. Make the pastry: sift the flour, sugar and salt into a mixing bowl. Cut the butter into small pieces and rub in with fingertips until the mixture resembles coarse breadcrumbs. Make a well in the middle.
2. Beat the egg yolks and the milk in a jug and pour into the well. Mix to a firm dough, first with a knife and then with one hand.* Turn on to a work surface and quickly make into a ball of dough. Chill for 30 minutes.
3. Put the milk, lemon and orange zests, cinnamon stick and vanilla seeds for the crème pâtissière into a small saucepan and heat to boiling point. Remove from the heat,

cover and leave to infuse until required.

4. Make the beetroot filling: either grate the beetroot on the coarsest side of a hand grater, or process in a food processor to very coarse breadcrumbs. Put into a small saucepan with the cloves, sugar, lemon and orange juices and the cassis. Cook over a medium heat, until all the liquid has evaporated. Leave to cool.

5. Preheat the oven to 200°C/400°F/gas mark 6, and put a baking sheet on the middle shelf to heat.

6. Cut the pastry into two-thirds and one-third. Roll out the larger piece on a floured work surface to 0.5cm/¼ inch thickness.

7. Use to line a 25cm/10 inch loose-bottomed flan tin (see p. 183). Chill again for 30 minutes.

8. Meanwhile, roll out the remaining pastry and stamp out 20 heart shapes with a 7.5cm/ 3 inch heart-shaped pastry cutter. Alternatively, use a 5cm/2 inch round pastry cutter. Chill until ready to use.

9. Bake the pastry case 'blind' (see p. 183) on the hot baking sheet for 10–15 minutes. Take the pastry case out of the oven, remove the 'blind beans' and return the pastry to the oven for a further 5 minutes or until the case is dried out but not completely cooked. Leave to cool.

10. Make the crème pâtissière: beat the yolks and the sugar in a small bowl until pale and creamy. Mix in the flours and beat again. Remove just the cinnamon stick from the infused milk (step 3) and stir the milk into the egg and flour mixture. Mix well.

11. Return the mixture to the pan and bring slowly to the boil, stirring continuously (it will go alarmingly lumpy. Do not worry: stir vigorously and the sauce will become smooth again). Allow to cool slightly. The crème pâtissière should be of pouring consistency. Add a little milk if necessary.

12. Assemble the tart: spread half the crème pâtissière over the base of the pastry case with the back of a spoon or a spatula. Scatter with the pine nuts. Spread over the beetroot mixture and cover with the remaining crème pâtissière.

13. Make a 'lid' of slightly overlapping pastry hearts or circles. Put the tart back into the oven for a further 20 minutes or until the pastry shapes are cooked and brown. Cool the tart in the flan tin on a wire rack.

14. Remove the tart from the flan tin, put on to a large serving plate and dust with icing sugar. Serve with crème anglaise or crème fraîche.

NOTE:

* If a food processor is available, mix the pastry ingredients, except the milk, until well combined. Add the milk through the feeder with the motor running.

Deep-fried Choux Pea Ring

SERVES 6

3 tablespoons clear honey
55g/2oz unblanched almonds, slivered
55g/2oz pistachios, slivered
110g/4oz dried pear or dried apricot, chopped
110g/4oz natural glacé cherries, cut into half
oil for deep-frying

FOR THE CHOUX PASTRY:
55g/2oz butter
150ml/5fl oz water
65g/2½oz plain flour, sifted
2 eggs
pinch of salt

1. Make the choux pastry following the recipe on p. 173.
2. Line two or three trays or baking sheets that will fit into the freezer with greaseproof paper.
3. Using a piping bag with a 5mm/¼ inch plain nozzle, pipe pea-sized balls of mixture, close together, on to the sheets of paper (they will swell to chick pea size when deep-fried). Continue until the mixture is finished. Put the trays or baking sheets into the freezer for 1 hour.
4. Heat 7.5cm/3 inches of oil in a deep saucepan until a cube of stale bread dropped in sizzles straight away.

5. Remove one tray of choux 'peas' from the freezer, loosen them from the greaseproof paper and tip them straight into the oil. Stir all the time to ensure even browning. Deep-fry for a few minutes or until pale golden brown. Remove from the oil with a slotted spoon and drain on paper towels. Repeat until all the 'peas' have been deep-fried. Then tip them all back into the oil and fry for a further 2 minutes until crisp and a deeper golden brown. Remove with a slotted spoon and leave to drain on fresh paper towels.
6. Melt the honey in a large saucepan over a moderate heat, then boil for 2–3 minutes, or until a drop will set on a cold plate. Remove from the heat, add the nuts and fruits (reserving some cherries and a few nuts for decoration) and the choux 'peas' and toss gently with a wooden spoon until well coated. Pack into a 1.1litre/2 pint ring mould and leave to cool.
7. To unmould: hold the mould over a flame for a few seconds to loosen the honey,* place a plate over the top and invert both together. The choux pea ring will drop on to the plate.
8. Decorate the top with the reserved cherries and nuts.

NOTE:
* Alternatively, stand the mould in a bowl of very hot water for a few seconds; dry the mould before inverting.

Chocolate and Chestnut Fudge Roulade

SERVES 8

225g/8oz dark chocolate, chopped into even-sized pieces
110g/4oz unsalted butter
450g/1lb can unsweetened chestnut purée
1 tablespoon rum
225g/8oz walnuts, finely chopped
150ml/5fl oz double cream
1 teaspoon natural vanilla essence
1 teaspoon rum
icing sugar for dusting

TO GARNISH:
marrons glacés (see p. 199)

1. Make a roulade case (see p. 184).
2. Melt the chocolate and butter in a bowl over a saucepan of simmering water. Remove from the heat and leave to cool.
3. Add the chestnut purée and rum to the chocolate mixture and beat until smooth. Stir in the chopped walnuts.*
4. Spoon the chocolate mixture into the Swiss roll tin and smooth the top with a palette knife or spatula. Refrigerate for 2 hours or overnight. Bring back to room temperature before trying to roll up the cake.
5. Whip the cream in a bowl with the vanilla essence and rum.
6. Put a piece of greaseproof paper on a work surface and sprinkle with icing sugar. Turn out the roulade on to the paper removing the paper used to line the tin. Spread evenly with cream.
7. Using the paper under the cake to help, roll it up firmly from the narrow end. Rest the cake on its seam. Wrap tightly with the greaseproof paper and refrigerate for 30 minutes.
8. Serve dusted with icing sugar and garnished with the marrons glacés.

NOTE:
* Instead of being incorporated in the roulade, the chopped walnuts can be used to cover the outside, at step 6, in place of the icing sugar.

◆ ◆

Banana and Lime Cheesecake

SERVES 4–6
FOR THE CRUST:
12 large digestive biscuits, crushed
55g/2oz butter, melted
½ teaspoon ground ginger

FOR THE FILLING:
450g/1lb curd cheese
3 tablespoons caster sugar
2 ripe bananas, mashed
grated zest and juice of 1 lemon
grated zest of 1 lime
150ml/5fl oz double cream, lightly whipped
or 150ml/5fl oz Greek yoghurt

FOR THE DECORATION:
thinly pared zest of 1 lemon
thinly pared zest of 1 lime

1. Make the crust: combine the ingredients in a bowl and use the mixture to line the base of a 20cm/8 inch loose-bottom sandwich tin, pressing it down firmly with the back of a wooden spoon. Chill for 30 minutes.

2. Make the filling: put the curd cheese and sugar into a bowl and beat with a wooden spoon. Add the mashed bananas, lemon juice and zest and the lime zest. Beat again. Fold in the cream or Greek yoghurt and pour on to the crust. Smooth the top with a palette knife.

3. Cover and chill for 3 hours.

4. Prepare the decoration: cut the pared lemon and lime zest into very thin strips. Bring a small saucepan of water to the boil, drop in the strips and boil for 2 minutes. Refresh under running cold water, drain and pat dry on paper towels. Allow to cool.

5. To serve: remove the cheesecake from the sandwich tin and transfer to a serving plate. Scatter the lemon and lime zest strips around the edge.

◆ ◆

Prune and Brandy Mousse

SERVES 6

225g/8oz prunes
290ml/10fl oz tea, boiling
1 tablespoon brandy
1 tablespoon water
7g/¼oz gelatine (for agar agar see p. 180)
3 eggs, separated
110g/4oz sugar
150ml/5fl oz double cream, lightly whipped

1. Put the prunes into a bowl with the tea and soak for a minimum of 30 minutes, or, preferably, overnight.

2. Transfer the prunes and soaking liquor to a saucepan and cook over a medium heat until soft. Drain and reserve the liquor. Stone the prunes.

3. Mix the flesh in a blender or food processor, adding some of the reserved liquor if necessary; the mixture should be of dropping consistency.

4. Put the brandy and water into a small saucepan, sprinkle over the gelatine and leave to soak for 5 minutes.

5. Whisk the egg yolks and sugar in a bowl set over, not in, a saucepan of simmering water (if using electric beaters heat is not required) until thick, pale and mousse-like. Remove from the heat and whisk until cool.

6. Add the prune purée to the egg yolk mixture.

7. Gently heat the gelatine until dissolved and completely clear; do not allow to boil. Mix into the prune mixture and stir gently until on the point of setting.

8. Fold in the cream. Whisk the egg whites until stiff but not dry. Stir 1 tablespoon of egg white into the prune mixture with a large metal spoon and then fold in the rest quickly but carefully.

9. Pour the mousse into a bowl and refrigerate.

10. Remove the mousse from the fridge 15 minutes before serving.

Creamed Cheeses with Fresh Figs and Honey

We have described how to serve this pudding very precisely as it looks pretty. Presentation is naturally a matter of taste and can be altered accordingly.

SERVES 4

110g/4oz ricotta cheese
110g/4oz mascarpone cheese
2 tablespoons icing sugar
1 tablespoon lemon juice
seeds from ½ vanilla pod
8 black-skinned figs
2 tablespoons clear honey
2–3 teaspoons hot water

TO GARNISH (OPTIONAL):
4 sprigs of purple fennel

1. Put the ricotta and mascarpone cheeses, the icing sugar, lemon juice, and vanilla seeds into a bowl and mix together. Add more icing sugar if preferred.
2. Using 2 tablespoons of the cheese mixture make a mound just off the centre of four plates. Cover and leave in the refrigerator until required.
3. Trim the stalks of four of the figs. Cut a cross through the stems to within 3.5cm/ 1½ inches of the bottom of each fig. With the forefinger and thumb of each hand, gently press the bottom of the figs inwards until they open like a flower.
4. Trim the stalks of the other four figs and slice each one lengthways, making about five

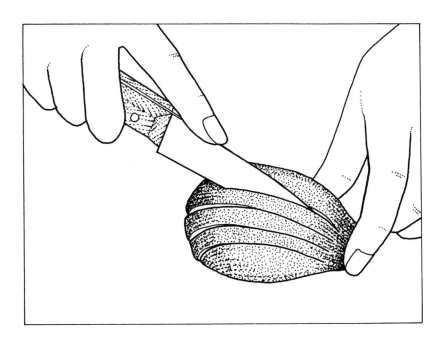

CREAMED CHEESES WITH FIGS & HONEY

or six cuts to within 5mm/¼ inch of the stalk. Press gently at the stalk end to fan.
5. Mix the honey with the hot water and glaze all the figs using a soft pastry brush.

6. To serve: put one of each of the figs with a mound of creamed cheese on each of four plates, and drizzle with the remaining honey. Garnish with a sprig of fennel.

♦ ♦

Mascarpone al Caffe

SERVES 4
225g/8oz mascarpone cheese
110g/4oz caster sugar
2 tablespoons freshly, finely ground coffee beans
4 tablespoons rum

TO SERVE:
tuiles au chocolat (see p. 168)

1. Put all the ingredients into a bowl and mix well with a wooden spoon. The mixture will be fairly stiff.
2. Spoon into four small glass bowls and serve with tuiles au chocolat.

♦ ♦

Sweet Ricotta Fritters

MAKES APPROXIMATELY 12 FRITTERS
340g/12oz ricotta cheese
2 egg yolks
55g/2oz plain flour
20g/¾oz butter, melted
grated zest and juice of 1 lemon
4 tablespoons clear honey
pinch of salt
oil for frying

1. Put the ricotta cheese, egg yolks, flour, butter, lemon zest, 1 tablespoon lemon juice,

2 tablespoons honey and a pinch of salt in a bowl and beat until well mixed. Leave to stand in a refrigerator for 30 minutes.
2. Heat 5cm/2 inches oil in a deep saucepan until a small cube of stale bread sizzles immediately it is added.
3. Fry tablespoons of the ricotta mixture for 3–4 minutes until golden brown, turning them if necessary. Remove from the oil and drain on paper towels. Transfer to a dish and keep warm. Repeat with the remaining ricotta mixture.
4. Put the remaining lemon juice and honey in a small saucepan and heat gently, stirring.
5. Serve the fritters immediately, drizzled with the honey sauce.

Caramelised Gnocchi with Apricot Sauce

SERVES 4
290ml/10fl oz milk
1 bay leaf
pinch of freshly grated nutmeg
55g/2oz semolina
225g/8oz dried apricots, soaked overnight in
  cold water to cover
170ml/6fl oz single cream
30g/1oz caster sugar

1. Slowly heat the milk with the bay leaf and grated nutmeg to boiling point. Remove from the heat, cover and leave to infuse for 10 minutes. Remove the bay leaf, add the sugar and bring to the boil again slowly.
2. Sprinkle in the semolina, stirring all the time, and cook, still stirring, until the mixture is thick, about 1 minute.
3. Spread the mixture in a 1cm/½ inch thick layer on a wet baking sheet. Leave to cool.
4. Put the apricots and their soaking liquor into a saucepan. Cover and cook gently for 5 minutes or until completely soft. Transfer to a blender or food processor and mix to a smooth sauce of dropping consistency. Pour into a shallow ovenproof serving dish and leave to cool.
5. Preheat the oven to 200°C/400°F/gas mark 6.
6. Cut the gnocchi into circles using a 3.5cm/1½ inch pastry cutter. Arrange, slightly overlapping, on the apricot sauce. Pour over the single cream and sprinkle with sugar. Bake for 15–20 minutes.
7. 10 minutes before the end of the cooking time, preheat the grill to maximum.
8. Place the gnocchi under the grill to caramelise the sugar.
9. Serve immediately.

◆ ◆ ◆ ◆ ◆ ◆ ◆ ◆ ◆ ◆ ◆ ◆ ◆ ◆ ◆ ◆ ◆ ◆ ◆ ◆

Baked Sauternes Creams

SERVES 4
110ml/4fl oz Sauternes
pinch of saffron strands or powder
290ml/10fl oz double cream
1 vanilla pod
3 egg yolks
1 egg
50g/1½oz caster sugar

TO GARNISH:
110g/4oz dried muscat grapes or large
Californian raisins, soaked for 2 hours in
Sauternes to cover

TO SERVE:
caramelised apple purée (see p. 200)

1. Preheat the oven to 150°C/300°F/gas mark 3. Oil four ramekins lightly and leave to drain, upside down, on paper towels.
2. Heat the Sauternes and saffron in a small saucepan to just below boiling. Turn off the heat and leave to infuse for 5 minutes.
3. Pour the cream into another saucepan. Scrape the seeds from the vanilla pod and

add them and the pod to the cream (the pod will be discarded; the seeds add interest to the creams). Heat gently to just below boiling. Turn off the heat and leave to infuse for 5 minutes.

4. Beat the egg yolks, egg and sugar together in a bowl until thick. Stir in the Sauternes mixture, then the warmed cream.

5. Strain into a jug and pour into the ramekins.

6. Stand the ramekins in a roasting tin. Pour in enough hot water to come half-way up the sides of the dishes and put on the middle shelf of the oven. Bake for 35–40 minutes or until the creams are set. Remove from the oven and allow to cool.

7. Serve at room temperature, with the caramelised apple purée, garnished with the soaked dried fruit.

◆ ◆

Damson Roulade

This recipe is adapted from one given to us by Nell Scott, who was a member of staff for a while. Its light texture and clean taste make it an ideal pudding to follow a rich main course.

SERVES 6–8
4 eggs, separated
110g/4oz caster sugar
55g/2oz plain flour
pinch of salt
450g/1lb damson purée (see p. 200)
3 tablespoons water
1 teaspoon gelatine (for agar agar see p. 180)

TO SERVE:
Greek yoghurt or crème fraîche

1. Preheat the oven to 200°C/400°F/gas mark 6. Make a roulade case (see p. 184).

2. Put the egg yolks into a bowl, add the sugar and whisk with electric beaters until the mixture is thick and pale.

3. Sift the flour and salt and fold into the egg mixture with half of the damson purée.

4. Whisk the egg whites in a large bowl until stiff but not dry (the mixture should form a soft peak when the whisk is lifted out).

5. Stir 1 tablespoon of egg white into the damson purée to loosen it. Then gently, but quickly, fold in the rest of the egg white with a large metal spoon.

6. Pour the mixture into the roulade case and spread evenly. Put on the middle shelf of the oven and bake for 15–20 minutes or until the roulade is light brown and feels firm to the touch. Remove from the oven and leave to cool in the tin.

7. Meanwhile, put the water into a small saucepan, and sprinkle on the gelatine and leave to soak for 5 minutes.

8. Gently heat the gelatine until dissolved and quite clear; do not allow to boil.

9. Put the remaining 225g/8oz damson purée into a bowl and stir in the warm gelatine. Leave to cool. The mixture will not solidify completely. Reserve 2 tablespoons to glaze the roulade.

10. Remove the roulade in its silicone lining from the Swiss roll tin to a flat surface. Peel down the sides of the paper case and trim the roulade. Spread the brown surface evenly

with the jellied damson purée.

11. Fold over the first 2.5cm/1 inch of the roulade and then roll up like a Swiss roll, using the silicone paper to roll tightly as you go. Roll straight on to the serving plate, leaving the seam underneath. Wrap tightly with the silicone paper to help keep its shape

while the roulade is setting. Refrigerate.

12. Brush the roulade with the reserved purée to glaze. If the glaze has become too firm, beat for a few minutes to soften.

13. Serve with Greek yoghurt or crème fraîche.

♦ ♦

Poached Tamarillos with Coconut Tapioca Timbales

SERVES 4

FOR THE TIMBALES:

570–860ml/1–1½ pints milk
110g/4oz creamed coconut, chopped
½ vanilla pod with seeds
45g/1½oz pearl tapioca
55g/2oz caster sugar

FOR THE TAMARILLOS:

4 tamarillos
170g/6oz caster sugar
570ml/1 pint water

1. Oil four timbales or ramekins lightly. Turn them upside down and leave on paper towels to drain off any excess oil.

2. Make the tapioca timbales: pour 570ml/1 pint milk into a medium saucepan, add the coconut and melt over a gentle heat. Scrape the seeds from the vanilla pod and put both the seeds and the pod into the milk. When the milk is hot but not boiling, add the

tapioca and cook over a low heat for 10–15 minutes, stirring frequently. Add the sugar and stir until dissolved. The consistency of the tapioca should be that of lightly whipped cream. Add a little cold milk if necessary.

3. Put the timbales or ramekins on a plate and spoon in the tapioca. Cover with cling film and place in a refrigerator until ready to use.

4. Prepare the tamarillos: bring a small but deep saucepan of water to the boil. Drop in the tamarillos, count to ten, remove them and plunge into a bowl of very cold water to prevent further cooking. Remove the skins. If the skin is still difficult to remove, repeat the process.

5. Put the sugar and water into a large, shallow saucepan and heat gently until the sugar has completely dissolved. Bring to the boil and reduce by half. Remove from the heat.

6. Leaving the stalks on, slice the tamarillos, making about 5–6 cuts lengthways, to within 5mm/¼ inch of the stalk. The fruit should remain in one piece. (See illustration on p. 139). Add the tamarillos to the syrup, using a fish slice. Fan them out and spoon over the syrup.

7. Reduce the heat and gently poach the tamarillos for 10–12 minutes*. Baste continually. The syrup will be reduced to a

thick, glossy sauce.

8. To serve: unmould the tapioca timbales on to four serving plates.

9. Remove the tamarillos carefully from the pan and place next to the tapioca timbales. Spoon the syrup over and around the tamarillos. Tamarillos are high in pectin so the syrup will set like jam.

NOTE:

* The length of time it takes to cook the tamarillos will depend on their state of ripeness. If they are cooked before the juices are fully reduced, remove carefully on to a plate and boil the liquid to the required consistency.

◆ ◆

Fresh Redcurrants, Brown Breadcrumbs and Crème Fraîche

This fruit pudding is an Austrian recipe. It is wonderfully fresh, and quite delicious. Though it may sound an unlikely combination, it does, after all, use similar ingredients to our summer pudding. It is very easy to put together and should not be passed over.

SERVES 4

450g/1lb redcurrants
225g/8oz fresh brown breadcrumbs
110g/4oz Demerara sugar
450g/1lb crème fraîche

TO GARNISH:
redcurrant leaves or mint leaves

1. Strip the redcurrants from the stalks using a fork. Do not rinse them unless necessary, in which case drain thoroughly on paper towels.

2. Mix the breadcrumbs and sugar in a bowl. Cover the bowl with cling film and set aside.

3. To serve: divide the redcurrants between four plates or bowls. Sprinkle each portion with 3 tablespoons of the breadcrumb mixture. Serve topped with a generous spoonful of crème fraîche and garnish with the redcurrant leaves or mint leaves.

NOTE:

* Redcurrants can be sour, so put a bowl of Demerara sugar on the table for those who do not find the pudding sweet enough.

Apples and Blackberries in Cassis Syrup

SERVES 4

4 Granny Smith apples, with stalks if
possible

FOR THE POACHING LIQUID:

225g/8oz blackberries
juice and 2 strips of peel from half a lemon
½ stick of cinnamon
2 strips of orange peel
110g/4oz sugar
150ml/5fl oz crème de cassis
150ml/5fl oz dry white wine

TO SERVE:

2 tablespoons of the poaching juices (see above)
yoghurt
225g/8oz blackberries

1. Put the poaching ingredients into a large shallow pan and simmer over a low heat until the sugar has dissolved.

2. Peel the apples, cut in half leaving the stalk on one half, and remove the cores with a melon baller or small spoon.

3. Add to the poaching liquid, cut side up, and cover with a lid.

4. Poach the apples over a low heat for about 15 minutes or until just tender. Baste frequently, using a wooden spoon to avoid damaging the fruit. Take the pan off the heat. Leave the fruit to cool in the liquid. The longer the apples are left in the poaching liquid the more coloured they will become.

5. Remove the apples with two wooden spoons and place, cut side down, on a plate. Strain the cooking liquid through a plastic or nylon sieve, return to a clean saucepan and simmer over a moderate heat until reduced to a thick syrup. Leave to cool.

6. To serve: put two apple halves on each of four plates and spoon the syrup over and around. Add a spoonful of yoghurt if wished or serve it separately.

7. Garnish with blackberries.

NOTE:

* This recipe also works well with pears; cook them for 20 minutes.

Star Fruit and Kumquats Poached with Star Anise

SERVES 4
FOR THE SYRUP:
285g/10oz granulated sugar
570ml/1 pint water
1 tablespoon lemon juice
4 whole star anise (to be kept for garnish)
4 sprigs of oregano

FOR THE FRUIT:
4 star fruit, sliced
12 kumquats, sliced

TO GARNISH:
4 sprigs of oregano
4 star anise (reserved from poaching)

1. Put the sugar and water into a wide-bottomed sauté pan and place over a low heat until the sugar has dissolved. Add the lemon juice, star anise and oregano.
2. Put the star fruit and kumquats into the poaching liquid and simmer over a low heat for about 8–10 minutes. Remove the star fruit with a slotted spoon on to a plate.
3. Leave the kumquats in the liquid and cook gently for a further 5 minutes, or until soft. Remove the kumquats in the same way as the star fruit. Continue to simmer gently until the liquid has reached a thick, syrupy consistency. Do not allow to boil as it will start to caramelise. Remove from the heat.
4. Take out and reserve the star anise. Discard the oregano. Return the star fruit and kumquats to the pan and carefully coat with the syrup. Allow to cool in the syrup.
5. Arrange on four serving plates and garnish each one with 1 star anise and a fresh sprig of oregano.

♦ ♦

Poached Fresh Figs with Mascarpone Mousse

SERVES 6
FOR THE MOUSSE:
2 tablespoons warm basic sugar syrup (see p. 179)
250g/9oz mascarpone cheese
seeds from 1 vanilla pod
2 tablespoons Amaretto

150ml/5fl oz Greek yoghurt
3 tablespoons water
15g/½oz gelatine
2 egg whites

FOR THE POACHED FIGS:
570ml/1 pint medium dry red wine
110g/4oz sugar
1 vanilla pod
1 cinnamon stick
2 strips of lemon peel
6 large ripe figs, trimmed

TO SERVE:
icing sugar

1. Oil six dariole moulds or ramekins lightly. Leave upside down on paper towels to drain.

2. Make the mousse: put the warm sugar syrup, mascarpone, vanilla seeds, Amaretto and Greek yoghurt into a large bowl and beat to a smooth cream using electric beaters or a hand whisk.

3. Put the water into a small saucepan, sprinkle over the gelatine and leave to sponge for 5 minutes.

4. Gently heat the gelatine until dissolved and completely clear; do not allow to boil. Pour into the mascarpone mixture quickly, stirring continuously. Leave until beginning to set.

5. Meanwhile, put the egg whites into a large bowl and whisk until they reach a soft peak consistency. Stir 1 tablespoon into the mascarpone mixture and then carefully fold in the rest with a large metal spoon.

6. Pour the mixture into the prepared moulds or ramekins and chill for at least 2 hours.

7. Poach the figs: gently heat the wine, sugar, vanilla pod, cinnamon stick and strips of lemon peel in a saucepan until the sugar has dissolved. Bring to the boil and simmer for 5 minutes. Remove from the heat.

8. Stand the figs upright in the syrup, cover and return the saucepan to the heat. Poach gently for 5–10 minutes, spooning the juices over the figs occasionally.

9. Remove the figs with a slotted spoon and put to one side. If necessary boil the poaching liquid to a syrupy consistency. Strain into a jug and leave to cool.

10. To serve: heat the grill until very hot. Unmould the mousses on to six plates, sprinkle generously with icing sugar and flash under the grill until the icing sugar starts to caramelise. This will not take long and should be watched VERY carefully. Do not leave the grill.

11. Cut the figs in half and place on each plate with the mousse. Pour over some wine syrup.

◆ ◆

Poached Pears with Ginger and Chinese Five Spice

SERVES 4

4 firm Comice pears, peeled carefully
85g/3oz caster sugar
5cm/2 inch piece of fresh ginger, peeled and
    coarsely chopped
7g/¼oz Chinese five spice, whole or powdered
150ml/5fl oz Stone's ginger wine
water

TO GARNISH:
2 pieces of stem ginger cut into julienne strips

1. Place the pears in a saucepan tall enough to accommodate them easily.

2. Add the sugar, ginger, Chinese five spice, ginger wine and enough water to cover the pears. Place a disc of wet greaseproof paper over the pears to keep them submerged. Cover with a close-fitting lid and cook over a low heat until the sugar has dissolved.

3. Bring to the boil, reduce the temperature and poach the pears until tender.* Test with a sharp knife or skewer.

4. Carefully remove the pears with a slotted spoon and put into a serving dish.

5. Strain the poaching liquid, return to the pan and boil until reduced to a syrup. Pour over the pears, and set aside to cool.

6. To serve: put 1 pear on each of four plates and spoon over some of the poaching syrup. Garnish with the stem ginger.

NOTE:
* Once the poaching liquid has been brought to the boil, the pears can be transferred to a low oven (130°C/250°F/gas mark 1) for 1–1½ hours or until cooked.

◆ ◆

Exotic Fresh Fruit Platter

The selection of fruit for this recipe is a matter of personal taste based on what is available. However, the watermelon is essential for the design of the dish. The fruit must be ripe.

SERVES 6

½ small watermelon, wiped
1 small pineapple
2 oranges
1 star fruit, wiped
6 fresh lychees
3 black-skinned figs, wiped carefully
3 passion fruit, wiped
110g/4oz fresh dates, stones removed

1. Leaving the skin on, cut the watermelon into 1cm/½ inch thick slices. Cut the slices in half horizontally to make wedge shapes. Reserve any juices in a jug, and set aside.

2. Remove the skin and the eyes from the pineapple with a sharp, serrated fruit knife. Cut into 1cm/½ inch thick slices. Remove and discard the cores; put the slices to one side. Add any juices to the reserved melon juice.

3. Remove the skin, pith and white membrane from the oranges with a sharp, serrated fruit knife. Slice the oranges horizontally, and put to one side. Add the juices to the reserved juices.

4. Slice the star fruit horizontally. Half-peel the lychees. Put aside.

5. Cut the figs, passion fruit and dates in half and put aside.

6. Arrange the fruit on a large oval platter in a fan shape, starting with a row of overlapping wedges of watermelon on the outside, then rows of pineapple, oranges, star fruit, and lychees, finishing with the halves of fig and passion fruit at the front. Finally, scatter over the fresh dates.

7. Before serving pour over the combined fruit juices.

Elderflower and Champagne Jellies

SERVES 4
425ml/15fl oz champagne
30g/1oz gelatine
150ml/5fl oz elderflower cordial (see p. 196)

TO GARNISH:
frosted elderflower florets*

TO SERVE:
lace biscuits (see p. 166)

1. Put 3 tablespoons champagne into a small saucepan, sprinkle on the gelatine and leave to soak for 5 minutes.
2. Gently heat the gelatine until dissolved and quite clear; do not allow to boil.
3. Mix the remaining champagne and the elderflower cordial in a large bowl and whisk in the gelatine with a hand-whisk until well blended. Pour into individual jelly moulds** (or champagne glasses) and refrigerate overnight.
4. Unmould the jellies: put the moulds into a bowl of hot water for a few seconds to loosen the jelly. Place a serving plate over the top of the mould and invert both together. There is no need to unmould jelly set in champagne glasses.
5. Garnish with a frosted elderflower head and serve with lace biscuits.

NOTES:
* To make frosted elderflower florets: break the flower heads into florets. Beat one egg white until beginning to froth. Brush the umbels lightly with some beaten egg white and then dredge with caster sugar. Put each floret into a coffee cup or small jar for support and leave to dry for 24 hours.
** The jelly may also be set in a 570ml/1 pint mould.

♦ ♦

Black Velvet Ice Cream

This recipe is a very good way of using up left-over champagne or sparkling wines. Do not be put off by the unusual combination of ingredients!

MAKES APPROXIMATELY 860ML/1½ PINTS
110ml/4fl oz water
4 tablespoons cornflour
110g/4oz caster sugar
pinch of salt
570ml/1 pint single cream
4 tablespoons condensed milk
150ml/5fl oz champagne or sparkling wine
150ml/5fl oz stout

TO SERVE:
shattered fragments of praline (see p. 201)

1. Put the water and cornflour into a medium-sized saucepan and mix together with a wooden spoon. Add the sugar, salt and cream and cook, stirring over a low heat for 5–8 minutes until the cornflour has thickened and the 'custard' is thick and creamy (do not allow the mixture to boil until it has begun to thicken). Remove from the heat.

2. Stir in the condensed milk and leave until cold. The mixture should be beaten well or mixed to a smooth cream in a food processor if it becomes lumpy on setting.

3. Stir in the champagne, or sparkling wine, and the stout, pour into a plastic container and freeze for 2 hours or until solid round the edges but soft in the centre.

5. Scoop the ice cream into a bowl and beat well or put into a food processor and mix until thick and smooth. Refreeze for a further 2 hours or until ready to serve.

6. Thirty minutes before serving, remove to a refrigerator to soften.

7. Serve decorated with shattered fragments of praline.

NOTE:

* This ice cream will be much creamier if made in an ice cream maker.

♦ ♦

Ratafia and Crème Fraîche Ice Cream

SERVES 4–6
450g/1lb crème fraîche
1 teaspoon natural almond essence
1 teaspoon natural vanilla essence
3–4 tablespoons icing sugar
2 egg whites
20 ratafia biscuits

1. Put the crème fraîche into a bowl and add the almond and vanilla essences. Do not cut down on the stated quantities of essences as freezing dilutes flavours. Sift in the icing sugar.

2. Transfer to a freezer-proof container, cover and freeze for 1–1½ hours.

3. When the ice cream is half frozen, remove from the freezer and mix gently in a food processor to break up the ice crystals.* Add the egg whites and process again briefly.

4. Stir in the ratafia biscuits. Taste and add more icing sugar or essence if necessary. Pour back into the container, cover and return to the freezer for at least 2 hours.

5. Thirty minutes before serving, move the ice cream from the freezer to the refrigerator.

NOTES:

* Do not mix the ice cream if too hard or it will curdle.

** To make individual servings, freeze in ramekins or teacups.

Honey and Greek Yoghurt Ice Cream

SERVES 4

4 egg yolks
4 tablespoons clear honey
290ml/10fl oz milk
500g/18oz Greek yoghurt

1. Put the egg yolks and honey into a bowl and whisk with electric beaters until pale, thick and creamy.
2. Warm the milk in a saucepan and then pour on to the yolk and honey mixture, stirring steadily.
3. Return the milk to the saucepan. Stir over a low heat until the mixture has thickened and will coat the back of a spoon. This will take about 5 minutes. Do not boil.
4. Pour into a large bowl and beat in the yoghurt using a wooden spoon.
5. Pour into a freezer-proof container, cover with a lid, and leave to become cold. Freeze for 2 to 3 hours, or until solid.
6. Remove from the freezer and allow to soften at room temperature. Place in a food processor and mix to remove the ice crystals. Return the mixture to the container, cover and return to the freezer for at least 2 hours.
7. Twenty minutes before serving, transfer the ice cream to the refrigerator.

NOTE:
* Yoghurt has a low fat content, so yoghurt-based ice creams are generally much creamier if made in an ice cream maker.

BREADS

Baguette
Ciabatta
Focaccia
Polenta Rolls
Quick Rosemary Bread
Granary and Pine Nut Soda Bread
Seeded Sweet Potato Bread
Tomato, Herb and Mozzarella Flatbread
Red Pepper Bread
Sun-dried Tomato and Olive Bread
Warm Cheddar and Pickle Quickbread
Corn Bread
Curried Pumpkin Bread
Smoked Tofu and Soy Sauce Bread
Coconut Bread

Baguette

MAKES 2 SHORT BAGUETTES
15g/½oz fresh yeast or 7g/¼oz easy-blend
  yeast
450g/1lb strong unbleached flour
290ml/10fl oz warm water
1 teaspoon salt

1. Cream the fresh yeast with 2 tablespoons of the warm water in a small bowl or a teacup.
2. Sift the flour and salt into a large bowl (stir in the easy-blend yeast, if using).
3. Add the fresh yeast, and water and mix to a sticky dough. Remove the dough to a lightly floured surface and knead for about 15–20 minutes or until it is smooth and elastic. Do not be worried that the dough is too sticky or be tempted to add more flour. As the dough is kneaded it will become easier to handle. Form the dough into a ball.*
4. Lightly oil a bowl, put the ball of dough into it and turn to coat with oil. Cover the bowl with cling film. Leave to rise in a warm, draught-free place for about 1½ hours or until doubled in size.
5. Flour two large baking sheets or two flat oven trays lightly.
6. Knock back the dough; transfer to a floured surface and knead again for 5 minutes. Divide the dough in half and, using both hands, roll each piece into a length to fit diagonally on to the baking sheets or oven trays.
7. Place a loaf on each baking sheet or oven tray, and make diagonal slashes at even intervals along each one. Spray, or sprinkle evenly, with water and leave in a warm place to rise again for 30 minutes or until almost doubled in size.
8. Meanwhile, preheat the oven to 220°C/425°F/gas mark 7.
9. Spray, or sprinkle evenly, with water again and put on the middle shelf of the oven. Spray or sprinkle with cold water every 3 minutes for the first 9 minutes (spraying helps to give a good crisp crust). Continue cooking for a further 20–25 minutes or until the bread is well browned and crisp. The underside should sound hollow when tapped.
10. Transfer to a wire rack to cool.

NOTE:
* At this stage the dough could be placed in a large plastic bag and left to rise in a refrigerator overnight. Seal the bag at the neck end to allow room for the dough to expand. Bring the dough back up to room temperature before proceeding with stage 5.

♦ ♦

Ciabatta

Ciabatta takes about 24 hours to make because the dough needs two slow risings and then a long proving period in order to allow the yeast to produce the characteristic large holes.

MAKES 4 LOAVES

FOR THE STARTER DOUGH:
7g/¼oz fresh yeast or ½ teaspoon easy-blend
  yeast
200ml/7fl oz warm water
340g/12oz strong unbleached flour

FOR THE CIABATTA:

20g/¾oz fresh yeast or 2 teaspoons easy-blend yeast

200–290ml/7–10fl oz warm water

5 tablespoons warm milk

4 tablespoons olive oil

560g/1¼lb strong unbleached flour

1 teaspoon salt

1. Make the starter dough: cream the fresh yeast with the warm water in a small bowl, and then sift in the flour (if using easy-blend yeast, add to the flour with the warm water) and mix to make a soft dough. Add more water if necessary. Knead for a few minutes. Lightly oil a bowl, put in the dough, turn to coat with oil and cover the bowl with cling film. Leave at room temperature for 12–24 hours until tripled in size.

2. Make the ciabatta: cream the fresh yeast with a little of the warm water, in a small bowl or a teacup. Knock back the starter dough, add the fresh yeast, the rest of the warm water, the warm milk and the olive oil and gently mix together.

3. Sift the flour and salt into a large bowl (add the easy-blend yeast, if using), gradually add the starter dough mixture and combine to form a soft dough. Transfer to a lightly floured surface and knead for about 20 minutes or until smooth and elastic. Form into a ball.

4. Lightly oil a bowl, put the ball of dough into it, turn to coat with oil and cover the bowl with cling film. Leave the dough to rise

in a warm, draught-free place for about 2 hours or until doubled in size.

5. Knock back the dough; transfer to a lightly floured surface and knead for a few minutes. Divide into four pieces and knead each into a ball.

6. Flour four baking sheets. Put one ball of dough on to one of the baking sheets and, using the hands and knuckles, stretch and prod the dough into a 2.5cm/1 inch thick rectangle, about 35 × 15cm/14 × 6 inches. Make final indentations with the knuckles. Repeat with the other three balls of dough.

7. Brush with olive oil and leave to rise again in a warm place for 30–40 minutes until the dough, although relatively flat, is slightly risen and rather uneven.

8. Meanwhile, preheat the oven to 220°C/425°F/gas mark 7.

9. Spray, or sprinkle, the loaves with cold water, put on the middle shelf of the oven and bake for 15–20 minutes, spraying or sprinkling with cold water every 3 minutes for the first 9 minutes (spraying is important for producing a good crisp crust). The bread will be cooked when it is brown and sounds hollow when tapped on the underside.

10. Cool on wire racks.

NOTES:

* If more convenient, bake the loaves in two batches. The second two loaves can be proving while the first two are baking.

** Ciabatta is best eaten on the day it is made, but it can be frozen.

Focaccia

MAKES 1 LOAF
15g/½ oz fresh yeast or 7g/¼ oz easy-blend yeast
290ml/10fl oz warm water
340g/12oz strong unbleached flour
1 teaspoon salt
6 tablespoons olive oil
1 tablespoon sea salt

1. Cream the fresh yeast with a little of the warm water, in a small bowl, or a teacup.
2. Sift the flour and salt into a large bowl (stir in the easy-blend yeast if using). Add the fresh yeast, water and olive oil and mix with a knife and then a hand to a soft dough.
3. Turn on to a lightly floured surface and knead for about 10 minutes or until smooth and elastic.*
4. Lightly oil a bowl, put the ball of dough into it and turn to coat with oil. Cover the bowl with cling film. Leave the dough to rise in a warm, draught-free place for 1½–2 hours or until doubled in size.
5. Knock back the dough; transfer to a lightly floured surface and knead for a few minutes. Put on to a floured baking sheet and stretch into a roughly-shaped rectangle about 30 × 15cm/12 × 6 inches and 2.5cm/1 inch thick. Using the handle of a wooden spoon or a finger, make deep indentations over the surface.
6. Brush generously with olive oil and leave to rise again in a warm place for about 30 minutes or until it is 5cm/2 inches high. Indent again, if necessary.
7. Meawhile, preheat the oven to 200°C/400°F/gas mark 6.
8. Sprinkle the loaf with sea salt and put on the middle shelf of the oven. Bake for approximately 25 minutes or until cooked and browned.
9. Serve warm.

NOTES:
* At this stage the dough can be placed in a large plastic bag and left to rise in a refrigerator overnight. Seal the bag at the neck to allow room for the dough to expand. Bring the dough back up to room temperature before proceeding with stage 5.
** Focaccia can be served by itself, but it is often served topped, or filled. The following suggestions can be used either on top (add at the end of stage 5 and proceed according to the recipe) or in the middle (cut the cooked loaf open horizontally and fill like a sandwich):
– Beef tomatoes, black olives and basil drizzled with olive oil.
– Artichoke hearts, grilled aubergine, rocket and mustard mayonnaise (filling only).
– Roasted peppers, roasted garlic and sun-dried tomatoes.
– Mozzarella, Gorgonzola and Parmesan cheeses.
– Fried onions, sage and Cheddar cheese.

Polenta Rolls

MAKES 6 ROLLS
30g/1oz fresh yeast or 15g/½oz easy-blend
  yeast
290ml/10fl oz warm water
285g/10oz plain flour
1 teaspoon salt
170g/6oz instant polenta
flour for kneading
1 egg, beaten to glaze

1. Cream the fresh yeast with a little of the warm water, in a small bowl or a teacup.
2. Sift the flour, salt and polenta into a large bowl (stir in the easy-blend yeast if using). Add the fresh yeast and water and mix with a fork to make a sticky dough that is just too wet to knead (add a little more water if it is dry enough to handle).
3. Cover the bowl with cling film and leave to rise in a warm, draught-free place for 1½–2 hours or until doubled in size and frothy.
4. Knock back the dough; transfer to a floured surface and knead for 20 minutes, working in as much flour as is needed to make a soft dough.
5. Flour a baking sheet. Divide the dough into six pieces and shape into rolls. Place on the baking sheet and leave to rise again in a warm place for 30 minutes or until doubled in size. The texture of these rolls is quite dense so do not hurry this stage.
6. Meanwhile, preheat the oven to 220°C/425°F/gas mark 7.
7. Brush the rolls with beaten egg, place on the middle shelf of the oven and bake for 20 minutes or until risen and pale brown and sound hollow when tapped on the underside.
8. Leave to cool on a wire rack. If a soft crust is required, cover the rolls with a tea towel whilst cooling.

◆ ◆

Quick Rosemary Bread

This recipe needs only one rising instead of the usual two. The heat of the oven is all that is required to make the bread rise once it has been shaped.

MAKES 1 LOAF
15g/½oz fresh yeast or 7g/¼oz easy-blend
  yeast
150ml/5fl oz warm water
340g/12oz strong unbleached flour
salt and freshly ground black pepper
1½ tablespoons finely chopped rosemary leaves
milk for glazing

1. Cream the fresh yeast with a little of the warm water, in a small bowl or a teacup. Sift the flour and seasonings into a large bowl (stir in the easy-blend yeast if using). Add the rosemary, fresh yeast, and the water and mix to a soft dough. If necessary, add more warm water. Knead for 5–10 minutes.
2. Lightly oil a bowl, put the dough into it and turn to coat with oil. Cover the bowl with cling film. Leave to rise in a warm, draught-free place for 1½–2 hours or until doubled in size.

3. Preheat the oven to 200°C/400°F/gas mark 6. Flour a baking sheet.

4. Knock back the dough: transfer to a lightly floured surface and knead for a few minutes. Form the dough into a ball and put on to the baking sheet. Cut the ball into eight wedges but do not separate the wedges out. Brush the dough with milk.

5. Put on the middle shelf of the oven and bake for 20–25 minutes or until golden brown and the loaf sounds hollow when tapped on the underside. Brush the glazed areas only with more milk 10 minutes before the end of cooking time.

6. Cool on a wire rack.

◆ ◆

Granary and Pine Nut Soda Bread

MAKES 2 LOAVES

110g/4oz plain flour
450g/1lb granary flour, plus extra for sprinkling
2 teaspoons baking powder
2 teaspoons bicarbonate of soda
110g/4oz coarse or fine bran
225g/8oz pine nuts
425ml/15fl oz plain yoghurt
290ml/10fl oz milk

1. Preheat the oven to 200°C/400°F/gas mark 6. Flour 2 baking sheets.

2. Sift both the flours, the baking powder and bicarbonate of soda into a large bowl. Return the cereal grains to the bowl and mix in the bran. Add the pine nuts, yoghurt and enough milk to make a soft but not too sticky, dough.

3. Transfer to a lightly floured surface and divide the dough in half. Transfer each half to the baking sheets and shape, with the minimum of kneading, into a round loaf. The dough should not look smooth.

4. Using the floured handle of a wooden spoon, make a deep cross in each loaf, almost dividing them into four sections. Sprinkle the top with granary flour.

5. Put the loaves in the oven and bake for 25–30 minutes, or until brown and hollow-sounding when tapped on the underside.

6. Leave to cool on a wire rack.

◆ ◆

Seeded Sweet Potato Bread

This recipe was given to us by 'C.J.' Jackson, Head Teacher at the School. It has a wonderful spiced flavour and nutty texture.

MAKES 1 LOAF

1 large sweet potato (about 225–285g/8–10oz)
30g/1oz fresh yeast or 15g/½oz easy-blend yeast
675g/1½lb plain flour
1 tablespoon salt
55g/2oz butter
200ml/7fl oz milk, warmed
2 eggs, beaten

1 tablespoon fennel seeds
1 tablespoon caraway seeds
1 tablespoon dill seeds
1 teaspoon cumin seeds
30g/1oz pumpkin seeds
2 teaspoons ground coriander
1 beaten egg to glaze

1. Preheat the oven to 190°C/375°F/gas mark 5.
2. Bake the sweet potato for approximately 1 hour or until soft. Leave until cool enough to handle.
3. Peel the sweet potato and push the flesh through a sieve with the back of a wooden spoon. Set aside.
4. Cream the fresh yeast with a little warm water in a small bowl.
5. Sift the flour and salt into a large bowl (stir in the easy-blend yeast, if using). Add the butter and rub in to resemble breadcrumbs.
6. Mix the fresh yeast with the warm milk and the eggs. Make a well in the centre of the flour, pour in the fresh yeast mixture (or just the milk and eggs), add the sweet potato,

and mix to a soft dough.
7. Transfer to a lightly floured surface and knead for 10 minutes, or until smooth and elastic.
8. Lightly oil a bowl, put the dough into it, turn to coat in oil then cover the bowl with cling film. Leave in a warm, draught-free place for about 1½ hours or until doubled in size.
9. Grease a 1kg/2lb loaf tin. Knock back the dough on a lightly floured surface. Flatten out the dough, sprinkle with the seeds and knead for a further 5 minutes or until the seeds are well distributed.
10. Shape the dough and put into the loaf tin. Cover with cling film and leave to rise again in a warm place for about 30 minutes or until almost doubled in size.
11. Meanwhile preheat the oven to 200°C/400°F/gas mark 6.
12. Glaze the bread and bake on the middle shelf of the oven for 35–40 minutes or until well risen and brown and the loaf sounds hollow when tapped on the underside.
13. Cool on a wire rack.

◆ ◆

Tomato, Herb and Mozzarella Flatbread

MAKES 1 LOAF
15g/½oz fresh yeast or 7g/¼oz easy-blend yeast
200ml/7fl oz warm water
400g/14oz strong unbleached flour
1 teaspoon salt

1 tablespoon chopped oregano
1 tablespoon chopped mint
1 tablespoon chopped thyme leaves
2 teaspoons chopped sage leaves
2 teaspoons chopped rosemary
110 ml/4fl oz olive oil

FOR THE FILLING:
400g/14oz tomatoes, peeled and sliced
225g/8oz mozzarella cheese, sliced
freshly ground black pepper

FOR THE TOP:
olive oil for brushing
20 black olives, pitted
55g/2oz Parmesan cheese, freshly grated

1. Cream the fresh yeast with a little of the warm water, in a small bowl or a teacup.
2. Sift the flour and salt into a large bowl (stir in the easy-blend yeast, if using). Add the fresh yeast, herbs, olive oil and water and mix well to make a soft, almost sticky, dough.
3. Transfer to a lightly floured surface and knead for 10 minutes or until the dough is soft and elastic. Form into a ball.
4. Lightly oil a bowl, put the ball of dough into it and turn to coat with oil. Cover the bowl with cling film. Leave to rise in a warm, draught-free place for 1½–2 hours or until doubled in size. Oil a baking sheet.
5. Knock back the dough: transfer to a lightly floured surface and knead for a few minutes. Divide in half. Put one half on to the baking sheet and flatten with the fingers to a 25cm/10 inch circle.
6. Cover with a layer of overlapping tomato slices, then a layer of mozzarella, leaving a

2.5cm/1 inch border. Season generously with freshly ground black pepper.
7. Make another 25cm/10 inch circle with the remaining dough. Place over the top of the tomato and mozzarella filling and seal the edges. They will stick together as the bread rises again. Make into a neat, round loaf.
8. Brush the dough with olive oil and then stud firmly with the black olives. Sprinkle with the Parmesan cheese. Leave to rise in a warm place for about 30 minutes or until almost doubled in size.
9. Meanwhile, preheat the oven to 200°C/400°F/gas mark 6.
10. Place the bread on the middle shelf of the oven and bake for 20 minutes. Lower the oven temperature to 190°C/375°F/gas mark 5 and bake for a further 30–35 minutes or until the bread is risen and golden brown. The bread is not cooked until it comes away cleanly from the baking sheet.
11. Cool on a wire rack for 10 minutes then transfer to a large plate.
12. To serve: cut into wedges.

◆ ◆

Red Pepper Bread

MAKES 1 LOAF
30g/1oz fresh yeast, or
   15g/½ oz easy-blend yeast
225ml/8fl oz warm water
450g/1lb strong unbleached flour
2 teaspoons salt
2 tablespoons olive oil
2 red peppers, grilled, peeled and diced (see
   p. 181)

4 tablespoons olive oil
2 sprigs of rosemary
1 tablespoon sea salt

1. Cream the fresh yeast with the water in a small bowl or a teacup.
2. Sift the flour and salt into a large bowl (stir in the easy-blend yeast, if using) and make a well in the centre. Add the fresh yeast (water if using easy-blend yeast) and the olive oil, and mix to a dough. Turn out

on to a lightly floured surface and knead for 8–10 minutes or until the dough is smooth and elastic.

3. Lightly oil a bowl, put the dough into it, turn to coat with oil, and cover the bowl with cling film. Leave to rise in a warm, draught-free place for about 1½ hours or until doubled in size.*

4. Knock back the dough on a floured surface and flatten it out. Sprinkle over the diced red pepper and knead for a few minutes until the pepper is evenly distributed throughout the dough. This may take a little time as the pepper is slippery. Shape into a flat round.

5. Flour a baking sheet, put the loaf on it and leave to rise again in a warm place for about 30 minutes until it has almost doubled its original size.

6. Meanwhile preheat the oven to 220°C/

425°F/gas mark 7.

7. Using a floured finger or handle of a wooden spoon, make indentations over the surface of the loaf. Drizzle over the olive oil, stud with spikes of rosemary and sprinkle with sea salt.

8. Place the bread on the middle shelf of the oven and bake for 30–35 minutes or until well risen, brown and the underside sounds hollow when tapped.

9. Cool on a wire rack.

NOTES:

* At this stage the dough could be placed in a large plastic bag and left to rise in a refrigerator overnight. Seal the bag at the neck end to allow room for the dough to expand. Bring the dough back up to room temperature before proceeding with stage 4.

** The dough can also be made into twelve rolls; bake for 15–18 minutes.

♦ ♦

Sun-dried Tomato and Olive Bread

MAKES 1 LOAF

2 tablespoons oil from a jar of sun-dried tomatoes
2 cloves of garlic, crushed
1 teaspoon chopped rosemary
340g/12oz plain flour
2 teaspoons baking powder
1 teaspoon bicarbonate of soda
1 teaspoon salt
1 tablespoon sugar
2 large eggs
290ml/10fl oz milk
3 tablespoons vegetable shortening, melted
55g/2oz sun-dried tomatoes, chopped

55g/2oz black olives, pitted and chopped
2 tablespoons capers, chopped
4 tablespoons finely chopped parsley
freshly ground black pepper
110g/4oz Parmesan cheese, freshly grated

1. Preheat the oven to 180°C/350°F/gas mark 4. Oil the bottom and sides of a 1kg/2lb loaf tin lightly.

2. Heat the sun-dried tomato oil in a small saucepan, add the garlic and rosemary and cook over a low heat for about 4–5 minutes. Do not allow to brown. Leave to cool.

3. Sift the flour, baking powder, bicarbonate of soda, salt and sugar into a bowl.

4. Put the eggs, milk, melted shortening and the garlic mixture in a large bowl and whisk

together. Stir in the flour mixture to make a stiffish batter.

5. Add the sun-dried tomatoes, olives, capers, parsley, pepper and Parmesan cheese and mix well.

6. Spoon the batter into the loaf tin and put on a baking sheet. Bake on the middle shelf of the oven for 35–40 minutes or until a skewer inserted into the middle comes out clean.

7. Remove from the oven, leave in the tin for 10 minutes and then transfer to a wire rack to cool.

♦ ♦

Warm Cheddar and Pickle Quickbread

Although this bread is best eaten warm, it is also good eaten cold and is ideal for picnics.

SERVES 4

340g/12oz plain flour, sifted
340g/12oz wholemeal flour, sifted
pinch of salt
1½ teaspoons baking powder
½ teaspoon bicarbonate of soda
60g/2½oz butter
handful of parsley, roughly chopped
150ml/5fl oz milk
55ml/2fl oz water

FOR THE FILLING:
4–5 tablespoons sweet pickle
1 large onion, very finely chopped
225g/8oz Cheddar cheese, grated
freshly ground black pepper

1. Preheat the oven to 200°C/400°F/gas mark 6.

2. Put both flours into a food processor* with the salt, baking powder, bicarbonate of soda and butter and mix until blended. Add the parsley and process again.

3. With the motor running, pour in the milk and water to make a soft dough. If necessary add a little more water.

4. Turn the dough on to a lightly floured surface, bring together and divide in half. Using hands or a rolling pin, make each half into two rough circles about 2cm/¾ inch thick.

5. Flour a baking sheet and transfer one of the circles of dough to it. Spread on the pickle with the back of a spoon, leaving a 1cm/½ inch border. Sprinkle with the onion and then all but 2 tablespoons of the Cheddar cheese. Season with black pepper.

6. Brush the edge of the dough with water and cover with the second circle of dough. Seal the edges, shape the bread into a neat circle and sprinkle over the remaining cheese.

7. Put the quickbread on the top shelf of the oven, bake for 10 minutes, then move it down to the middle shelf and continue baking for another 30 minutes or until crisp and well browned.

8. Leave to cool on a wire rack for 10 minutes before serving.

NOTE:
* To make the bread by hand, sift the dry ingredients into a bowl. Dice the butter and rub into the dry ingredients. Mix in the parsley. Make a well in the centre and add the milk and enough water to make a soft dough. Continue with stage 4.

Corn Bread

MAKES 1 LOAF
110g/4oz plain flour
30g/1oz caster sugar
1 tablespoon baking powder
½ teaspoon salt
1 teaspoon harissa paste* or hot chilli powder
170g/6oz polenta or coarse yellow cornmeal
2 eggs
6 tablespoons vegetable oil
110g/4oz cottage cheese
5 tablespoons plain or Greek yoghurt
55g/2oz mature Cheddar cheese, grated

1. Oil a 1kg/2lb loaf tin lightly. Line the bottom of the tin with a piece of greaseproof paper cut to fit, and oil again.
2. Preheat the oven to 200°C/400°F/gas mark 6.
3. Sift the flour, sugar, baking powder, salt and chilli powder, if used, into a bowl. Stir in the polenta or cornmeal.
4. Put the harissa paste, if used, the eggs, oil, cottage cheese, yoghurt and Cheddar cheese into another bowl and beat together.
5. Add to the dry ingredients and mix well. Alternatively, mix all the ingredients in a food processor.
6. Pour into the loaf tin, place on a baking sheet and put on the middle shelf of the oven. Bake for about 25 minutes or until a skewer inserted into the middle of the loaf comes out clean.
7. Leave in the tin for 10 minutes then remove and place on a wire rack to cool.

NOTE:
* Harissa is a fiery Tunisian spice paste (it is now sometimes available in powder form). Available from some Middle Eastern shops, specialist delicatessens and Mail Order (see p. 250).

◆ ◆

Curried Pumpkin Bread

MAKES 2 LOAVES
225g/8oz plain flour
225g/8oz polenta or coarse yellow cornmeal
2 teaspoons baking powder
1 teaspoon bicarbonate of soda
45g/1½oz caster sugar
85g/3oz unsalted butter
2 onions, finely chopped
½ teaspoon ground turmeric
½ teaspoon ground coriander
½ teaspoon ground cumin
½ teaspoon cayenne pepper
1½ teaspoons salt
20g/¾oz cumin seeds, toasted
1 × 425g/15oz can of pumpkin purée
3 eggs
150ml/5fl oz buttermilk

1. Preheat the oven to 180°C/350F/gas mark 4. Grease two 450g/1lb loaf tins and put on a baking sheet.
2. Sift the flour, polenta or cornmeal, baking powder, bicarbonate of soda and sugar into a bowl.
3. Melt 30g/1oz of the butter in a frying pan and add the onions, turmeric, coriander, ground cumin, cayenne pepper and salt. Cook over a low heat for 5 minutes, stirring

all the time. Let the mixture cool and add the cumin seeds. Melt the remaining butter in a small saucepan. Put the pumpkin purée, eggs, buttermilk, melted butter and onion mixture into a large bowl. Whisk together.

4. Make a well in the flour mixture, add the pumpkin and onion mixture, stirring well to form a batter. Pour into the loaf tins.

5. Put on the middle shelf of the oven and bake for 40–45 minutes or until the breads spring back when touched.

6. Remove from the oven and allow to cool for 10 minutes in the tin. Then take out of the tins and leave to cool on a wire rack.

◆ ◆

Smoked Tofu and Soy Sauce Bread

This recipe is adapted from one in Mark Gregory's and Yuzaburo Mogi Kikkoman's *Cooking Japanese Style* (Martin Books). It is quite unusual and has a wonderful savoury taste. It is best eaten on the day it is made.

MAKES 1 LOAF

65ml/2½fl oz soy sauce
1 onion, finely chopped
30g/1oz fresh yeast or 15g/½oz easy-blend yeast
200ml/7fl oz warm water
55g/2oz butter, melted
1 large egg, beaten
55g/2oz Gruyère cheese, grated
285g/10oz plain flour
225g/8oz wholemeal flour
225g/8oz smoked tofu, crumbled
½ bunch spring onions, chopped
1 tablespoon sesame seeds

1. Put the soy sauce into a small saucepan with the onion. Cook slowly until the onion is soft.

2. Cream the fresh yeast with the warm water, add the melted butter, almost all of the egg (reserving some for the glaze) and the grated cheese. Whisk well.

3. Put the flours into a large mixing bowl (stir in the easy-blend yeast, if using). Make a well in the centre and pour in the fresh yeast batter (or, if using easy-blend yeast, the melted butter, some of the egg and the grated cheese). Beat well and add the soy sauce and onion mixture.

4. Transfer to a lightly floured surface and knead for about 10–15 minutes until firm and elastic.

5. Lightly oil a bowl. Put the dough into the bowl, turn to coat with oil and cover the bowl with cling film. Leave in a warm draught-free place for about 1 hour or until doubled in bulk.

6. Grease a baking sheet. Knock back the dough on a floured surface and knead into a smooth ball. Press out the dough into a rectangle 25 × 30cm/10 × 12 inches. Sprinkle with the tofu and spring onions and roll up as you would a Swiss roll. Put on the baking sheet. Cover with cling film and leave to rise again in a warm place for about 40 minutes or until doubled in bulk.

7. Meanwhile, preheat the oven to 190°C/ 375°F/gas mark 5.

8. Brush the bread with the reserved beaten egg and sprinkle with the sesame seeds.

9. Put on the middle shelf of the oven and bake for 30–40 minutes or until golden brown and the underside sounds hollow when tapped. Leave to cool on a wire rack.

Coconut Bread

MAKES 1 LOAF

*15g/½oz fresh yeast or 7g/¼oz easy-blend
    yeast*
290ml/10fl oz warm coconut milk
450g/1lb strong unbleached flour
1½ teaspoons sugar
1 teaspoon salt
100g/3½oz creamed coconut, grated
1 egg, lightly beaten
beaten egg to glaze

1. Lightly oil the bottom and sides of a 1kg/
2lb loaf tin.
2. Cream the fresh yeast with a little of the
coconut milk, in a small bowl or a teacup.
3. Sift the flour, sugar and salt into a large
bowl (stir in the easy-blend yeast, if using).
Add the fresh yeast, coconut milk, sugar,
grated creamed coconut and the egg and mix
to a soft dough, first with a fork and then
with the hand.
4. Transfer to a floured surface and knead
for about 15 minutes or until smooth, shiny
and elastic.* Form into ball.
5. Lightly oil a bowl, put the ball of dough

into it and turn to coat with oil. Cover the
bowl with cling film. Leave to rise in a warm,
draught-free place for about 1½–2 hours
until doubled in size.
6. Knock back the dough on a lightly
floured surface and knead for a few minutes.
Shape and put into the loaf tin. Cover with
cling film and leave to rise again in a warm
place for 30–40 minutes.
7. Meanwhile, preheat the oven to 200°C/
400°F/gas mark 6.
8. Brush the loaf with beaten egg. Put the tin
on the middle shelf of the oven and bake for 10
minutes. Turn the heat down to 190°C/
375°F/gas mark 5 and bake for a further 25
minutes or until the bread is brown and sounds
hollow when the bottom is tapped.
9. Leave to cool on a wire rack.

NOTE:
* At this stage the dough could be placed in a
large plastic bag and left to rise in a refrigerator
overnight. Seal the bag at the neck end to allow
room for the dough to expand. Bring the dough
back up to room temperature before proceeding
with stage 6.

BISCUITS

Lace biscuits
Langues de Chat
Sponge Fingers
Tuiles à l'Orange
Tuiles Amandines
Tuiles au Chocolat
Venetian Biscuits
Orange Flower Biscuits

Lace Biscuits

MAKES 30–40
55g/2oz unsalted butter
55g/2oz caster sugar
3 tablespoons liquid glucose*
55g/2oz plain flour

1. Preheat the oven to 200°C/400°F/gas mark 6.
2. Melt the butter in a saucepan over a low heat and leave to cool. Add the sugar, glucose and flour and mix thoroughly. Set aside.
3. Cut four pieces of silicone paper to fit two baking trays. Line each tray with one sheet, reserving the other two sheets for covering the biscuit mixture later on.
4. Roll teaspoons of the mixture into cherry-sized balls. Place three balls on each baking tray, keeping them well apart to allow for spreading. Cover with the reserved sheet of silicone paper and squash the balls into a flat round shape. The uncooked mixture should be paper thin and sandwiched between the two layers of silicone.
5. Bake the biscuits on the top shelf of the oven for 4–5 minutes, until golden brown.
6. Slide the biscuits and paper on to a work surface. Flatten with the bottom of a saucepan or a suitable alternative. Leave to cool. Repeat with the second tray.
7. Peel off the top sheet of silicone paper very carefully, and transfer the biscuits from the bottom sheet on to a wire rack, again very carefully as the biscuits are fragile.
8. Repeat with the remaining mixture, using the same sheets of silicone paper.
9. Store the biscuits carefully between layers of greaseproof paper in an airtight container. They will become soft and sticky if left exposed to the air for more than 2 hours.

NOTE:
* Available at any good chemist.

◆ ◆

Langues de Chat

MAKES 30–40
100g/3½oz butter
100g/3½oz caster sugar
3 egg whites
100g/3½oz plain flour, sifted

1. Preheat the oven to 200°C/400°F/gas mark 6. Grease a baking sheet or line with silicone paper.
2. Soften the butter with a wooden spoon and add the sugar gradually. Beat until pale and fluffy.
3. Whisk the egg whites slightly and add gradually to the mixture, beating thoroughly between each addition.
4. Fold the flour into the mixture with a metal spoon. Put into a forcing bag fitted with a medium-sized plain nozzle. Pipe into fingers the thickness of a pencil and about 5cm/2 inches long.
5. Tap the baking sheet on the table to release any over-large air bubbles from the fingers. Bake on the middle shelf of the oven for 5–7 minutes or until biscuit-coloured in the middle and brown at the edges.
6. Leave to cool slightly, then lift off the baking sheet with a palette knife. Cool completely before putting into an airtight container.

Sponge Fingers

MAKES 30

6 eggs
140g/5oz caster sugar
110g/4oz plain flour, sifted
30g/1oz arrowroot, sifted

1. Preheat the oven to 200°C/400°F/gas mark 6. Line two large baking sheets with silicone baking paper. Draw parallel lines 12.5cm/5 inches apart on the paper.
2. Separate five of the eggs. Whisk the yolks with the whole egg and 110g/4oz of the caster sugar in a large bowl using electric beaters, until they are nearly white.
3. Whisk the egg whites until stiff and gradually whisk in the remaining caster sugar.
4. Fold the egg whites into the egg yolk and sugar mixture. Carefully fold in the flour and arrowroot.
5. Fit a 5mm/¼ inch plain nozzle into a piping bag and fill the bag with the mixture. Pipe 12.5cm/5 inch fingers between the parallel lines on the baking paper. The fingers should be just touching.
6. Put on the top shelf of the oven and bake for about 10 minutes or until the fingers have risen and are biscuit-coloured.
7. Invert the fingers on to a clean tea towel. Immediately and carefully peel off the paper. Turn the sponge fingers on to a wire rack to cool.

◆ ◆

Tuiles à l'Orange

MAKES 25

2 egg whites
110g/4oz caster sugar
55g/2oz butter, melted
55g/2oz plain flour, sifted
grated zest of 1 orange

1. Preheat the oven to 190°C/375°F/gas mark 5. Grease two or three baking sheets or line with silicone paper.*
2. Whisk the egg whites until stiff. Add the sugar and whisk thoroughly.
3. Gradually fold the butter and flour into the meringue mixture. Fold in the orange zest.
4. Spread out teaspoonfuls very thinly on the baking sheet, keeping them well apart to allow for spreading during cooking. Bake on the middle shelf of the oven for 5–6 minutes, until golden brown.
5. Oil a rolling pin or the handle of a large wooden spoon. Loosen the tuiles from the baking sheet while still hot and pliable and immediately curl them over the rolling pin or round the wooden spoon handle. When they are quite firm, slip them off, leave until cold, and store in an airtight container.

NOTE:
* Using silicone paper guarantees that the tuiles will not stick.

Tuiles Amandines

MAKES ABOUT 25
2 egg whites
110g/4oz caster sugar
55g/2oz plain flour
½ teaspoon of natural vanilla essence
30g/1oz blanched almonds, cut into fine shreds
55g/2oz butter, melted

1. Preheat the oven to 180°C/350°F/gas mark 4. Lightly grease at least three baking sheets and a rolling pin or line the baking sheets with silicone paper.*
2. Place the egg whites in a bowl. Beat in the sugar with a fork. The egg white should be frothy but by no means snowy. Sift in the flour and add the vanilla and almonds. Mix with the fork.
3. Cool the butter (it should be melted but not hot) and add it to the mixture. Stir well.
4. Place the mixture in teaspoonfuls at least 12.5cm/5 inches apart on the baking sheets and flatten well.
5. Bake in batches on the middle shelf of the oven for about 6 minutes or until a good brown at the edges and pale biscuit-coloured in the middle.
6. Leave to cool on the baking sheet for a few seconds then lift the biscuits off carefully with a palette knife. Lay them, while still warm and pliable, over the rolling pin to form them into a slightly curved shape. As soon as they are cold put them into an airtight tin or plastic bag to keep them crisp.

NOTE:
* Using silicone paper guarantees that the tuiles will not sick.

◆ ◆

Tuiles au Chocolat

MAKES ABOUT 25-30 TUILES
30g/1oz light brown sugar
55g/2oz caster sugar
3 egg whites
40g/1½oz plain flour
1 tablespoon cocoa powder
pinch of salt
pinch of mixed spice
3 tablespoons double cream
55g/2oz unsalted butter, melted

1. Preheat the oven to 180°C/350°F/gas mark 4. Place two shelves at the top of the oven. Line three baking sheets with silicone paper.
2. Put the sugars and egg whites into a large bowl and whisk with electric beaters to a thick, soft meringue.
3. Sift the remaining dry ingredients and fold into the meringue with a metal spoon.
4. Add the cream and melted butter and stir gently to mix. Refrigerate for 20 minutes.
5. Spread teaspoonfuls of the mixture very thinly on the baking sheets, keeping the circles well apart to allow for spreading during cooking.
6. Put the baking sheets in the top of the oven and bake for 6-7 minutes or until beginning to brown at the edges.
7. Oil a rolling pin or the handle of a

wooden spoon. Working quickly, loosen the tuiles from the silicone paper with a palette knife and, while still hot and pliable, curl them over the rolling pin or round the spoon handle.* Leave until cold, then remove and store them in an airtight container.

NOTES:

* If the tuiles become too rigid to curl over the

rolling pin or round the handle of the wooden spoon, put them back into the oven for a few minutes to soften again.

** Do not remove the tuiles from their airtight container until ready to serve as they soften very quickly once in contact with the air.

*** If some of the mixture remains unused, transfer into a plastic container and freeze for another occasion.

♦ ♦

Venetian Biscuits

MAKES ABOUT 24

110g/4oz blanched almonds
450g/1lb plain flour
pinch of salt
1 teaspoon baking powder
140g/5oz granulated sugar
85g/3oz plain chocolate, chopped into small
    pieces
30g/1oz dried apricots, chopped into small pieces
15g/½oz pistachios, chopped into small pieces
4 large eggs, lightly beaten
1 egg white

1. Preheat the oven to 190°C/375°F/gas mark 5. Grease a baking sheet.
2. Place the almonds on the baking sheet and bake in the oven until golden brown. Cool slightly. Chop two-thirds and grind the remaining third finely.
3. Sift the flour, salt and baking powder into a bowl. Add the sugar, chocolate, toasted almonds, dried apricots and pistachios, and mix well.

4. Make a well in the centre and add the beaten eggs. Gradually incorporate the dry ingredients into the eggs. The dough should be firm.
5. Divide the dough into four and roll each piece into a sausage shape, approximately 2cm/¾ inch in diameter and 20cm/8 inches long.
6. Place the rolls on the baking sheet, leaving at least 5cm/2 inches between them. Lightly whisk the egg white until just frothy and brush over the tops of the rolls.
7. Bake on the middle shelf of the oven for 20 minutes.
8. Remove the rolls from the oven, lower the temperature to 105°C/225°F/gas mark ½. Slice the rolls at a 45-degree angle at 1cm/½ inch intervals and return the biscuits individually to the baking sheet. Put back into the oven for a further 30 minutes. Allow to cool completely before serving.

NOTE:

* The biscuits are meant to be eaten after being dipped in a liqueur, e.g Amaretto or grappa.

Orange Flower Water Biscuits

MAKES ABOUT 30–35
170g/6oz butter
110g/4oz icing sugar
110g/4oz cornflour
170g/6oz self-raising flour
zest of 1 lemon
1 tablespoon orange flower water

1. Preheat the oven to 190°C/375°F/gas mark 5. Grease two baking sheets lightly.
2. Put the butter and icing sugar into a bowl and cream until soft and light. Sift the cornflour and self-raising flour together on to the butter mixture and cut and fold until well combined. Add the lemon zest and orange flower water.
3. Fit a 1cm/½ inch star nozzle into a piping bag, fill with the biscuit mixture and pipe five shapes on to the baking sheets.* Make sure that the biscuits are well spaced to allow for spreading. Repeat until all the mixture is used.
4. Bake on the middle shelf of the oven for 12–15 minutes until an even golden brown.
5. Leave to cool slightly before transferring to a cooling rack.

NOTES:
* Alternatively the mixture can be divided into 25 walnut-sized balls, and either flattened with the back of a fork, or pressed into cylinders or ovals.
** For a crunchy texture, sprinkle generously with granulated sugar before baking.

BASIC RECIPES
AND TECHNIQUES

Vegetable Stock
Rich Shortcrust Pastry
Pâte Sucrée
Choux Pastry
Rough Puff Pastry
Puff Pastry
Suet Pastry
Filo or Strudel Pastry
French Pancakes
Fresh Pasta
Shaping Pasta by Hand
Crème Pâtissière
Crème Anglaise (English Egg Custard)
Uncooked Marzipan
To Make Sugar Syrup
Sugar Temperatures
To Make Vanilla Sugar
Agar Agar
Cooking Asparagus
Peeling Peppers
Preparing and Cooking Spinach
Melba Toast
To Line a Flan Tin
To Bake Blind
To Make a Roulade Case

Vegetable Stock

MAKES 290–425ml/10–15fl oz

4 tablespoons oil
1 onion, roughly chopped
1 leek, roughly chopped
1 large carrot, roughly chopped
2 sticks of celery, roughly chopped
a few cabbage leaves, roughly shredded
a few mushroom stalks
2 cloves of garlic, crushed
a few parsley stalks
6 black peppercorns
sea salt
1 large bay leaf
6 tablespoons dry white wine
570ml/1 pint water

1. Heat the oil in a large saucepan. Add the vegetables, cover and cook gently for 5 minutes or until softening.
2. Add the peppercorns, salt, bay leaf, wine and water and bring to the boil. Reduce the heat and simmer for 30 minutes or until the liquid is reduced by half.
3. Strain the stock through a sieve, pressing hard to remove as much of the liquid as possible. Discard the vegetable pulp. Allow to cool and skim off any fat.
4. Use as required.

NOTE:
* The stock can be kept, covered, in the refrigerator for up to 1 week. It can also be frozen.

◆ ◆

Rich Shortcrust Pastry

225g/8oz plain flour
pinch of salt
110g/4oz butter, chopped
1 egg yolk
3 tablespoons very cold water

1. Sift the flour with the salt.

2. Rub in the fat until the mixture looks like coarse breadcrumbs.
3. Mix the egg yolk with the water, then add to the mixture. Mix to a firm dough, first with a knife, then with one hand. It may be necessary to add more water, but the pastry should not be too damp. (Though crumbly pastry is more difficult to handle, it produces a shorter, lighter result.)
4. Wrap and chill for 30 minutes before using.

Pâte Sucrée

225g/8oz plain flour
salt
110g/4oz butter, softened
4 egg yolks
110g/4oz sugar
3 drops of natural vanilla essence

1. Sift the flour on to a board with a pinch of salt. Make a large well in the centre and put the butter into it. Place the egg yolks and sugar on the butter with the vanilla essence.
2. Using the fingertips of one hand, mix the butter, yolks and sugar together. When mixed to a soft paste, draw in the flour and knead until the pastry is just smooth.
3. If the pastry is very soft, chill before rolling or pressing out to the required shape. In any event the pastry must be allowed to relax for 30 minutes either before or after rolling out, but before baking.

◆ ◆

Choux Pastry

85g/3oz butter, chopped
200ml/7fl oz water
105g/3¾oz plain flour, well sifted
salt
3 eggs

1. Put the butter and water together in a heavy saucepan. Bring slowly to the boil so that by the time the water boils the butter is completely melted.
2. Immediately the mixture is boiling really fast, tip in all the flour and draw the pan off the heat.
3. Working as fast as you can, beat the mixture hard with a wooden spoon; it will soon become thick and smooth and leave the sides of the pan. Beat in a pinch of salt.
4. Stand the bottom of the saucepan in a bowl or sink of cold water so the mixture cools quickly.
5. Beat in the eggs, a little at a time, until the mixture is soft, shiny, smooth and is of a dropping consistency (see p. 203) – not too runny. If the eggs are large, it may not be necessary to add all of them.
6. Use as required.

Rough Puff Pastry

225g/8oz plain flour
pinch of salt
140g/5oz butter
very cold water

1. Sift the flour and salt into a cold bowl. Cut the butter into knobs about the size of a sugar lump and add to the flour. Do not rub in but add enough water to just bind the paste together. Mix first with a knife, then with one hand. Knead very lightly.
2. Wrap the pastry and leave to relax for 10 minutes in the refrigerator.
3. On a floured board, roll the pastry into a strip about 30 × 10cm/12 × 4 inches long. This must be done carefully: with a heavy rolling pin, press firmly on the pastry and give short sharp rolls until the pastry has reached the required size. The surface of the pastry should not be over-stretched and broken.
4. Fold the strip into three and turn so that the folded edge is to your left, like a closed book.
5. Again roll out into a strip 1cm/½ inch thick. Fold in three again and leave, wrapped, in the refrigerator for 15 minutes.
6. Roll and fold the pastry as before, then chill again for 15 minutes.
7. Roll and fold again, by which time the pastry should be ready for use, with no signs of streakiness.
8. Roll into the required shape.
9. Chill again before baking.

◆ ◆

Puff Pastry

225g/8oz plain flour
pinch of salt
30g/1oz vegetable shortening
150ml/5fl oz very cold water
140–200g/5–7oz butter

1. If you have never made puff pastry before use the smaller amount of butter: this will give a normal pastry. If you have some experience, more butter will produce a lighter, very rich pastry.
2. Sift the flour with a pinch of salt. Rub in the vegetable shortening. Add the water and mix with a knife to a doughy consistency. Turn on to the table and knead quickly until just smooth. Wrap and leave in the refrigerator for 30 minutes to relax.
3. Lightly flour the work surface or a board and roll the dough into a rectangle about 10 × 30cm/4 × 12 inches long.
4. Tap the butter lightly with a floured rolling pin to get it into a flattened block about 9 × 7.5cm/3½ × 3 inches. Put the butter on the rectangle of pastry. Fold the third of the pastry closest to you over the butter then bring the top third down. Press the sides together to prevent the butter escaping. Give the pastry parcel a 90° anti-clockwise turn so the folded, closed edge is on your left.
5. Tap the pastry parcel with the rolling pin to flatten the butter a little; then roll out quickly and lightly until the pastry is three times as long as it is wide. Fold it very evenly in three as before. Turn the pastry 90° anti-clockwise so the folded, closed edge is on

your left. Again press the edges firmly with the rolling pin. Roll out again to form a rectangle as before.

6. The pastry has now had two rolls and folds, or 'turns' as they are called. It should be put to rest in a cool place for 30 minutes or so. The rolling and folding must be repeated twice more, the pastry again rested, and then again given two more 'turns'. This makes a total of six. If the butter is still very streaky, roll and fold it once more.

7. Use as required.

◆ ◆

Suet Pastry

As suet pastry is most often used for steamed puddings, instructions for lining a pudding basin are included here.

340g/12oz self-raising flour
salt
170g/6oz shredded vegetable suet
water to mix

1. Grease a 1.1 litre/2 pint pudding basin.
2. Sift the flour with a good pinch of salt into a bowl. Stir in the shredded suet and add enough water to mix, first with a knife, and then with one hand, to a soft dough.
3. On a floured surface, roll out two-thirds of the pastry into a round about 1cm/½ inch thick. Sprinkle the pastry evenly with flour.
4. Fold the round in half and place the open curved sides towards you.

5. Shape the pastry by rolling the straight edge away from you and gently pushing the middle and pulling the sides to form a bag that, when spread out, will fit the pudding basin.
6. With a dry pastry brush, remove all excess flour and place the bag in the well-greased basin.
7. Fill the pastry bag with the desired mixture.
8. Roll out the remaining piece of pastry and use it as a lid, damping the edges and pressing them firmly together.
9. Cover the basin with buttered greaseproof paper, pleated in the centre, and a layer of pleated tin foil. (Pleating the paper and foil allows the pastry to expand slightly without bursting the wrappings.) Tie down firmly to prevent water or steam getting in during cooking.

Filo or Strudel Pastry

285g/10oz plain flour
pinch of salt
1 egg
150ml/5fl oz water
1 teaspoon oil

1. Sift the flour and salt into a bowl.
2. Beat the egg and add the water and oil. First with a knife and then with one hand, mix the water and egg into the flour, adding more water if necessary to make a soft dough.
3. The paste now has to be beaten: lift the whole mixture up in one hand and then, with a flick of the wrist, slap it on to a lightly floured board. Continue doing this until the paste no longer sticks to your fingers, and the whole mixture is smooth and very elastic. Put it into a clean floured bowl. Cover and leave in a warm place for 15 minutes.
4. The pastry is now ready for rolling and pulling. To do this, flour a tea towel or large cloth on a table top and roll out the pastry as thinly as you can. Now put your hand (well floured) under the pastry and, keeping your hand fairly flat, gently stretch and pull the pastry, gradually and carefully working your way round until the paste is paper thin. (You should be able to see through it easily.) Trim off the thick edges.
5. Use immediately, as strudel pastry dries out and cracks very quickly. Brushing with melted butter or oil helps to prevent this. Or the pastry sheets may be kept covered with a clean, dry cloth.

NOTE:
* If the paste is not for immediate use wrap it well and keep refrigerated or frozen. Flour the pastry surfaces before folding up. This will prevent sticking.

♦ ♦

French Pancakes

MAKES ABOUT 12
110g/4oz plain flour
pinch of salt
1 egg
1 egg yolk
290ml/10fl oz milk or milk and water mixed
1 tablespoon oil, plus extra for frying

1. Sift the flour and salt into a bowl and make a well in the centre, exposing the bottom of the bowl.
2. Put the egg and egg yolk and a little of the milk into the well in the flour.
3. Using a wooden spoon or a whisk, mix the egg and milk, or milk and water, and then gradually draw in the flour from the sides as you mix.
4. When the mixture reaches the consistency of thick cream, beat well and stir in the oil.
5. Add the rest of the milk, or milk and water – the consistency should now be that of thin cream.
6. Cover the bowl and refrigerate for about 30 minutes. This is done so that the starch cells will swell, giving a lighter result.
7. Prepare a pancake pan or frying pan by heating well and wiping out with oil.

Pancakes are not fried in fat like most foods – the purpose of the oil is simply to prevent sticking.

8. Pour in about 1 tablespoon of the batter and swirl about the pan until evenly spread across the bottom.

9. Cook for 1 minute, then, using a palette knife and fingers, turn the pancake over and cook again until the underside is brown. Pancakes should be extremely thin, so if the first one is too thick, add a little extra milk to the batter. The first pancake is unlikely to be perfect, and is often discarded.

10. Transfer to a tea towel or plate.** Repeat with the remaining batter.

NOTES:

* Batter can also be made by placing all the ingredients in a blender and mixing for a few seconds, but take care not to over-mix or the batter will be bubbly.

** Pancakes can be kept warm in a folded tea towel, on a plate over a saucepan of simmering water, in the oven, or in a warmer. If allowed to cool, they may be reheated by being briefly returned to the frying pan or by warming in an oven.

** Pancakes freeze well, but should be separated by pieces of greaseproof paper. They may also be refrigerated for a day or two.

♦ ♦

Fresh Pasta

450g/1lb plain flour or 000 Italian pasta flour
pinch of salt
4 eggs
1 tablespoon oil

1. Sift the flour and salt on to a wooden board. Make a well in the centre and drop in the eggs and oil.

2. Using the fingers of one hand mix together the eggs and oil and gradually draw in the flour. The mixture should be a very stiff dough.

3. Knead for about 15 minutes or until smooth and elastic. Wrap in polythene and leave to relax in a cool place for 1 hour.

4. Roll one small piece of dough out at a

time until paper thin. Cut into required shapes.

5. Allow to dry; hang noodles over the clean handle of a broom suspended between two chairs; lay small shapes on a wire rack or dry tea-towel. Leave for at least 30 minutes before boiling.

NOTES:

* If more or less pasta is required the recipe can be altered on a pro-rata basis, for example a 110g/4oz quantity of flour calls for a pinch of salt, 1 egg and a scant tablespoon of oil.

** To make pasta in a food processor, put the dry ingredients, eggs and oil into the bowl and process until the mixture resembles coarse, moist crumbs, and comes together when pushed between two fingers.

Shaping Pasta by Hand

Cut the ball of dough into four and roll out one piece at a time, using a rolling pin, until the pasta is paper thin.

Tagliatelle: sprinkle the pasta lightly with flour and roll up like a Swiss roll. Alternatively, cut the pasta into a rectangle, fold the longer outside edges into the middle (so they meet), then fold again lengthways so there are four layers. Cut into narrow strips. Unravel each strip and allow to dry by hanging them over the clean handle of a broom, suspended between two chairs.

Cannelloni: cut the pasta into 12.5cm/5 inch squares. Spoon on a line of filling, roll up and place, seam side down, in an ovenproof dish.

Lasagne: cut the pasta into oblong sheets, 17.5cm × 10cm/7 × 4 inches. Dry on sheets of silicone paper.

Ravioli: cut the pasta into strips 5cm/2 inches wide. Place spoonfuls of the filling at 3.5cm/1½ inch intervals, moisten the pasta and cover with another long pasta strip and seal between and around the filling. Cut into required shape with a pastry or pasta cutter. Dry on silicone paper after filling.

Spaghetti and macaroni can only be made using a pasta machine.

◆ ◆

Crème Pâtissière

MAKES 290ml/10fl oz
290ml/10fl oz milk
2 egg yolks
55g/2oz caster sugar
20g/¾oz flour
20g/¾oz cornflour
few drops of natural vanilla essence

1. Scald the milk
2. Beat the egg yolks with the sugar until pale, then mix in the flours.
3. Strain in the milk, stirring thoroughly.
4. Pour into the milk pan and bring slowly to the boil, stirring continuously. (The sauce will go alarmingly lumpy, but don't worry; keep stirring and it will get smooth.) Allow to cool slightly and add the vanilla essence.

Crème Anglaise (English Egg Custard)

MAKES 290ml/10fl oz
290ml/10fl oz milk
1 tablespoon sugar
*1 vanilla pod or few drops of natural vanilla
  essence*
2 egg yolks

1. Put the milk, sugar and vanilla pod if using, in a saucepan and bring slowly to the boil.
2. Beat the yolks in a bowl.
3. Remove the vanilla pod and slowly pour the milk on to the egg yolks, stirring steadily. Return to the pan.
4. Stir over a gentle heat until the mixture is thick enough to coat the back of a spoon; this will take about 5 minutes. Do not boil. Pour into a cold bowl.
5. Add the vanilla essence if using.

◆ ◆

Uncooked Marzipan

MAKES 1kg/2lb
225g/8oz caster sugar
225g/8oz icing sugar, plus extra for dusting
450g/1lb ground almonds
2 egg yolks
2 whole eggs
2 teaspoons lemon juice
6 drops of vanilla essence

1. Sift the sugars together into a bowl and mix with the ground almonds.
2. Mix together the egg yolks, whole eggs, lemon juice and vanilla essence. Add to the sugar mixture and beat briefly with a wooden spoon.
3. Lightly dust the working surface with icing sugar. Knead the paste until just smooth (overworking will draw the oil out of the almonds, giving too greasy a paste).
4. Wrap well and store in a cool place.

◆ ◆

To Make Sugar Syrup

1. Measure 285g/10oz sugar and 570ml/1 pint water into a large, deep, clean, thick-bottomed saucepan.*
2. Heat gently, stirring occasionally, until the sugar has dissolved.
3. Bring to the boil without stirring.**
4. Continue boiling until the syrup is the required concentration.
5. Use as required.

NOTES:
* The proportion of sugar to water is not critical as long as there is enough water to allow the sugar to dissolve before beginning to boil. However, too much water at the start will take longer to evaporate (and there will be an unnecessary waste of energy).
** Stirring causes sugar crystals to form on the sides of the pan. Should this happen, dip a clean pastry brush into some hot water and brush round the sides of the pan to dissolve the crystals.

SUGAR TEMPERATURES

Stage	Temperatures	Use
Thread	106–113°C/223–236°F	Syrup
Soft ball	112–116°C/234–240°F	Fondant; fudge
Firm ball	118–121°C/244–250°F	Soft toffee
Hard ball	121–130°C/250–266°F	Nougat
Soft crack	132–143°C/270–290°F	Pulled sugar
Hard crack	149–154°C/300–310°F	Hard toffee
Caramel	160–177°C/320–350°F	Pralines

A sugar thermometer is easily obtained from any good kitchen shop.

◆ ◆

To Make Vanilla Sugar

Fill a large jar with caster or granulated sugar.

Cut a vanilla pod into three pieces and bury them in the sugar. Leave to flavour the sugar for 1 week. Top up with more sugar as the vanilla sugar is used, and shake to mix.

◆ ◆

Agar Agar

Agar agar is a seaweed, but looks like a natural sponge. It is cooked, pressed, freeze-dried and then flaked or powdered for use in the kitchen. The powder is approximately three times more dense than the flakes, and 1 teaspoon powder is equivalent to 1 tablespoon flakes:

All the recipes in this book requiring a setting agent specify gelatine, which we find easier to use. Agar agar's setting qualities are affected by the nature of the food to which it is added. For example, agar agar works well with lemons, but fruits such as pineapple, fig, mango and peach break down its setting ability. For this reason, it is not possible to give a general conversion ratio of gelatine to agar agar. Each recipe will require a specific amount, depending upon the reaction of the agar agar to the particular food. It will be a matter of trial and error. As a general guide:

To set 570ml/1 pint:	use 1 teaspoon powder or 1 tablespoon flakes
To make 570ml/1 pint of soufflé mixture:	use 1 teaspoon powder or 1 tablespoon flakes
To make a firm jelly:	use 2 teaspoons powder or 2 tablespoons flakes

METHOD:
1. Soak the agar agar in the full liquid measurement specified in the recipe, in a saucepan; leave powder for 5 minutes, flakes for 10–15 minutes.

2. Dissolve the agar agar in the pan over a

medium heat, stirring continuously. Turn up the heat and boil for 2–3 minutes, continuing to stir to prevent sticking. Use as required. (Agar agar may be re-boiled without impairing its setting ability.)

3. If properly prepared, agar agar sets quickly on contact with anything much cooler than itself. Therefore, the ingredients to which it is added must be no colder than room temperature. To test whether it is ready for use, spoon a small quantity on to a cold plate: a skin should form very quickly, and wrinkle if a finger is pulled over the surface.

NOTE:
* Vegetable stock may be set with agar agar and used as aspic.

♦ ♦

Cooking Asparagus

The most important thing to remember when cooking asparagus is that the tips cook more quickly than the woody stems. The concentration of heat, therefore, must be under or around the bottom of the spears. If an asparagus kettle is not available, we have found that the following methods work just as well. Whichever method is used, the cooking time will vary depending on the thickness of the asparagus. The average cooking time for finger-thick asparagus is 8 – 10 minutes. In any event the asparagus is cooked when the tips are firm but the point of a knife will slide in.

A. Stand the bundles of asparagus in as tall a saucepan as is available. Pour in boiling water to come half-way up the stems. Add a pinch of salt. Cover with foil, folding it down around the bundles to stabilize them and then over the sides of the saucepan. Make pinprick holes in the foil to allow **some** steam to escape.

B. Lay the asparagus loose in a roasting tin and cover with boiling, salted water. Cook over a moderate heat with the woody ends of the spears directly over the heat and the tips away from it.

C. Stand the asparagus bundles in a saucepan and pack with new potatoes to come half-way up the stems. Pour in boiling water, add salt, and loosely cover with foil. Make pinprick holes for **some** steam to escape. The potatoes will taste delicious, but they will require longer cooking than asparagus, so remove the asparagus when done.

♦ ♦

Peeling Peppers

There are four ways of peeling peppers.

STEAMING:
Cut the peppers into quarters and remove the stalks, cores and seeds.

Put the pepper quarters into a steamer or colander, cover and place over a saucepan of boiling water. Steam for about 20 minutes. Put the pepper quarters into a plastic bag and leave until cool enough to handle. Peel off and discard the skin.

MICROWAVE:

Cut the peppers into quarters and remove the stalks, cores and seeds.

Put the pepper quarters into a plastic bag and microwave for 4 or 5 minutes at maximum heat. Remove from the microwave and leave until cool enough to handle. Peel off and discard the skin.

This method is advised if keeping the colour is important.

GRILLING:

Preheat the grill until very hot. Cut the peppers into quarters and remove the stalks, cores and seeds. Place, skin side up, under the grill and cook until the skin is quite black. Put the quarters into a plastic bag and leave until cool enough to handle. Peel off and discard the skin.

Grilled peppers have a delicious flavour, but they will not be brightly coloured.

BAKING:

Preheat the oven to 200°C/400°F/gas mark 6.

Put the whole peppers on a baking sheet and place in the oven for about 20–30 minutes or until quite soft. Put the peppers into a plastic bag and leave until cool enough to handle. Peel off the skin and remove the seeds; discard skin and seeds.

Baking affects the colour of the peppers and is an extravagant way of peeling them, unless the oven is already on.

NOTE:

* The steam which builds up inside the plastic bag loosens the skin and makes it easy to remove.

◆ ◆

Preparing and Cooking Spinach

1. Remove the stalks, including any thick veins in the leaves.
2. Wash thoroughly in several changes of water.
3. Put the wet leaves into a pan, add a sprinkling of salt, cover and cook over a moderate heat for 5–7 minutes, shaking the pan occasionally to prevent sticking and burning, until the spinach is wilted and still bright green.
4. Drain thoroughly. Remove excess water by squeezing the spinach between two plates; repeat until the spinach is dry.
5. The spinach will reduce by about half during cooking.

Melba Toast

6 slices of white bread

1. Preheat the grill. Preheat the oven to 150°C/300°F/gas mark 2.
2. Toast the bread on both sides until evenly browned.
3. While the toast is still hot, quickly cut off the crusts and split the bread in half horizontally.
4. Put the toast in the oven and leave until dry and brittle.

NOTE:
* Melba toast is undoubtedly best served straight from the oven but it can be kept for a day or two in an airtight tin; it will lose its flavour if kept longer.

♦ ♦

To Line a Flan Tin

1. Roll out the pastry on a lightly floured surface to about 2.5mm/⅛ inch thick and 5cm/2 inches larger than the flan tin.
2. Using a floured rolling pin, carefully slip one side of the pastry over the pin to give the pastry support when it is moved.
3. Carefully position the pastry centrally over the flan tin.
4. Using an index finger, ease the pastry into the tin, without stretching it. The pastry should fit neatly without folds or creases.
5. Fold the edge of the pastry over the flan tin. Using a rolling pin, roll off the excess pastry.

♦ ♦

To Bake Blind

All pastry (except suet) needs to be baked at a high temperature: 200°C/400°F/gas mark 6. However, some fillings (especially custard-based) need to be cooked at low temperatures. Unless the pastry is partly cooked beforehand, therefore, it will be soggy and unpleasant to eat

Line the raw pastry case with a double sheet of greaseproof paper and fill with dried beans, rice, ceramic balls, or even pebbles or coins (these are referred to as 'blind beans').

They prevent the pastry base bubbling up, and the sides from shrinking during cooking.

When the pastry is half-cooked (after about 15 minutes) the 'blind beans' are removed. If the pastry case is to be filled, it should be returned to the oven, to dry out, for a further 5–8 minutes when it will have lost its translucent, raw look and be pale in colour; if it is not to be filled, then it will need a further 9–12 minutes in the oven to finish its cooking.

To Make a Roulade Case

There are three ways to make a roulade case:

1. Using a roasting tin:
   a) Fit a double layer of lightly oiled greasproof paper into a roasting tin measuring 27.5 × 20cm/11 × 8 inches, arranging and folding the corners to make a rectangular case.
   b) Do not allow the paper to come more than 5cm/2 inches above the top of the tin. This could prevent the top of the roulade from cooking evenly.

2. Using a Swiss roll tin without a paper case:
   Line the base of the Swiss roll tin with silicone or lightly oiled greaseproof paper cut to fit. Lightly oil the sides of the tin.

3. Using a paper case:
   a) Cut greaseproof paper and silicone paper into sheets measuring 25 × 35cm/ 10 × 14 inches; put them together, with the silicone paper on top. Centre a sheet of A4 paper (20 × 30cm/8 × 12 inches) on the silicone paper: there will be an allowance of approximately 5cm/2 inches on each side.
   b) Fold the edges of the greaseproof and silicone paper against the edges of the A4 paper, using it as a template.
   c) Remove the A4 paper and re-crease the fold lines so that the folded edges stand upright.
   d) Fold the corners and secure with paper clips.
   e) Put the paper case on to a flat baking sheet.

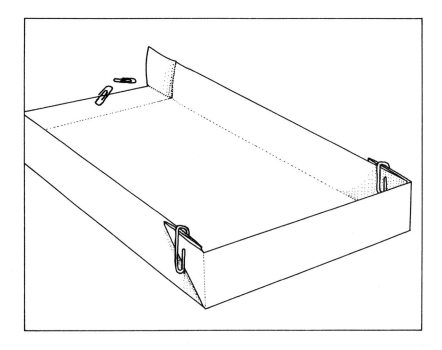

ROULADE CASE

MISCELLANEOUS

Thyme pastry
Lemon Shortcrust Pastry
Walnut Pastry
Sun-dried Tomato and Polenta Pastry
Poppy Seed Pasta
Three Cheese Filling for Pasta Shapes
New Potatoes en Papillotes
Potato Galettes
Spicy Potatoes
Fragrant Yellow Coconut Rice Cones
Parsnip, Wild Rice and Walnut Fritters
Wild Rice and Batter Dollops
Braised Chestnuts
Braised Red Cabbage
Marjoram-scented Roast Button Onions
Spinach with Barley and Fresh Ginger
Preserved Lemons
Elderflower Cordial
Spiced Macaroni Crisps
Vegetable Crisps
Panforte
Eccles Cakes
Marrons Glacés
Damson Purée
Caramelised Apple Purée
Praline

Thyme Pastry

225g/8oz plain flour
salt and freshly ground black pepper
110g/4oz butter, chopped
2 tablespoons thyme leaves, unchopped
2 tablespoons dry white wine
very cold water (optional)

1. Sift the flour, salt and pepper into a large bowl. Rub in the butter with the fingertips until the mixture resembles breadcrumbs. Add the thyme leaves.

2. Add the wine and mix to a firm, but not damp, dough, first with a knife, and then with one hand. Add water only if required. A crumbly pastry may be more difficult to handle but will produce a lighter result.
3. Use as required.

NOTES:
* Any herb can be used in this recipe. Rosemary should be chopped finely.
** The pastry can also be made in a food processor (see p. 187).

♦ ♦

Lemon Shortcrust Pastry

170g/6oz plain flour
pinch of salt
1 teaspoon grated lemon zest
30g/1oz vegetable shortening or butter, chopped
55g/2oz butter, chopped
2 tablespoons very cold water

1. Sift the flour with the salt. Add the grated lemon zest.

2. Rub in the fats until the mixture looks like breadcrumbs.
3. Add the water to the mixture. Mix to a firm dough, first with a knife, and finally with one hand. It may be necessary to add more water, but the pastry should not be too damp. (Though crumbly pastry is more difficult to handle, it produces a shorter, less tough result).
4. Wrap and chill for 30 minutes before using.

NOTE:
* The pastry can also be made in a food processor (see p. 187).

Walnut Pastry

225g/8oz plain flour
pinch of salt
110g/4oz butter, chopped
140g/5oz ground walnuts
45g/1½oz sugar
beaten egg

1. Sift the flour and salt into a bowl. Rub in the butter until the mixture resembles coarse breadcrumbs.

2. Stir in the walnuts and sugar and add enough beaten egg (probably half an egg) to just bind the mixture together. Knead lightly.

3. Wrap and chill for 30 minutes before using.

NOTE:

* If you have a food processor, simply mix all the ingredients together until lightly combined. Chill before use.

♦ ♦

Sun-dried Tomato and Polenta Pastry

This pastry has to be made in a food processor because the sun-dried tomatoes, which are one of the binding agents, must be finely chopped. The crust is formed by pressing the mixture on to the bottom and up the sides of the flan tin.

170g/6oz plain flour
pinch of salt
110g/4oz coarse polenta or cornmeal
2 teaspoons cumin seeds
½ teaspoon cayenne pepper
55g/2oz butter
8 whole halves of sun-dried tomatoes plus their
*   oil to make the total weight up to 85g/3oz*
2 tablespoons cold water (optional)

1. Put all the ingredients, except the water, in a food processor and process until the mixture is well combined, looks like coarse breadcrumbs and will stick together when pressed with the fingertips. Add the cold water only if necessary.

2. Wrap and chill for 30 minutes before using.

Poppy Seed Pasta

This pasta can be used as tagliatelle or to make ravioli. Fill with the braised pumpkin and lentil mixture (see p. 67), three cheese filling (see below), or any finely chopped cooked leftovers.

450g/1lb plain flour or 000 Italian pasta flour
pinch of salt
2 tablespoons poppy seeds
3 eggs
1 egg yolk, plus white, if necessary
1 tablespoon oil (optional)

1. Sift the flour and salt on to a flat surface and mix in the poppy seeds. Make a well in the centre, add the whole eggs and the egg yolk, and the oil, if using.
2. Using the fingers of one hand, mix together the eggs, and oil, if using, and gradually draw in the flour and poppy seeds to make quite a firm dough.
3. Knead for about 15 minutes or until smooth and elastic. Wrap in cling film and chill for 1 hour.
4. Shape as required by hand (see p. 154), or using a pasta machine.**
5. Cook in plenty of boiling salted water for 2–3 minutes.

NOTES:
* Pasta is easily made in a food processor. Put the dry ingredients, the eggs and egg yolk and oil, if using, into the bowl and process until the mixture resembles coarse, moist breadcrumbs and comes together when pinched between two fingers. The dough should be quite firm.
** To shape pasta using a machine, cut the ball of dough into four pieces and roll one piece at a time through the machine on setting 1, folding the dough in half each time, until soft and elastic. This will take up to 10 'rolls'. Process the pasta through from setting 1 to setting 6 and then use as required.

◆ ◆

Three Cheese Filling for Pasta Shapes

This filling is very simple and can be used for any pasta shape. This quantity will fill 450g/1lb pasta.

1 spring onion, finely sliced
110g/4oz feta cheese, grated
110g/4oz ricotta cheese
55g/2oz freshly grated Parmesan cheese
8 large basil leaves, chopped
1 teaspoon tomato purée
1 egg yolk
salt and freshly ground white pepper

1. Mix all the ingredients in a bowl until well combined. The mixture should be stiff.
2. Use as required.

New Potatoes en Papillotes

SERVES 4

55g/2 oz unsalted butter, cut into eight
450g/1lb very small new potatoes, scrubbed
sea salt
4 sprigs of tarragon or rosemary
4 large cloves of garlic, peeled and left whole

1. Preheat the oven to 200°C/400°F/gas mark 6.
2. Cut four 22.5cm/9 inch and four 24cm/ 9½ inch discs of greaseproof paper. Smear one piece of butter over each disc.

3. Divide the potatoes into four portions. Put one portion on a larger disc of greaseproof paper with a herb sprig and a garlic clove. Place a smaller greaseproof paper disc over the top and seal the edges. Repeat three more times.
4. Place the four parcels on a baking sheet, put on the middle shelf of the oven and bake for about 20–30 minutes (the cooking time will depend on the size of the potatoes). Gently press the potatoes to test but do not puncture the bags.
5. Serve the papillotes, unopened, immediately.

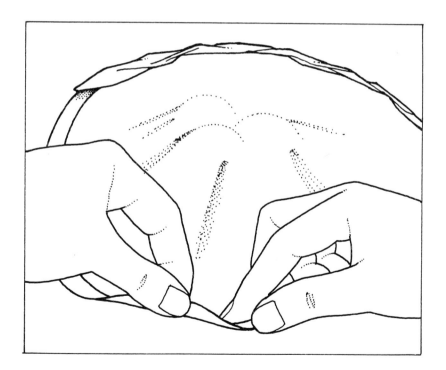

NEW POTATOES EN PAPILLOTES

Potato Galettes

Potato galettes can be served as an accompanying vegetable; they also make an interesting base on which to present other food (see lentil, caper and parmesan patties on croûtes pp. 52/3).

SERVES 4

4 waxy potatoes, coarsely grated
2 tablespoons flour
salt and freshly ground black pepper
oil for frying

1. Combine the potatoes, flour and seasoning in a bowl and mix well.

2. Heat 1cm/½ inch of oil in a large frying pan. Add tablespoons of the mixture, spreading them with a fork into circles about 5cm/2 inches in diameter.* Fry over a medium heat for about 10 minutes, or until crisp and brown.

3. Remove from the pan and drain on paper towels. Keep warm while frying the remaining mixture.

NOTE:

* Do not make the galettes too compact, but try to create a lacy effect using two forks, otherwise the potato will brown before it is cooked through.

♦ ♦

Spicy Potatoes

SERVES 6–8

45g/1½oz ghee or clarified butter
1kg/2lb potatoes, cut into 1cm/½ inch cubes
2 teaspoons ground turmeric
½ teaspoon chilli powder
1 bay leaf
1 teaspoon garam masala
1 teaspoon ground black pepper
salt

1. Melt the ghee or clarified butter in a large pan. Add the potato cubes, ground turmeric, chilli powder and bay leaf. Fry over a low heat, stirring constantly, for 5–8 minutes; take care not to break up the potatoes.

2. Add the garam masala, pepper, and salt to taste. Cover and cook gently for 10 minutes or until the potatoes are tender.

3. Remove the lid, increase the heat and cook, turning frequently, until the potatoes are brown and crisp on all sides; do not allow the potatoes to burn.

4. Serve immediately.

Fragrant Yellow Coconut Rice Cones

This is a Thai recipe and the traditional Thai method of cooking the rice is first to steam it, then to cook it with the flavourings (in this instance, coconut milk infused with turmeric) and, finally, to steam it again. However, we have simplified the method, cooking the rice by the risotto method. The rice is served shaped into cones or balls.

SERVES 4

1 tablespoon peeled and grated turmeric, or
  1 teaspoon ground turmeric
150ml/5fl oz water
55g/2oz long-grain rice
170g/6oz Thai sticky rice, pudding rice or
  arborio (risotto) rice
1 × 400g/14oz can of coconut milk
1 stalk of lemon grass, tender part only, crushed
2 bay leaves
2 lime leaves (or grated zest of 1 lime)
salt
juice of 1 lime

TO SERVE:

selection of stir-fried vegetables tossed in chilli,
  lime leaf and coconut sauce (see p. 124)

1. Soak the grated turmeric in 2 tablespoons water for 5 minutes; strain the liquid and reserve. If using ground turmeric, soak in 3 tablespoons of water.
2. Pour the 150ml/5fl oz water into a saucepan and bring to the boil. Add the two rices and cook for 10 minutes, stirring all the time.
3. Add the turmeric water, coconut milk, lemon grass, bay leaves, lime leaves or grated lime zest, and the salt and bring back to the boil. Stir over a medium heat until all the liquid has been absorbed and the rice is cooked to a sticky consistency.
4. Take off the heat. Remove the lemon grass, lime and bay leaves, then add the lime juice and season to taste.
5. Form spoonfuls of the mixture into the required shape, using wet hands.
6. Serve with a selection of stir-fried vegetables tossed in chilli, lime leaf and coconut sauce.

NOTE:

* Fresh turmeric and lime leaves are available in many good supermarkets. Sticky rice is obtainable in Asian food markets or by mail order (see p. 250). However, arborio rice or pudding rice can be used instead. Do not use an 'easy cook' rice as the starch has been reduced and in this recipe starch is necessary to make the rice stick together. Mixing sticky arborio or pudding rice with long-grain rice makes the end result less glutinous, but it is still sufficiently sticky to allow the rice to be shaped.

Parsnip, Wild Rice and Walnut Fritters

These fritters can be served instead of potatoes; if the parsnips and walnuts are very finely diced, they also make delicious canapés. The fritters can be made ahead of time and reheated in the oven.

SERVES 4–6 (MAKES 20)
FOR THE BATTER:
110g/4oz flour
1 egg
1 egg yolk
65ml/2½ fl oz milk
85g/3oz butter, melted

1kg/2lb parsnips, cut into small chunks
85g/3oz walnuts, roughly chopped
110g/4oz wild rice, cooked
2 tablespoons finely chopped parsley
salt and freshly ground black pepper
oil for frying

1. Make the batter: mix all the batter ingredients in a blender until smooth. If a blender is not available, see p. 176. Leave to stand in the refrigerator for 30 minutes. This will produce a lighter batter.
2. Put the parsnip chunks into a steamer* and place over a saucepan of boiling water. Cover and steam for 10 minutes or until cooked. Leave to cool.
3. Put the batter, parsnips and the other ingredients into a large bowl and mix well.
4. Heat about 6.5cm/2½ inches oil in a deep saucepan until a cube of stale bread starts to sizzle immediately it is dropped in.
5. Carefully drop spoonfuls of the parsnip mixture into the oil and fry for 5–8 minutes until pale golden brown (they will continue to cook once removed from the oil). Remove with a slotted spoon and drain on paper towels. Keep warm. Repeat until all the mixture is used.

NOTE:
* If a steamer is not available, use a sieve and cover both the sieve and the saucepan with foil.

◆ ◆

Wild Rice and Batter Dollops

These 'pancakes' can be used as a base for toppings, such as fried eggs, grilled tomatoes or pâtés. At the School we make a canapé version topped with soured cream and salmon roe.

SERVES 4–6
FOR THE BATTER:
110g/4oz plain flour
1 egg
1 egg yolk

200 ml/7fl oz milk
1 tablespoon oil

225g/8oz wild rice, cooked
2 tablespoons finely chopped parsley
1 tablespoon grated fresh ginger
salt and freshly ground black pepper
oil for frying

1. To make the batter: mix the flour, egg, egg yolk, milk and oil to a batter in a blender. Alternatively, make according to instructions on p. 176.
2. Mix the rice, parsley, ginger, seasoning and batter in a bowl.

DAMSON ROULADE

Poached Tamarillos with Coconut Tapioca Timbales

Deep-fried Choux Pea Ring

Apples, Pears and Blackberries in Cassis Syrup

ELDERFLOWER AND CHAMPAGNE JELLIES

PRUNE AND MACADAMIA CARAMEL TART

Star Fruit and Kumquats Poached with Star Anise

BREADS

3. Chill for 30 minutes. This allows the starch cells to swell, which gives a lighter result.

4. Heat about 1cm/½ inch oil in a shallow frying pan over a moderately high heat. Drop in tablespoons of the mixture, spread thinly with a fork to 7.5cm/3 inch circles and cook for 4–5 minutes, turning once. Remove with a slotted spoon and drain on paper towels. Keep warm. Repeat until all the mixture has been used, adding more oil as necessary.

◆ ◆

Braised Chestnuts

These chestnuts go particularly well with chestnut crown roast (see p. 89)

SERVES 8
30g/1oz butter
1 onion, coarsely chopped
1 clove of garlic, crushed
1 small carrot, coarsely chopped
4 sticks of celery, coarsely chopped
1 leek, washed and coarsely chopped
2 cloves
2 bay leaves
1 teaspoon juniper berries, lightly crushed
1 tablespoon tomato purée
110g/4oz pitted prunes
225g/8oz vacu-packed chestnuts or canned whole chestnuts*
290ml/10fl oz water
290ml/10fl oz full-bodied red wine
3 big sprigs of thyme
2 good sprigs of parsley
salt and freshly ground black pepper

1. Melt the butter in a saucepan over a low heat. Add the onion and cook for about 10 minutes. Turn up the heat and add the garlic, vegetables, cloves, bay leaves and juniper berries and cook, stirring to prevent burning, for about 10 minutes or until beginning to brown. Add the tomato purée, prunes and chestnuts and cook for a few minutes.

2. Add the water, wine, thyme and parsley and bring to the boil. Reduce the heat and simmer for about 20 minutes until thickened but still runny. Stir occasionally but take care not to break up the chestnuts. Leave to infuse in the cooking juices, if liked, until ready to serve.

3. Strain the chestnuts and vegetables through a sieve and reserve the liquor. Remove the chestnuts (and the prunes if using in the chestnut crown roast) from the strained mixture and set them aside. Discard the remaining vegetables, the bay leaves and spices.

4. Heat the liquor in a saucepan and reduce by boiling rapidly until syrupy. Add the chestnuts and warm thoroughly.

NOTE:
* Dried chestnuts can also be used; they are available in good health food shops. Soak and cook the whole packet, and freeze what is not required to use on another occasion. Cook for approximately 1 hour at stage 3.

Braised Red Cabbage

SERVES 6

1 small red cabbage
1 onion, sliced
30g/1oz butter
1 small cooking apple, peeled, cored and sliced
1 small dessert apple, peeled, cored and sliced
1 tablespoon clear honey
2 teaspoons brown sugar
2 teaspoons red wine vinegar
pinch of ground cloves
salt and freshly ground black pepper

1. Shred the cabbage and discard the hard stalks. Rinse well.
2. Fry the onion in the butter in a large saucepan until it begins to soften.
3. Add the drained but still wet cabbage, the apples, honey, sugar, vinegar and cloves, and season with salt and pepper.
4. Cover tightly and cook very slowly for 1 hour, mixing well and stirring every 15 minutes or so, or until the whole mass is soft and reduced in bulk (during the cooking it may be necessary to add a little water).
5. Taste and add more salt, pepper or sugar if necessary.

♦ ♦

Marjoram-scented Roast Button Onions

SERVES 4

675g/1½lb button onions
30g/1oz butter
1½ tablespoons olive oil
salt and freshly ground black pepper
2 tablespoons coarsely chopped marjoram

1. Preheat the oven to 180°C/350°F/gas mark 4.
2. Put the onions into a bowl and cover with boiling water. Leave for 5 minutes. Drain.
3. Peel the onions and carefully shave the root end (if too much of the root end is removed the onions will fall apart during cooking).
4. Put the onions into an ovenproof dish or roasting tin, dot with the butter, drizzle with the olive oil and season with the salt and freshly ground black pepper.
5. Roast for 20 minutes, turning the onions occasionally. Sprinkle the marjoram over the onions and continue roasting for about 10 minutes or until the onions are cooked through but still holding their shape.
6. Serve immediately in a warm serving dish.

Spinach with Barley and Fresh Ginger

SERVES 4

570ml/1 pint vegetable stock (see p. 172)
225g/8oz pearl barley, rinsed
55g/2oz butter
salt and freshly ground black pepper
1 large clove of garlic, crushed
2.5cm/1 inch piece fresh ginger, peeled and
  grated
675g/1½lb spinach, cooked and drained (see
  p. 182)

1. Put the vegetable stock into a large saucepan, add the pearl barley and cook, stirring occasionally, for approximately 35 minutes or until soft but firm to the bite. Drain, if necessary. Return the barley to the pan, add 30g/1oz of the butter and stir to coat it evenly. Season to taste and keep warm.
2. Melt the remaining butter in a saucepan, add the garlic and ginger. Cook over a low heat for 1 minute then add the spinach. Season to taste. Reheat, stirring carefully, taking care not to break up the spinach.
3. Add the barley and toss gently with the spinach until thoroughly hot. Adjust the seasoning and transfer to a serving dish.

◆ ◆

Preserved Lemons

Use the lemon slices to flavour bean hotpots, casseroles or tagines, but remove them before serving.

6 lemons, sliced
salt
paprika pepper or chilli powder
4–6 whole cloves
1 cinnamon stick, broken in half
150–290ml/5–10fl oz extra virgin olive oil

1. Place the slices of lemon in a colander, sprinkle with salt and leave for 24 hours.
2. Wipe off surplus salt and arrange a few lemon slices in the bottom of a 570ml/1 pint Kilner jar. Sprinkle with about ½ teaspoon paprika pepper or chilli powder. Arrange another layer of lemon slices on top and sprinkle with paprika pepper or chilli powder in the same way. Repeat with the remaining slices of the lemon, adding the cloves and halved cinnamon stick during the layering.
3. Pour in enough olive oil to cover completely. Gently tap the jar on a hard surface to get rid of air bubbles. Cover with two layers of greaseproof paper and leave in a cool place for at least 3 weeks.

NOTE:
* Limes can also be preserved in this way and would be a suitable flavouring for any oriental dish.

Elderflower Cordial

MAKES 2.5 LITRES/4½ PINTS
20 elderflower umbels (heads)
900g/2lb light brown sugar
900g/2lb white sugar
85g/3oz citric acid
3 lemons, halved
1¾ litres/3 pints cold, boiled water

1. Put the ingredients into a plastic bucket and leave, covered, for 5 days. Stir every now and again to help dissolve and distribute the sugar.
2. Strain through a sieve lined with a piece of muslin, or a jam strainer. The syrup should be clear and free of any particles.
3. Pour into plastic or glass bottles and store in a dark place. The cordial will keep indefinitely.

NOTE:
* The cordial is ready for immediate use and should be served diluted with iced water.

◆ ◆

Spiced Macaroni Crisps

SERVES 4
225g/8oz macaroni, cooked but not rinsed
2 tablespoons corn oil
1 tablespoon curry powder
1 tablespoon garam masala
1 tablespoon ground coriander
2 tablespoons chilli powder
2 teaspoons salt
oil for deep frying

1. Toss the cooked macaroni in 2 tablespoons corn oil and spread on a tray lined with paper towels. Cover loosely and allow to dry out for at least 4 hours, preferably overnight.
2. Put the spices and salt into a large bowl and mix together.
3. Coat the dried macaroni in more corn oil if necessary and toss in the spices. Fork through the macaroni to separate and coat thoroughly.
4. Pour 7.5cm/3 inches oil into a wok or shallow sauté pan and heat until a cube of stale bread dropped in sizzles immediately it is added. Fry the macaroni for about 5 minutes until golden brown, separating the pieces with a long-handled fork to prevent sticking; take care not to brown them too much as they will continue to cook and become crisp after they have been removed from the hot oil.
5. Remove from the oil with a slotted spoon. Drain on paper towels and allow to cool.
6. The crisps can be stored in an airtight container for several days. Refresh quickly in a hot oven if wished.

Vegetable Crisps

It is difficult to cut slices fine enough for crisps from any vegetable by hand: mandolins make the job much easier. Look out for Japanese mandolins; they can be obtained inexpensively. These delicious unusual crisps will make the investment worth while. Suitable vegetables include sweet potatoes, butternut squash, raw beetroot, parsnips, celeriac, aubergines, courgettes, lotus roots, and, of course, potatoes (see below for special preparation notes).

chosen vegetable, prepared
oil for deep frying
salt

1. Slice the vegetable very thinly using a mandolin and put the slices into a bowl of cold water.
2. Fill a deep, thick-bottomed saucepan with 7.5cm/3 inches oil and heat over a moderately high heat until a cube of stale bread sizzles immediately it is dropped in.
3. Drain the vegetable slices, dry thoroughly on paper towels, and cook, in batches, for 2–3 minutes or until crisp and golden brown.* This will depend on the thickness of the chips: they should snap when cold. Remove with a slotted spoon and drain on paper towels. Toss with salt.
4. Store in an airtight container.

NOTE:
* The chips will become soggy if there is any moisture left in them after cooking. If they begin to burn before they have become crisp, turn down the heat a little. They can be refreshed in a medium hot oven before serving.

BUTTERNUT SQUASH
Peel the squash, cut in half and remove the seeds.

AUBERGINES
Slice the aubergines thinly. Sprinkle the slices with salt and leave to disgorge their juices for 30 minutes. Rinse carefully and pat thoroughly dry with paper towels.

COURGETTES
Slice the courgettes thinly. Sprinkle with salt and leave to disgorge their juices for 30 minutes. Rinse carefully and pat thoroughly dry with paper towels.

CELERIAC
Slice the peeled celeriac thinly and cut the slices into smaller pieces, if wished.

LOTUS ROOT
Lotus root is available sliced in cans and vacu-packs, from Asian shops, see p. 250 for mail order supplies.

1. Dry thoroughly with paper towels then slice the lotus root thinly (with care).

POTATO
The flavour of potato crisps can be made more interesting by cooking them in oil that has been heated and infused with garlic or chillies.

Panforte

This is a delicious recipe for home-made panforte. Serve with coffee after dinner.

MAKES APPROXIMATELY 40 PIECES
4 sheets of rice paper
225g/8oz blanched almonds, roasted
225g/8oz whole hazelnuts, roasted
285g/10oz prunes, stoned
285g/10oz plump raisins
285g/10oz good quality mixed peel
1 tablespoon ground cinnamon
1 tablespoon mixed spice
225g/8oz plain flour
350g/12oz caster sugar
285g/10oz clear honey

1. Preheat the oven to 170°C/325°F/gas mark 3. Line the bottom of a Swiss roll tin with rice paper cut to fit. Do not grease the tin first.
2. Mix all the ingredients, apart from the sugar and honey, in a bowl.
3. Dissolve the sugar and honey in a small saucepan over a low heat. Turn the heat up and boil to 112°C/234°F, the soft ball stage (see p. 180). Remove from the heat, add to the dry ingredients and mix well.
4. Transfer the mixture to the Swiss roll tin, spreading it with the back of a metal spoon. Cover the top with rice paper cut to fit, pressing it down to make it stick. Flatten by running a rolling pin across the top of the tin.
5. Put the tin on to a baking sheet and place on the middle shelf of the oven for about 20 minutes until set; do not allow to brown.
6. Leave in the tin to cool for a few minutes. While still warm and soft, mark out diamond shapes in the panforte with a sharp knife. The panforte will become firm as it cools.
7. When cool, invert the tin on to a flat surface to remove the panforte; give it a sharp tap if necessary. Turn the panforte the right way up and cut into pieces following the markings. Store in an airtight container.

◆ ◆

Eccles Cakes

MAKES 6
rough puff pastry made with 225g/8oz flour (see p. 174)

FOR THE FILLING:
15g/½oz butter
55g/2oz brown sugar
110g/4oz currants
30g/1oz chopped mixed peel
½ teaspoon ground cinnamon
¼ teaspoon ground nutmeg
¼ teaspoon ground ginger
grated zest of ½ lemon
1 teaspoon lemon juice

FOR THE GLAZE:
1 egg white, lightly beaten
caster sugar

1. Preheat the oven to 220°C/425°F/gas mark 7.
2. Roll the pastry to the thickness of a coin. Cut out six rounds 12.5cm/5 inches in diameter. Put aside to relax.
3. Make the filling: melt the butter in a pan and stir in all the other filling ingredients. Set aside to cool.
4. Place a good teaspoon of filling in the

centre of each pastry round.

5. Damp the edges of the pastry and press together in the centre, forming a small ball. Turn the balls over and lightly roll them until the fruit begins to show through the pastry.

6. With a sharp knife, make three small parallel cuts on the top.

7. Brush the top of the Eccles cakes with the egg white, and sprinkle with caster sugar.

8. Place on a wet baking sheet and bake on the middle shelf of the oven for 20 minutes, or until lightly browned.

♦ ♦

Marrons Glacés

These chestnuts take time to prepare, but are much nicer than those that are commercially prepared.

1kg/2lb large chestnuts in their skins
570ml/1 pint milk
1 vanilla pod
570ml/1 pint water
450g/1lb granulated sugar
225g/8oz liquid glucose*

1. Cut a slit in the skin of each chestnut then put them into a large saucepan and cover with water. Bring to the boil and simmer gently for 5 minutes. Remove from the heat.

2. Remove the chestnuts one by one and peel, taking care to remove the inside membrane of the chestnut as well as the skin (it is easier to peel the chestnuts whilst they are still hot).

3. Put the chestnuts into a clean saucepan, pour over the milk and add the vanilla pod. Bring to the boil and cook the chestnuts over a low heat for 5 minutes, or until completely soft but not breaking up. Lift out of the milk with a slotted spoon and leave to drain on kitchen paper. Rinse the vanilla pod and reserve.

4. Make the syrup: put the water, sugar and liquid glucose into a saucepan. Dissolve the sugar over a low heat, then bring to the boil. Simmer for 5 minutes. Add the chestnuts to the pan with the vanilla pod and bring back to the boil. Simmer for a further minute. Pour the chestnuts and syrup into a bowl and leave to cool overnight.

5. The following day, return the chestnuts and syrup to the pan, bring back to the boil and simmer for 1 minute. Cool overnight. Repeat this process once more the following day.

6. Put a wire rack over a tray. Remove the chestnuts from the syrup with a slotted spoon and leave to drain on the wire rack overnight.

7. Put the marrons into petit four cases and store in a cool, dry place.

NOTE:
* Liquid glucose is obtainable at any good chemist. It is sometimes known as glucose syrup.

Damson Purée

1 kg/2lb damsons, halved and stoned
225g/8oz granulated sugar
150ml/5fl oz water

1. Put the damsons, sugar and water into a heavy saucepan. Cover and simmer gently for about 20 minutes, or until the damsons have become a soft pulp. If the purée is too wet, reduce, by boiling rapidly, to thicken it, stirring occasionally, but take care as it will splash.

3. For a smooth purée, put the fruit into a food processor or blender and mix to the required smoothness.

NOTE:
* Any fruit purée can be made by this method. Most fruit contains a lot of water and therefore requires only just enough to moisten and start to draw out the juices from the fruit. The amount of sugar needed will depend on the ripeness of the fruit, 110g/4oz to 450g/1lb is a general guide.

The aim is to finish with a thick mixture of sweetened fruit low in water content.

◆ ◆

Caramelised Apple Purée

This purée is the accompaniment for baked Sauternes creams (see p. 141) but can be served on its own.

SERVES 4
110g/4oz granulated sugar
110ml/4fl oz Sauternes
1 tablespoon water
2 large cooking apples, peeled and cored

1. Put the sugar, half the Sauternes and the water into a small saucepan and heat gently, stirring, until the sugar has dissolved. Raise the heat and boil, without stirring, until the syrup is golden brown. Remove from the heat and pour in the remaining Sauternes. Take care, it will splutter. Return to a low heat to dissolve the hardened caramel.
2. Add the apples and cook slowly to a thick purée, stirring now and again. This will take anything up to 20–25 minutes. The apple should be glossy and caramel-coloured. If a fine purée is required, pass the apple through a sieve.

Praline

55g/2oz unblanched almonds, with skins on
55g/2oz granulated sugar

1. Line a baking sheet with silicone paper.
2. Put the almonds and sugar in a thick-bottomed saucepan and put over a gentle heat. As the sugar begins to melt, stir carefully with a metal spoon to coat the almonds. Continue cooking until the mixture is thoroughly caramelized (browned).
3. Quickly tip on to the silicone paper and leave to cool.
4. When the praline is completely cold, break into fragments or pound to a coarse powder in a mortar, or a blender.
5. Store in an airtight container.

DICTIONARY OF COOKING TERMS AND KITCHEN FRENCH

Bake 'blind': To bake a flan case while empty. In order to prevent the sides falling in or the base bubbling up, the pastry is usually lined with paper and filled with 'blind beans'. See below.

Bain-marie: A baking tin half-filled with hot water in which terrines, custards, etc. stand while cooking. The food is protected from direct fierce heat and cooks in a gentle, steamy atmosphere. Also a large container that will hold a number of pans standing in hot water, used to keep soups, sauces, etc. hot without further cooking.

Baste: To spoon over liquid (sometimes stock, sometimes fat) during cooking to prevent drying out and to promote flavour.

Bavarois: Creamy pudding made with eggs and cream and set with gelatine.

Beignets: Fritters.

Beurre manié: Butter and flour in equal quantities worked together to a soft paste, and used as a liaison or thickening for liquids. Small pieces are whisked into boiling liquid. As the butter melts it disperses the flour evenly through the liquid, thereby thickening it without causing lumps.

Blind beans: Dried beans, peas, rice or pasta used to temporarily fill pastry cases during baking.

Bouquet garni: Parsley stalks, small bay leaf, fresh thyme, celery stalk, sometimes with a blade of mace, tied together with string and used to flavour stews etc. Removed before serving.

Braise: To bake or stew slowly on a bed of vegetables in a covered pan.

Caramel: Sugar cooked to a toffee.

Clarified butter: Butter that has been separated from milk particles and other impurities which cause it to look cloudy when melted, and to burn easily when heated.

Concasser: To chop roughly.

Consommé: Clear soup.

Coulis: Essentially a thick sauce, e.g. *coulis de tomates* (thick tomato sauce); raspberry coulis (raspberry sauce).

Court bouillon: Liquid used for cooking fish.

Cream Sugar: To beat ingredients together, such as butter and sugar when making a sponge cake.

Crêpes: Thin French pancakes.

Croquettes: Pâté of mashed potato and possibly pulses or cheese, formed into small balls or patties, coated in egg and breadcrumbs and deep-fried.

Croustade: Bread case dipped in butter and baked until crisp. Used to contain hot savoury mixtures for a canapé, savoury or as a garnish.

Croûte: Literally crust. Sometimes a pastry case, sometimes toasted or fried bread, as in scrambled eggs on toast.

Croûtons: Small evenly sized cubes of fried bread used as a soup garnish and occasionally in other dishes.

Dariole: Small castle-shaped mould used for moulding rice salads and sometimes for cooking cake mixtures.

Déglacer: To loosen and liquefy the fat, sediment and browned juices stuck at the bottom of a frying pan or saucepan by adding liquid (usually stock, water or wine) and stirring while boiling.

Deglaze: See Déglacer.

Dégorger: To extract the juices from meat, fish or vegetables, generally by salting. Usually done to remove indigestible or strong-tasting juices.

Dépouiller: To skim off the scum from a sauce or stock: a splash of cold stock is added to the boiling liquid. This helps to bring scum and fat to the surface, which can then be skimmed more easily.

Dropping consistency: The consistency where a mixture will drop reluctantly from a spoon, neither pouring off nor obstinately adhering.

Duxelles: Finely chopped raw mushrooms, sometimes with chopped shallots, often used as a stuffing.

Egg wash: Beaten raw egg, sometimes with salt, used for glazing pastry to give it a shine when baked.

Emulsion: A stable suspension of fat and other liquid, e.g. mayonnaise, hollandaise.

Entrée: Traditionally a dish served before the main course, but usually served as a main course today.

Entremet: Dessert or sweet course, excluding pastry sweets.

Farce: Stuffing.

Fecule: Farinaceous thickening, usually arrowroot or cornflour.

Flamber: To set alcohol alight. Usually to burn off the alcohol, but frequently simply for dramatic effect. (Past tense flambé or flambée; English: to flame.)

Flame: See Flamber.

Fleurons: Crescents of puff pastry, generally used as a garnish.

Fold: To mix with a gentle lifting motion, rather than to stir vigorously. The aim is to avoid beating out air while mixing.

Frappé: Iced, or set in a bed of crushed ice.

Glaze: To cover with a thin layer of melted jam (for fruit flans) or syrup (for rum baba), butter or oil.

Gratiner: To brown under a grill after the surface of the dish has been sprinkled with breadcrumbs and butter and, sometimes, cheese. Dishes finished like this are sometimes called gratinée or au gratin.

Hors d'oeuvre: Usually simply means the first course. Sometimes used to denote a variety or selection of many savoury titbits served with drinks, or a mixed first course (*hors d'oeuvres variés*).

Infuse: To steep or heat gently to extract flavour, as when infusing milk with onion slices.

Julienne: Vegetables or citrus rind cut in thin matchstick shapes or very fine shreds.

Knock down or knock back: To punch or knead out the air in risen dough so that it resumes its pre-risen bulk.

Knock up: To slightly separate the layers of raw puff pastry with the blade of a knife to facilitate rising during cooking.

Liaison: Ingredients for binding together and thickening sauce, soup or other liquid, e.g. roux, beurre manié, egg yolk and cream, blood.

Macédoine: Small diced mixed vegetables, usually containing some root vegetables. Sometimes used of fruit meaning a fruit salad.

Macerate: To soak food in a syrup or liquid to allow flavours to mix.

Mandolin: Frame of metal or wood with adjustable blades set in it for finely slicing cucumbers, potatoes, etc.

Marinade: The liquid used for marinating. Usually contains oil, onion, bay leaf and vinegar or wine.

Marinate: To soak vegetables before or after cooking in acidulated liquid containing flavourings and herbs.

Marmite: French word for a covered earthenware soup container in which the soup is both cooked and served.

Mirepoix: The bed of braising vegetables described under Braise.

Moule-à-manqué: French cake tin with sloping sides. The resulting cake has a wider base than top, and is about 2.5cm/1 inch high.

Napper: To coat, mask or cover, e.g. éclairs nappées with hot chocolate sauce.

Needleshreds: Fine, evenly cut shreds of citrus rind (French julienne) generally used as a garnish.

Noisette: Literally 'nut'. Usually means nut-brown, as in beurre noisette, i.e. butter browned over heat to a nut colour. Also hazelnut.

Nouvelle cuisine: Style of cooking that promotes light and delicate dishes often using unusual combinations of very fresh ingredients, attractively arranged.

Panade or panada: Very thick mixture used as a base for soufflés, etc., usually made from milk, butter and flour.

Paner: To egg and crumb any ingredients before frying.

Papillote: A wrapping of paper in which ingredients are cooked to contain the aroma and flavour. The dish is brought to the table still wrapped up. Foil is sometimes used, but as it does not puff up dramatically, it is less satisfactory.

Parboil: To half-boil or partially soften by boiling.

Parisienne: Potato (sometimes with other ingredients) scooped into small balls with a melon baller and, usually, fried.

Pass: To strain or push through a sieve.

Pâte: The basic mixture or paste, often used of uncooked pastry, dough, uncooked meringue, etc.

Pâté: A savoury paste of vegetables (or meat).

Pâtisserie: Sweet cakes and pastries. Also, cake shop.

Praline: Almonds cooked in sugar until the mixture caramelizes, cooled and crushed to a powder. Used for flavouring desserts and ice cream.

Prove: To put dough or a yeasted mixture to rise before baking.

Purée: Liquidized, sieved or finely mashed fruit or vegetables.

Ragout: A stew.

Reduce: To reduce the amount of liquid by rapid boiling, causing evaporation and a consequent strengthening of flavour in the remaining liquid.

Refresh: To hold boiled vegetables under a cold tap, or to dunk them immediately in cold water to prevent their cooking further in their own steam, and to set the colour of green vegetables.

Relax or rest: Of pastry: to set aside in a cool place to allow the gluten (which will have expanded during rolling) to contract. This lessens the danger of shrinking in the oven. Of batters: to set aside to allow the starch cells to swell, giving a lighter result when cooked.

Roux: A basic liaison or thickening for a sauce or soup. Melted butter to which flour has been added.

Scald: Of milk: to heat until on the point of boiling, when some movement can be seen at the edges of the pan but there is no overall bubbling.
Of muslin, cloths, etc.: to dunk in clean boiling water, generally to sterilize.

Season: Of food: to flavour, generally with salt and pepper.
Of iron frying pans, griddles, etc.: to prepare new equipment for use by placing over high heat, generally coated with oil and sprinkled with salt. This prevents subsequent rusting and sticking.

Slake: To mix flour, arrowroot, cornflour or custard powder to a thin paste with a small quantity of cold water.

Sweat: To cook gently, usually in butter or oil, but sometimes in the food's own juices, without frying or browning.

Terrine: Pâté or minced mixture, baked or steamed in a loaf tin or earthenware container.

Timbale: A dish that has been cooked in a mini pudding-basin mould, or a dish served piled up high.

Velouté: A white sauce made from a roux and stock, and usually finished with cream.

Vol-au-vent: A large pastry case of puff pastry, with high sides and a deep hollow centre into which is placed a savoury filling.

Well: A hollow or dip made in a pile or bowlful of flour, exposing the tabletop or the bottom of the bowl, into which other ingredients are put prior to mixing.

Zest: The thin-coloured skin of an orange, lemon, or lime used to give flavour. It is very thinly pared without any of the bitter white pith.

DIET

Everyone in normal health who eats sensible amounts of a variety of well-cooked foods should have a nutritionally sound diet; vitamin and mineral supplements are, therefore, unnecessary. People who do not eat meat or fish need to pay slightly more attention to ensuring they are having enough vitamins B_6 and B_{12} and a good range of protein foods. Eating plenty of fresh fruit and vegetables is essential for everyone; they are more nutritious if they are eaten raw.

A varied diet will include in the right proportions:–	
Foods rich in Carbohydrates	e.g. Grains, pulses, potatoes
Foods rich in Protein	e.g. Dairy products, pulses, nuts and seeds
Small percentage of Fat	e.g. Animal-based lard and butter, vegetable oils
Vitamins	
Minerals	
Water	

CARBOHYDRATES

Needed for	– Principal source of energy
	– Provide taste and texture
	– Vital supplies of fibre

Sources of carbohydrate: potatoes, rice and other cereals, pulses, fruits and vegetables. These should account for the major portion of a day's food intake.

PROTEIN

Essential for	– Satisfying hunger
	– Growth
	– Repair

Sources of protein: nuts, seeds, pulses, grains, dairy products and eggs. There is a tendency to consume more protein than the body actually requires. Excess is converted and stored as fat. Note: Proteins are made of amino acids, eight of which are essential. Vegetable proteins do not contain all eight. Different foods are deficient in different amino acids. It is, therefore, important to eat two or more sources of vegetable protein, or vegetable protein with a dairy product or eggs, either at the same meal or during the same day.

FATS

Needed for – Protecting vital organs
             – Insulation
             – Fat soluble vitamins
             – Energy

Sources of fats: fat on meat, butter, margarine, lard, suet, oils, cheese, nuts, processed foods, pastry, cakes and biscuits. Fats are twice as fattening, weight for weight, as carbohydrates. Very little fat is needed for good health and too much saturated fat can be damaging, paricularly for the heart.
Note: On the whole, animal-based fats are higher in saturated fats than vegetable sources.

VITAMINS

Needed for – Regulation of growth
             – General good health
A balanced diet should provide the recommended daily requirements.

About twenty different vitamins have been isolated, and each one has its own important roles to play in the body. Some vitamins are fat soluble and can be stored by the body, in the liver and fatty tissue; others are water soluble and cannot be stored for long. Furthermore, they can be leached out of food during cooking, and may be destroyed by heat, or they can deteriorate during storage. Attention should therefore be paid to how food is stored, prepared and cooked.

Fat Soluble Vitamins

VITAMIN A	VITAMIN D	VITAMIN E	VITAMIN K
Role: Resistance to disease; healthy hair, skin, mucous membranes; night vision; bone growth; teeth development; reproduction.	*Role:* Absorption of calcium and phosphorous for bones and teeth.	*Role:* An important antioxidant.	*Role:* Clotting of blood.
Sources: Dark leafy greens, broccoli, dried apricots, carrots, pumpkin, dairy products, eggs.	*Sources:* Margarine, eggs, butter, cheese, sunlight on skin.	*Sources:* Vegetable oils, wholegrains, nuts, green vegetables, egg yolks, milk.	*Sources:* Green vegetables, wholegrains, potatoes.

Major Water Soluble Vitamins

VITAMIN B COMPLEX (e.g. thiamin (B_1), riboflavin (B_2) niacin (B_3, B_6, B_{12})	VITAMIN C
Role: Needed when carbohydrates are present in the diet; helping the nervous system and metabolism; formation of red blood cells	*Role:* Vitality; growth and repair; health of capillaries, bones and teeth; protection of other vitamins from oxidation; increases amount of iron absorbed; helps absorption of calcium (large doses may have anti-histamine effect).
Sources: Nuts, seeds, wholegrains, brewer's yeast, yeast extract, fortified cereals, milk, eggs.	*Sources:* Fruit, vegetables.

'ACE' Vitamins (antioxidants)

These are thought to protect against serious disease, coronary heart disease, and cancer. Food containing the 'ACE' vitamins should be consumed daily.

VITAMIN A (Beta – carotene)	VITAMIN C	VITAMIN E
Sources: Brightly-coloured vegetables.	*Sources:* Fruit, vegetables.	*Sources:* Vegetable oils, sunflower products, leafy green vegetables, wholegrains, egg yolks, milk.

Minerals

Needed for – Maintenance of healthy bones and teeth
       – Regulation of composition of body fluids
       – Assisting body enzymes, and proteins to function

Many foods contain minerals and in a varied, balanced diet there is little likelihood of deficiency. Care should be taken, though, to ensure adequate supplies of iron and calcium.

IRON	CALCIUM
Role: Muscle action; makes red blood cells; (vitamin C helps absorption). *Sources:* Yeast, egg yolks, wholegrains, cereals, parsley.	*Role:* Building bones/teeth; blood clotting; functioning of muscles, nerves. *Sources:* Dairy products, especially cheese, sesame seeds, white bread.

WATER

Water is not a nutrient but is vital.

Body tissue consists of 60% water
Body processes take place in a fluid medium
Water is the basis of the body's fluids, blood plasma, lymph fluid, tissue fluid
Vitamins and minerals must dissolve into water for metabolism
Water is needed for elimination of excess salts and waste products

PULSES

Pulses are the edible seeds of leguminous plants: peas, beans and lentils. They may be bought fresh but are more usually found dried. There are many different varieties, which vary in size, colour and taste. For example, mung beans are tiny, round and green, red kidneys beans are oval, shiny and maroon while butter beans are white and large. Pulses can be cooked and served on their own, but are more often mixed with other ingredients. They are used widely throughout the world and are increasingly to be found in modern European cookery.

NUTRITION

Pulses are an important source of B vitamins, minerals (such as iron, potassium and calcium), carbohydrate and protein. When eaten with a grain, pulses form a complete protein, providing the eight essential amino acids.

Nutritional Analysis of Two Typical Pulses

100g DRIED/RAW		MUNG BEANS	ADUKI BEANS
Energy	KJ	1188	1158
	Kcal	279	272
Fats	Total	1.1g	0.5g
	Sat.	0.3g	None
	Mono.	0.1g	None
	Poly.	0.5g	None
Protein		23.9g	19.9g
Carbohydrate		46.3g	50.1g
(Sugar)		1.5g	1.0g
Fibre		10.0g	11.1g
Cholesterol		None	None
Thiamin (B_1)		0.36mg	0.45mg
Riboflavin (B_2)		0.26mg	0.22mg

cont.

Niacin (B$_3$)	2.1mg	2.6mg
Vitamin (B$_6$)	0.38mg	None
Sodium	12.0mg	5.0mg
Calcium	89.0mg	84.0mg
Iron	6.0mg	4.2mg
Phosphorus	360.0mg	380.0mg
Magnesium	150.0mg	130.0mg
Potassium	1250.0mg	1220.0mg

BUYING AND STORING

The common varieties of pulses are widely available in supermarkets; the more unusual varieties can be found in healthfood or Asian shops. It is difficult to tell from looking at a packet whether the contents are fresh. It is advisable, therefore, to buy pulses from outlets which have a high turnover of stock. Dried pulses should be stored in an airtight container and should be used within six months. After cooking, they may be kept in a refrigerator for a few days, or frozen for up to three months.

PREPARATION

Care should be taken to sort through pulses and remove any particles of stone or grit, especially with the smaller varieties. Wash thoroughly in several changes of cold water. Pulses packed by large, reputable companies should not need any preparation.

SOAKING

The purpose of soaking pulses is to replace the water lost during the drying process. The soaking time will depend on the size of the pulse; chick peas, which are large and dense, should be soaked in cold water for at least 2 hours, while lentils require no soaking (see chart pp. 213–215).

Soaking time can be halved if the pulses are put into a pan of water, brought to the boil, simmered for 3 minutes then removed from the heat and left to soak in the hot water.

COOKING

The water in which the pulses have been soaked will contain leached-out minerals and can be used to cook them. However, if flatulence is a concern, boil the pulse for 5 minutes, drain it then cook completely in fresh water.

In order to kill harmful toxins, kidney beans should be boiled rapidly for 10–15 minutes, soya beans for 1 hour.

To prevent scum from forming during cooking a tablespoon of oil can be added to the pulse. Salt should not be added during cooking as this toughens the skin, and cooking times are considerably lengthened. Bicarbonate of soda reduces the cooking time but it is not recommended as it kills the vitamins and minerals, and can leave a bitter after-taste.

Pulses tend to taste better if they are cooked very slowly either on the hob or in a low oven (170°F/325°F/gas mark 3).

Using a pressure cooker at 15lbs pressure (full/high setting) reduces the cooking times by 75% and there is also less leaching of vitamins and minerals.

SPROUTED PULSES

Sprouting produces succulent shoots. These change the nutritional structure of the pulse, increasing existing vitamin levels, producing vitamin C, and reducing the carbohydrate content. Although special sprouting dishes can be bought, the same result can be achieved with a glass jar.

1. Put 2 tablespoons of the chosen pulse into a glass jar.
2. Fill the jar with warm water. Swirl it around a few times and then pour the water away.
3. Fill the jar again with warm water, leave to stand for 24 hours and then drain.
4. Add enough warm water to cover the beans, swirl and drain. Store the jar in a warm, dark place.
5. Repeat stage 4, morning and evening every day for five days, by which time the pulse will have sprouted. After this time, store in a refrigerator and eat within 48 hours.

NAME	APPROX. SOAKING TIME	APPROX. COOKING TIME	SPROUTING	USES	COMMENTS
ADUKI BEAN	1 hr	30–60 mins	3–5 days	Salads, stuffings, whole in sauces, oriental dishes.	Do not over-spice as they have their own strong flavour.
BLACK-EYED BEAN (or pea)	1 hr	30–60 mins	3–5 days	Spicy casseroles, mixed bean salad, sprouted for salads.	Sprouting produces an almost bitter taste.

cont.

BORLOTTI BEAN	1–2 hrs	1–1½ hrs	–	Spicy casseroles, Italian dishes, soups, mixed bean and pasta salads.	
BROAD BEAN (fava bean)	1–2 hrs	1½–2 hrs	–	Richly-flavoured stews/ casseroles.	Available fresh and dried; floury texture.
BUTTER BEAN	2–4 hrs	1½–2hrs	–	Richly flavoured stews/ casseroles, as a vegetable.	Floury texture when cooked.
CANNELLINI BEAN	2–3 hrs	1½hrs	–	Soups, salads, stews.	
CHICK PEA (garbanzo)	5–8 hrs	2 hrs	3–4 days	Hummus, spicy salads and stews, curries, Mediterranean dishes, soups.	Bitter when over-sprouted; dense so soak and cook thoroughly.
FLAGEOLET	2–3 hrs	1–1½hrs	3–5 days	Mixed bean salads, as a vegetable, sprouted for salads.	Use with subtly-flavoured dishes.
HARICOT BEAN	2–3 hrs	1–1½hrs	3–5 days	Slow-cooking stews and casseroles, soups, salads.	

cont.

LENTIL
  RED
  YELLOW
  GREEN
  BROWN
  PUY (blue)
	None
	"
	"
	"
	"
		5–8 mins
		(whole)
		
		20–30mins
		10–15mins
		"
			2–5 days
			
			(whole lentils
			only).
				Red/yellow:
				puréed, soups,
				dhal. Green
				and brown:
				stuffings,
				pasta sauces,
				as a vege-
				table. Puy: as
				a vegetable.
					Absorb other
					flavours well.
					Red and yellow
					disintegrate on
					cooking. Green
					and brown
					keep shape.
					Puy keep shape.

MUNG BEAN	1 hr	30–45mins	3–5 days	Oriental and Indian dishes, soups, casseroles, puréed.	Found whole, split, with skin removed; sprout- ing produces 'bean sprout'.
PEA Marrowfat	1 hr	30–45mins	–	Soups, mushy peas.	Green variety used in pease pudding.
KIDNEY BEAN Red & Black	2–3 hrs	1½–2 hrs	–	Spiced Mexican dishes, salads, pâtés.	Keep shape and colour well when cooked; cook separately (tends to colour other pulses); boil for 10–15 minutes to rem- ove dangerous toxins.
SOYA BEAN	5–8 hrs overnight	3–4 hrs	5 days	Needs well- flavoured sauces, soups, casseroles, salads, fermented black beans used in oriental- cooking.	High in protein, easily digested when cooked. By- products: soya milk, soya flour, bean curd (tofu), soya oil, soy sauce, miso (fermented soya bean paste).

GRAINS

Grains are the fruits of cereals. Types of cereal will vary according to climatic conditions. For example, wheat, oats and barley are grown in a cooler climate; rice needs warmer, wet conditions. Cereals are a staple food: wheat and rice make an important contribution to diets throughout the world. A grain is divided into three parts: outer husk, endosperm (the bulk of the grain), and the germ. Grains come in many forms: whole, with or without husk, rolled, crushed, flaked, partially cooked, and milled into flour. Therefore, grains are a versatile food.

NUTRITION

Grains are an important source of carbohydrate. They also contain protein, iron and B vitamins. For human consumption, grains are mostly sold processed. As with any food, processing affects the balance of nutrients and changes the taste.

NAME	USES	COMMENTS
BARLEY		
Whole (pot)	Thickener in stews/ casseroles; served as alternative to rice.	Has a nutty flavour when cooked.
Pearl	Added to soups; served hot or cold instead of rice.	Outer husk removed, therefore cooks quicker than whole barley.
Flakes	Added to muesli; decoration for bread.	
Flour	Combined with wheat flour to make bread and pastry.	Low in gluten.
Malted	Used in distilling.	
BUCKWHEAT		Related to rhubarb.
Groats	Roasted or plain; cooked as a staple; used for stuffing and croquettes.	Triangular grain.

cont.

Flour	Traditionally used in 'blinis' (Russian buckwheat pancakes).	Flour has distinctive mealy flavour, is an unusual grey colour, with dark speckles.
BULGAR WHEAT (burghul; pourgouri)	Salads (e.g. tabouleh), used like couscous or served instead of potatoes or rice.	Wheat grains are partially cooked, dried and cracked.
CORN, MAIZE		
Cornmeal	Cornbread, spoon bread, muffins.	
Cornflour	Thickening agent for sweet and savoury sauces; added to biscuits for soft texture.	Flour has velvety texture.
Polenta	Used as cornmeal.	Italian origin.
MILLET	Cooked in water or stock and served like rice; used as thickening agent in soups and stews.	Swells dramatically – use sparingly; allow 45g/1½oz per person.
OATS		Cooking produces jelly-like texture caused by release of water soluble fibre and pectins; gluten content low.
Jumbo flakes	Muesli; decoration for breads or added to bread doughs, savoury crumbles.	Bran intact, oat partially crushed.
Rolled oats	Quick porridge, flapjacks.	Bran removed, quickest to cook.
Oatmeal	Traditional Scottish cookery – porridge, athol brose, oat cake biscuits, instead of seasoned flour.	Endosperm cut to various sizes: pinhead (coarse), rough, medium, fine, superfine.
Oat bran	Alternative to wheat bran.	
RICE		Staple food of half the world's population; grows on marshy, flooded land.
American long-grain	Curries; stuffings and savoury dishes.	Swells substantially during cooking; dry and fluffy when cooked.

Arborio	Risotto.	Italian rice has four grades: superfino, fino, semifino, ordinario.
Basmati	Curries, pilaus, biryanis and Middle Eastern dishes.	Means fragrant, aromatic; needs plenty of rinsing; grains remain separate; brown and white available.
Brown	May be substituted whenever white rice is used.	Wholegrain (bran intact); available in all grain sizes; longer cooking time and more liquid required.
Flaked	Milk puddings; may be added to muesli.	Rolled for quick cooking; white and brown available.
Ground rice	Puddings, pastry, biscuits.	Like semolina, but paler; added to pastry, giving a sandy texture.
Pudding rice	Milk puddings.	Absorbs plenty of liquid; gives a creamy consistency.
Rice flour	Thickening agent, added to pastry, biscuits, cakes, puddings, pasta dough.	Very finely ground powder; white and brown available.
Sticky rice	Chinese, Japanese and Thai dishes.	Short or medium grain; high starch content; black (un-polished) and white (polished).
Wild rice	Mixed with other rices for rice dishes, stuffings, accompaniments.	Not actually rice, but an aquatic grass. Absorbs four times its volume of liquid; cooking time 35–60 minutes; high in protein, contains all essential amino acids; high in fibre, low in calories, gluten free.

WHEAT

Whole grain	Cooked like rice; sprouted; added to breads; salads.	If sprouted, carbohydrate content reduced and vitamin C level increased.
Kibbled	Decoration for bread.	Cracked, coarsely ground wheat grain.

Stoneground flour	Bread-making, can be substituted for white flour.	Traditional method of milling (less damage done to grain); nutritionally higher quality; may need more liquid than white flour.
Wholewheat flour	As above.	Labelled 100%. No part of grain removed during milling.
Wholemeal flour	For lighter baking than wholewheat flour.	Broad bran flakes removed (80–85% of whole grain remains).
Granary flour	Breads.	Whole grains sprouted, toasted and added to wholewheat flour.
White flour	Cakes, pastry, biscuits, yeast cookery, pasta.	Bran and wheatgerm removed, Soft wheat: plain or self-raising (cake/sponge flour). Hard wheat: strong flour high in protein and gluten.
Wheatgerm	Added to cakes and breads.	Sold in stabilised form to prevent rancidity. Full of protein, B and E vitamins.
Wheat bran	Enriches breads, crispbreads and breakfast cereals; decoration for bread.	Outer layer of grain; sold as broad or fine grade bran.
Semolina	Gnocchi, dumplings, milk puddings, biscuits, mixed with strong flour for pasta.	Ground from durum wheat (hard wheat); higher in protein and gluten than soft wheat; pale yellow.
Couscous	Salads, like rice and bulgar wheat.	Semolina grains rolled and coated with fine wheat flour. Soak first, then steam or cook like rice.

POTATOES

In Britain potatoes are often classified according to when they are harvested:

First earlies (new): end May–July

Second earlies (new): August–March

Main crop : September–May

The growing season for early potatoes is short. They are harvested when the tubers are immature; the skin is not 'set' and can be rubbed off easily, and they should be eaten soon after purchase as they do not keep well.

Main crop varieties are lifted when fully mature and will keep through to next year's harvest if correctly stored.

The three most popular varieties of main crop potatoes grown in Britain are, in descending order, Maris Piper, Record and Cara.

NUTRITION

Potatoes provide an inexpensive source of carbohydrate, protein, vitamin C, iron, thiamin, niacin and dietary fibre.

	New Potatoes raw per 100g	Old Potatoes raw per 100g
Energy KJ	298	318
Kcal	70	75
Fat Total	0.3g	0.2g
Protein	1.7g	2.1g
Carbohydrate	16.1g	17.2g
(Sugar)	(1.3g)	(0.6g)
Fibre	1.0g	1.3g
Thiamin (B_1)	0.15mg	0.21mg
Niacin (B_3)	0.40mg	0.60mg

cont.

Vitamin B$_6$	0.44mg	0.44mg
Vitamin C	16.0mg	11.0mg
Sodium	11.0mg	7.0mg
Phosphorous	34.0mg	37.0mg
Magnesium	14.0mg	17.0mg
Potassium	320.0mg	360.0mg
Chloride	57.0mg	66.0mg

BUYING & STORING

Look for potatoes that are well-shaped, firm and free from blemishes. Avoid those with green patches as these indicate exposure to light and the production of toxins (non-deadly poisons) under the skin. Buy new potatoes in small quantities as they do not keep well.

Always remove potatoes from the plastic bag in which they have been sold.

Main crop potatoes will keep well if they are stored, unwashed, in a dark, cool, frost-free, airy place away from smells. Light turns potatoes green, and warmth and dampness can cause them to sprout, shrivel and rot.

BOILING

As a general rule, old potatoes should be put in cold water and brought to the boil as this helps to prevent breakdown of the fragile outer layers. However, a potato recommended for boiling can break up even when cooked correctly, if conditions in which it was grown were particularly dry. New potatoes can be put into boiling water as they are naturally more waxy and will not disintegrate.

SELECTION OF POTATO VARIETIES

NAME	CROP	USES	COMMENTS
ARRAN PILOT	First early.	Salads, chipped, baked.	White skin and flesh; waxy texture when cooked.
ASPERGE *La Ratte/ Cornichon*	Second early.	Salads, steamed.	Yellow skin; creamy flesh; waxy texture when cooked.
CARA	Main.	All rounder.	Large; round; white skin; pink eyes; creamy flesh; creamy texture when cooked.

cont.

CHARLOTTE	Second early.	Salads, steamed, boiled.	Pale yellow skin and flesh; good flavour waxy texture when cooked.
DESIRÉE	Main.	All rounder.	Red skin; pale yellow flesh; waxy texture when cooked.
ESTIMA	Second early.	Baked, chipped, boiled.	Pale yellow skin and flesh; waxy texture when cooked.
GOLDEN WONDER	Main.	Salads, baked, mashed.	Brown skin; pale yellow flesh; floury texture when cooked.
KING EDWARD	Main.	All rounder.	Large; pale skin with pink patches; creamy flesh; floury texture when cooked.
MARIS BARD	First early.	Salads, boiled, baked when mature.	White skin and flesh; waxy texture when cooked.
MARIS PIPER	Main.	All rounder.	Thin white skin; cream coloured flesh; floury texture when cooked.
PENTLAND DELL	Main.	All rounder.	Long oval shape; white flesh and skin; firm texture when cooked.
PENTLAND JAVELIN	First early.	Salads, boiled, steamed.	Smooth white skin; white flesh; waxy texture when cooked.
PENTLAND SQUIRE	Main.	Baked, roasted, chipped, mashed.	White skin (russetted); white flesh; floury texture when cooked.

PINK FIR APPLE	Main.	Salads, boiled.	Pink skin; pinky-yellow flesh; new potato characteristics; waxy texture when cooked.
ROMANO	Main.	Baked, boiled, roasted, chipped.	Red skin; creamy flesh; waxy texture when cooked.
RECORD	Main.	Grown mainly for processing, such as crisps, waffles etc.	Short oval; yellow skin; pigments on exposure to light; yellow flesh; firm; slightly waxy texture.
ULSTER SCEPTRE	First early.	Salads, boiled.	Elongated oval shape; white skin and flesh; very waxy; firm texture when cooked.
WILJA	Second early.	Boiled, baked, chipped.	Rough yellow skin; pale yellow firm flesh; slightly dry but firm texture when cooked.

MOST SUITABLE COOKING METHODS

BOILING	MASHING	BAKING
Cara	Golden Wonder	Arran Pilot
Charlotte	King Edward	Cara
Desirée	Maris Piper	Estima
Estima	Pentland Dell	Golden Wonder
King Edward	Pentland Squire	King Edward
Maris Piper	Romano	Maris Piper
Maris Bard	Wilja	Pentland Dell
Pentland Javelin	Desirée	Romano
Pentland Squire		Wilja
Pink Fir Apple		Desirée
Romano		
Ulster Sceptre		
Wilja		

CHIPPING	ROASTING	SALADS
Arran Pilot	King Edward	Asperge
King Edward	Maris Piper	Desirée
Maris Piper	Pentland Dell	Golden Wonder
Maris Bard	Romano	Maris Bard
Pentland Dell	Wilja	Pentland Javelin
Romano	Desirée	Pentland Squire
Desirée		Wilja
		Charlotte
		Pink Fir Apple
		Ulster Sceptre

STEAMING	PROCESSING
Asperge	Record
Pentland Javelin	
Ulster Sceptre	
Wilja	

FUNGI

Fungi are a class of plant which feeds off living, dead or decaying organic matter. The part above the ground is the fruiting body of the plant; the part beneath the soil has a network of filaments (mycelium) through which the fungus draws its nutrients.

WARNING

On NO account pick or eat fungi unless they can be POSITIVELY identified. There are many different types; only a few are edible; the remainder are poisonous and may be deadly.

HABITAT

Dark damp areas; forest floors rich in leaf mould.

HARVEST

Some wild fungi, such as morels, mature in spring but the majority are collected in the autumn. They should be picked first thing in the morning to avoid damage by dew. Cultivated mushrooms are available all year round.

NUTRITION

Mushrooms are low in salt, and have no cholesterol, carbohydrate or fat. They therefore have few calories. They contain vegetable protein and many valuable vitamins – principally, thiamin, riboflavin, niacin and vitamin B_{12}. They also contain minerals such as phosphorus, magnesium, potassium and chloride.

TYPICAL ANALYSIS

Cultivated mushroom per 100g

Energy	KJ 55
	Kcal 15
Fat	Total: 0.5g
	Sat.: 0.1g
	Mono.: Trace
	Poly.: 0.3g
Protein	1.8g
Carbohydrate	0.4g
(Sugar)	(0.2g)
Fibre	1.1g
Minerals	
Phosphorus	80mg
Magnesium	9mg
Potassium	320mg
Chloride	69mg
Vitamins	
Thiamin (B_1)	0.09mg
Riboflavin (B_2)	0.31mg
Niacin (B_3)	3.20mg

STORING

Cultivated mushrooms should not be kept for more than three days in a refrigerator. Wild mushrooms should be eaten the day they are picked.

Mushrooms can be preserved by drying, pickling in vinegar or oil, and freezing if they are first blanched or sautéed.

PREPARATION

Mushrooms readily absorb water so they should not be washed; instead, wipe with damp paper towels. Stubborn dirt, or grit and sand trapped in crevices can be removed with a soft brush. Trim the stem, if necessary.

COOKING

Mushrooms contain a lot of water, which they will exude if cooked slowly; salt also encourages water to be given up.

DRIED MUSHROOMS

Many varieties are available dried, such as ceps (porcini), morels and chanterelles. They can be used to enrich sauces, soups, stuffings etc. They should be soaked in water for about 20 minutes before use.

CULTIVATED MUSHROOMS (*Agraricus bisporus*)

BUTTON:
The immature stage, when the round cap first surfaces. It has almost no stem and a mild flavour.

CLOSED CAP:
Here the membrane has broken although the gills are still not visible.

OPEN CAP:
The cap has darkened in colour and the brown gills are just visible underneath.

FLAT CAP:
Fully mature, the mushroom cap has opened out completely. The gills are darker and the flavour is mature and distinctive.

WILD MUSHROOMS

NAME	HABITAT	USES	COMMENTS
Beefsteak fungus Ox tongue fungus (*Fistulina hepatica*)	On trees such as oak and chestnut.	General all purpose, especially sautéing.	Found in summer; good flavour and texture.
Wood Blewitt (*Lepista nuda*)	Under deciduous trees or conifers; grassy pastures and woods.	Fried; baked; Japanese dishes.	Found October–December; stem, cap and gills are lilac blue; traditionally picked in Britain.

cont.

Cep (Fr: cèpe, It: porcini) (*Boletus edulis*)	Beech woods; woodland clearings; under coniferous trees.	Sautéed, marinated.	Found in summer and autumn; round, brown cap with thick white stem; rich flavour, soft texture; available dried.
Chanterelle (Fr: Girolle) (*Cantharellus cibarius*)	Woods, especially beech.	Dishes that require long gentle cooking; French dishes.	Found in summer and winter; deep yellow/apricot cap; fluted edge; slight smell and taste of apricots; becomes peppery when cooked; needs longer cooking than most fungi; is not easily cultivated; available dried and canned.
False Chanterelle (*Hygrophoropsis avrantiaca*)	As above.	As above.	Found July-December; similar to chanterelles; well formed gills; inferior quality; liable to cause indigestion.
Field mushroom (*Agaricus campestris*)	Open grassy areas.	General all purpose.	Found in summer and autumn; similar to cultivated varieties.
Hedgehog fungus Rubber brush (Fr: Pied de mouton) (*Hydnum repandum*)	All types of woodland.	Sautéed, sauces, risottos, egg, dishes.	Found in autumn/ early winter; gathered commercially; has spines and not gills; pale colour; retains bulk after cooking.

cont.

Horse mushroom (*Agaricus arvensis*)	Open fields.	As for cultivated mushrooms.	Found in autumn; large, yellow, white; resembles cultivated varieties; concentrated flavour.
Jew's Ear (*Auricularia auricula-judae*)	Tree stumps.	Can be used in place of its relative cloud ear in Chinese cooking.	Found in summer and autumn; forms series of shallow oval cups; gelatinous – needs several changes of rinsing water; available dried; flavour inferior to cloud ears.
Morel (Fr: morille) (*Morchella esculenta* and *Morchella elata*)	Woodland clearings.	Stuffed, baked, stews.	Found in spring and early summer in many parts of Britain; dark brown honeycombed cap; never eat raw; available dried and canned.
Oyster mushroom (Fr: pleurotte) (*Pleurotus ostreatus*)	Logs and tree stumps; elms.	Sauces, sautéed, pasta dishes, feuilletées, egg dishes, oriental dishes.	Found January – late spring; wild and cultivated; pale fawn/grey, peacock blue, yellow and pink; available dried, requires minimal soaking.
Parasol mushroom (*Lepiota procera*)	Sandy meadows.	Baked.	Found July – November; tall stem, brown scales on cream cap; good flavour; stalks tough and fibrous; available dried.

cont.

Puff ball Giant puff ball (*Langermannia gigante*)	Woodlands and meadows.	Sautéed, soups, sauces.	Found late summer/ autumn; grows from golf to football size (eventually explodes); inedible after cricket ball size; white with no obvious stalk.
Shiitake Black Forest/Flower/ winter mushroom (*Lentinula edoes*)	Cultivated in Britain, Holland and USA.	Sauces, sautéed, oriental dishes where strong flavour required.	Found in autumn; pronounced scent and flavour; enhanced by cooking; tan cap, white gills and tough stem; available fresh or dried; also cultivated.
Truffles	Near roots of oak/ beech trees. Oak groves planted to encourage growth.	Sophisticated vegetable dishes, egg dishes, sauces, garnish.	Found in autumn, pigs and dogs used to find them; never served whole; expensive.
Périgord truffle (*Tuber melanosporum*) White truffle (*Tuber magnatum*)	As above. As above. Northern Italy.	Eggs dishes, subtly flavoured dishes. Grated on pasta, risotto, egg dishes, in fondues.	As above; knobbly black tuber; used raw.
Summer truffle (*Tuber aestivum*)	Beech trees, chalky soil.	As for superior varieties.	Found late summer/ autumn; inferior; rare; only truffle found in Britain.

NUTS AND SEEDS

Nuts and seeds are usually sold dried, but are occasionally available fresh (green).

Most nuts are high in protein, carbohydrate and fat and are, therefore, calorific. Nuts bought in the shell should be heavy for their size, and show no signs of blemish. Nuts in the shell keep better than shelled ones. Shelled nuts should be bought in small quantities and used relatively quickly.

NAME	ORIGIN	NUTRITION (per 100g)		COMMENTS
ALMOND	Middle East, China, Japan, Spain, Italy, Portugal, North Africa, California, Australia.	Energy KJ Kcal Fat Tot. Sat. Mono. Poly. Protein Carbo. Good source of vitamin E	2534 612 55.8g 4.7g 34.4g 14.2g 21.1g 6.9g	There are two types: sweet and bitter; the latter is poisonous if eaten raw. Almonds may be bought: whole (with or without brown skins); split into halves; flaked (or finely sliced); nibbed; ground (like breadcrumbs).
BRAZIL	Brazil, Venezuela, Chile, Africa.	Energy KJ Kcal Fat Tot. Sat. Mono. Poly. Protein Carbo.	1295 314 55.8g 7.5g 11.9g 10.6g 6.5g 1.4g	Season: Nov–Feb; the fruit when ripe splits open revealing 20 Brazil 'nuts' which are actually seeds.

cont.

CASHEW	South America, India, East Africa.	Roasted and Salted:		Taste improved by roasting; popular in Chinese and Indian dishes.
		Energy KJ	2533	
		Kcal	611	
		Fat Tot.	50.9g	
		Sat.	10.1g	
		Mono.	29.4g	
		Poly.	9.1g	
		Protein	20.5g	
		Carbo.	18.8g)	
CHESTNUT (Sweet)	France, Italy, Spain.	Energy KJ	719	Not to be confused with horse chestnut. Steamed or boiled. Sweetened/ unsweetened purée; preserved by drying/ baking in syrup (marron glacé). May be ground for flour.
		Kcal	170	
		Fat Tot.	2.7g	
		Sat.	0.5g	
		Mono.	1.0g	
		Poly.	1.1g	
		Protein	2.0g	
		Carbo.	36.6g	
COCONUT	Tropical regions.	Creamed Block:		Available forms: *Milk*: available canned or made by adding boiling water to fresh or dessicated flesh. *Desiccated*: the flesh is shredded and dried; may be sold as strands, chips or shreds. *Creamed*: hard block which may be added straight to a dish or melted with boiling liquid.
		Energy KJ	2760	
		Kcal	669	
		Fat Tot.	68.8g	
		Sat.	59.3g	
		Mono.	3.9g	
		Poly.	1.6g	
		Protein	6.0g	
		Carbo.	7.0g	
HAZELNUT	Turkey, USA, Italy, Spain, England (Kent).	Energy KJ	2685	Available all year round; may be used whole, roasted or ground; 'oils' quickly if over-handled; good source of calcium,
		Kcal	650	
		Fat Tot.	63.5g	
		Sat.	4.7g	
		Mono.	50.0g	
		Poly.	5.9g	

cont.

		Protein	14.1g	phosphorus, magnesium and potassium; produces oil.
		Carbo.	6.0g	
MACADAMIA	Australia, California, Hawai, Latin America.	Energy KJ	3082	Sold in shells; roasted, salted.
		Kcal	748	
		Fat Tot.	77.6g	
		Sat.	11.2g	
		Mono.	60.8g	
		Poly.	1.6g	
		Protein	7.9g	
		Carbo.	4.8g	
PEANUT	South America, West Africa, India, China and most hot countries.	Energy: KJ	2341	May be roasted, dry-roasted, salted or spiced; nutritious and cheap by-products: ground-nut oil (arachide); peanut butter.
		Kcal.	564	
		Fat Tot.	46.1g	
		Sat.	8.2g	
		Mono.	21.1g	
		Poly.	14.3g	
		Protein	25.6g	
		Carbo.	12.5g	
		High Niacin B_3		
		Vitamin E		
PECAN	USA.	Energy KJ	2843	Can replace walnuts.
		Kcal	689	
		Fat Tot.	70.1g	
		Sat.	5.7g	
		Mono.	42.5g	
		Poly.	18.7g	
		Protein	9.2g	
		Carbo.	5.8g	
PINE NUT	Mediterranean coastline, especially Spain.	Energy KJ	2840	Expensive to harvest, therefore a luxury item.
		Kcal	688	
		Fat Tot.	68.6g	
		Sat.	4.6g	
		Mono.	19.9g	
		Poly.	41.1g	
		Protein	14.0g	
		Carbo.	4.0g	
		Good source of vitamin E		

PISTACHIO	Middle East, Mediterranean.	Unshelled weight:		The greener the kernel the better the flavour and keeping quality; roasted or salted in shells.
		Energy KJ	1370	
		Kcal	331	
		Fat Tot.	30.5g	
		Sat.	4.1g	
		Mono.	15.2g	
		Poly.	9.8g	
		Protein	9.9g	
		Carbo.	4.6g	
WALNUT	France, Italy, Germany, California; Central Asia.	Energy KJ	2837	Available all year round; fresh known as 'wet' – use quickly; produces oil.
		Kcal	688	
		Fat Tot.	68.5g	
		Sat.	5.6g	
		Mono.	12.4g	
		Poly.	47.7g	
		Protein	14.7g	
		Carbo.	3.3g	

SEEDS

NAME	ORIGIN	USES
ALFALFA	Non-organic: Italy, France Organic: USA	Decoration; sprouted for salads.
LINSEED	Non-organic: UK Organic: USA	Decoration; added to breads.
NASTURTIUM	UK	Pickles; used like capers (unopened buds of plant native to Mediterranean region).
NIGELLA	UK, Middle East, India	Decoration; added to breads, Indian and Middle Eastern dishes.
POPPY	Spain, Hungary	Decoration for breads and pastry; used in bread dough; dry-roasted; added to dressings.
PUMPKIN	Non-organic: China	Salads; breads; mix with nuts for roasts and pâtés; sprouted.

SESAME	Non-organic: China Organic: USA	Good source of calcium. Decoration for breads and pastry; used in Chinese cooking; roasted and ground for tahini and halva. Sesame oil.
SUNFLOWER	Organic and non-organic: USA	Good source of vitamin E. Breads; salads.

HERBS

The flavour of herbs comes from their essential oils, which are released when cooked or crushed. Generally speaking, only the leaves are used. Robust leaves such as parsley, are usually finely chopped; more delicate leaves like basil and mint are normally roughly chopped; thyme and other small leaves are often used whole.

Herbs should be used when very fresh. They can, however, be stored in a plastic bag in the salad drawer of a refrigerator for a few days.

TO DRY HERBS

Pick the herbs before they have flowered, on a sunny day. Take care not to bruise them as this releases the oils. Blanch briefly in boiling water, then refresh in cold water. Tie into small bunches and hang by the stem in a dry airy room with low humidity (i.e. not the kitchen). Herb leaves can also be dried by placing them on trays in a very low oven, turning occasionally. They should be stored in airtight containers in a cool cupboard, and used within 6 months.

As a general guide, 1 teaspoon dried herbs is equivalent to 1 tablespoon fresh herbs.

TO FREEZE HERBS

Herbs should be blanched and refreshed and put into bags before freezing. Different varieties may be packed together to make a bouquet garni, otherwise they should be bagged separately. Herbs may also be frozen in ice cube trays: mix 1 tablespoon of chopped herbs with about 1 tablespoon of water and freeze.

TO MAKE HERB OILS

Fill a clear, glass bottle with freshly picked herbs, such as tarragon or basil (basil is particularly good if used with a couple of cloves of garlic). Top up with a good quality olive oil. Cover and leave for 2–4 weeks. Strain if liked. If leaving the herbs in the oil, don't allow them to become exposed to the air as they can go mouldy. As the oil is used, top up the bottle with fresh oil, though in time this will dilute the flavour.

TO MAKE HERB VINEGARS

Fill a glass bottle with freshly picked herbs such as tarragon, rosemary or a mixed bunch. Cover with cider or white wine vinegar, close the bottle with a cork or acid-proof cap and leave for 2–4 weeks. Strain if liked. Herbs can stay in the vinegar but their colour will fade and the last 1cm/½ inch will probably be a bit cloudy.

NAME	USES	COMMENTS
BASIL Genoa basil Sweet basil	Mediterranean dishes; with any summer vegetables; salads; infusions; pesto sauce.	Varieties include purple, opal, neapolitana, lemon, anise, cinnamon, and spice basil; leaves should be torn and not chopped.
BAY	General flavouring; added to sugar, rice puddings, baked egg custard. Used whole and removed before serving.	Basic ingredient of bouquet garni; best fresh, but mostly available dried.
BORAGE	Salads; summer punches.	Use flowers for garnish/ decorations; leaves very coarse.
CHERVIL	Salads, as a garnish.	One of the classic '*fines herbes*'; delicate aniseed taste; does not store or dry well.
CHIVES	Use with potato, egg, green salads, soups, sauces; use chopped or whole for garnishing.	One of the classic '*fines herbes*'; delicate onion flavour; add at end of cooking; freezes well but does not dry.
CORIANDER (Chinese parsley, Cilantro, Greek parsley)	Sauces; dressings; curries; salads.	Leaves, stalk and root used; use sparingly; leaves should be roughly chopped, roots chopped and mixed with other root vegetables.
DILL	Classic combination: dill and cucumber, use with potatoes, in soups and butters.	Feathery leaves have a slight aniseed flavour.

cont.

FENNEL	Mediterranean dishes.	Aniseed flavour.
GARLIC	Cloves used whole or crushed, whole bulbs roasted and served as vegetable.	Crushed with salt for smooth paste; raw garlic very strong, cooked garlic mild.
MARJORAM	Rich tomato sauce for pasta, gnocchi, pizza; soups; potato, pepper and onion and mushroom dishes.	Oregano (wild marjoram) can be substituted; both very perfumed, oregano has stronger flavour.
MINT	New potatoes; sauces; dressings; puddings; chocolates; fruit compotes.	Over 40 varieties, most common are: spearmint, peppermint, pineapple mint, apple mint, lemon; tear leaves.
PARSLEY	Sauces; rice dishes; salads; garnish (finely chopped).	Most widely used herb; two varieties: curly leaved and flat-leaved (Italian parsley); provides colour, carotene, vitamin C, iron and minerals.
ROSEMARY	Sauces; stuffings; vegetables.	Only leaves used, finely chopped; strong flavour, use sparingly.
SAGE	Cheese, tomato and egg dishes; breads; pasta.	Strong flavour, use sparingly.
SORREL	With subtle dishes and sauces; soup; cooked like spinach.	Resembles young spinach leaves; leaf has sharp lemon flavour; acidity will curdle milk.
TARRAGON	Basic ingredient of classic sauces, e.g. béarnaise; salads, dressings, vegetables; flavouring for mustard; vinegar.	One of the classic 'fines herbes'; slight aniseed flavour; French tarragon has a finer flavour than Russian variety.
THYME	Basic ingredient in bouquet garni; sauces; marinades.	Many cultivated varieties, e.g. common, lemon, orange and caraway.

SPICES

Spices are the dried seed, pod, berry, root, bark, bud or sap of plants noted for their powerful aromatic qualities. They are available whole or ground. Wherever possible buy small quantities of whole spices as, once ground, the flavour fades. Most spices can be ground with a pestle and mortar or in a small electric grinder, although some spices, such as fenugreek, are impossible to grind at home. Store spices in small airtight containers in dark, dry and cool conditions.

Spices should be cooked to extract maximum flavour. When used ground they should be fried in a little oil for 1 minute before adding the main ingredients. If they are to be added at the end of cooking time, they should be dry-roasted first.

NAME	USES	COMMENTS
ALLSPICE Jamaica pepper	Added to peppermill for extra seasoning; used instead of cloves; flavouring for vinegar; pickling; marinades and baking.	Dried berry; evergreen of myrtle family; not a pepper.
ANISEED	Indian dishes.	Fruit often substituted with star anise; Pernod.
CARAWAY	Traditional English baking: seed cake, breads, biscuits.	
CARDAMOM	North African and Indian cooking; milk puddings; ice creams.	Plants of ginger family; native to Sri Lanka; cream or green pods with black seeds inside; use whole or ground.

cont.

CELERY	Soups; sauces; vegetable dishes; ground with salt for celery salt.	From head of celery plant.
CHINESE FIVE SPICE	Oriental cooking; flavouring for syrups.	A combination of anise pepper, cassia, fennel seeds, star anise and cloves; powder or whole spices.
CINNAMON	Baking; fruit dishes; custards.	Bark of laurel; native of Sri Lanka; available whole (dried quills of bark) and powdered.
CLOVES	Traditional in Christmas pudding, mincemeat, hot-cross buns; sweet and savoury dishes; pickles; chutneys; infusions.	Dried flower buds of evergreen myrtle; cultivated in Zanzibar; used whole or ground.
CORIANDER	Stuffings; pickles; chutneys; dressings; breads.	Cultivated in Southern Europe, Africa, India, Mexico; toasted whole and then crushed.
CUMIN	Rice and couscous dishes; curries; vegetables dishes.	Cultivated in North Africa and India; used whole or ground, toasted or untoasted.
DILL SEED	Cucumber and root vegetable dishes.	Similar in appearance to fennel seeds but not the same aroma and taste.
FENNEL	Mediterranean-style dishes.	Aniseed aroma; less harsh than caraway.
FENUGREEK	Curry powders.	Member of pea family; very hard and difficult to grind; can be sprouted.
GARAM MASALA	Curries.	Combination of spices generally available in powdered form.
GINGER	Cakes, biscuits.	Finest quality dried root ginger comes from Jamaica; available fresh, powdered, crystallised and candied.

cont.

JUNIPER	Gin; savoury dishes; Christmas cakes; puddings.	Berries ripen every second year; highly aromatic.
LEMON GRASS	Thai and South East Asian dishes; infusions; can replace lemon zest.	Only white part of fresh stalk used, crushed; available fresh and dried.
MACE	Infusions (whole mace); mincemeat (ground). Interchangeable with nutmeg	Hard, lacy casing of nutmeg seed.
MIXED SPICE (Pudding spice)	Rich fruit cakes; puddings; biscuits.	Combination of sweet spices: cinnamon, cloves, nutmeg, sometimes coriander, occasionally allspice.
MUSTARD SEED	Dressings; mayonnaise; cheese sauces; decoration on and in breads; condiment.	Condiment since AD 300; English white mustard grown in Cambridge and Essex, very fine; black grown in Lincolnshire and Yorkshire; add to sauces only at final stage as flavour is quickly lost when heated.
NUTMEG	Traditional in Christmas cakes; puddings; accompaniment to spinach, milk and cheese dishes.	Loses aroma quickly when ground.
PEPPER Cayenne	Eggs, cheese dishes, hot spicy dishes.	Hottest pepper spice; pod and seed ground.
Chilli	Hot, Mexican dishes.	A ground mixture of peppers.
Paprika	Hungarian, Austrian and Spanish dishes.	Ground seeds of particular variety of sweet pepper; Hungarian is best; Spanish version called *pimentón*; mildest form of pepper spice.

cont.

PEPPERCORNS

Black and white	General seasoning.	Loses flavour once ground; white pepper (inner part of ripe berries) is hottest; black pepper (not completely ripe when picked and outer husk left on) is milder but more aromatic; white and black peppercorns ground together known as *mignonette* pepper.
Green	Sauces.	Immature berries; generally sold canned or in jars, in brine; soft and mild; use whole or crushed.
Pink	Sauces.	Pink berry (from poison ivy); mildly toxic in large quantities; used whole or crushed.
SAFFRON	Spanish, Moroccan, Indian dishes.	85,000 flowers make 450g/1lb, so very expensive.
TURMERIC	Moroccan, Indian dishes.	Related to ginger family; bright yellow when ground; substitute for saffron when colour is needed (not the same flavour).
VANILLA BEAN	Sweet and savoury sauces; flavouring for vanilla sugar and milk-based puddings.	Pod from climbing orchid; ancient plant used by Aztecs; best beans from Mexico; takes 4–5 months to dry and treat: natural vanilla essence; vanilla flavouring poorer quality.

DAIRY PRODUCTS

Cow's milk

TYPE OF MILK	NUTRITION per 100g		INFORMATION
PASTEURISED Silver top	Energy KJ	268	Pasteurisation kills harmful bacteria in milk but will not prevent later contamination.
	Kcal	64	
	Fats	3.8g	
	Protein	3.1g	
	Carbohydrate	4.7g	
HOMOGENISED Red top	As above		Milk undergoes pasteurisation then homogenisation, which distributes the fat throughout the milk.
SEMI-SKIMMED Silver and red striped top	Energy KJ	190	Taste is less rich due to reduced fat content.
	Kcal	45	
	Fats	1.6g	
	Protein	3.2g	
	Carbohydrate	4.9	
SKIMMED Blue and silver checked top	Energy KJ	136	Not suitable for small children; burns easily; beware when making sauces.
	Kcal	32	
	Protein	3.2g	
	Fat	0.1g	
	Carbohydrate	4.9g	
CHANNEL ISLAND/ JERSEY Gold top	Energy KJ	327	Fat content can vary from 4–8%; it is the best milk to use for milk puddings.
	Kcal	78	
	Protein	3.6g	
	Fat	5.1g	
	Carbohydrate	4.8g	

cont.

UNPASTEURISED (raw, untreated)	As pasteurised		All milk has to pass strict *brucellosis* tests; used widely in cheese making; less available.
BUTTERMILK	Energy KJ	165	By-product of butter-making; thin and unstable; best used in baking.
	Kcal	40	
	Protein	4.3g	
	Carbohydrate	5.5g	
DRIED SKIMMED	Energy KJ	1482	Once reconstituted use as skimmed milk.
	Kcal	348	
	Fat	0.6g	
	Protein	36.1g	
	Carbohydrate	52.9g	
CONDENSED	Energy KJ	1406	Thick and sweet; may be purchased unsweetened and sweetened, which is very sweet.
	Kcal	333	
	Fat	10.1g	
	Protein	8.5g	
	Carbohydrate	55.5g	
EVAPORATED	Energy KJ	629	Just over twice as concentrated as milk; characteristic 'cooked' flavour; unsweetened; can be used in sweet and savoury dishes.
	Kcal	151	
	Fats	9.4g	
	Protein	8.4g	
	Carbohydrate	8.5g	

CREAM

Cream is available in many different forms:

TYPE OF CREAM	NUTRITION per 100g		INFORMATION
SINGLE	Energy KJ	817	Fat content too low for whipping; curdles when subjected to high heat.
	Kcal	198	
	Fat	19.8g	
	Protein	2.6g	
	Carbohydrate	4.1g	
WHIPPING	Energy KJ	1539	Higher fat content; use cold bowl and whisk for good volume; does not hold its shape; is not a substitute for double cream.
	Kcal	373	
	Fat	39.3g	
	Protein	2.0g	
	Carbohydrate	3.1g	

cont.

DOUBLE	Energy KJ	1848	If over-whipped will turn to
	Kcal	449	butter; can be boiled.
	Fat	48.0g	
	Protein	1.7g	
	Carbohydrate	2.7g	
CLOTTED	Energy KJ	2413	Traditionally produced in
	Kcal	586	Devon, Cornwall and
	Fat	63.5g	Somerset and served with
	Protein	1.6g	scones.
	Carbohydrate	2.3g	
SOURED	Energy KJ	789	Homogenised cream with
	Kcal	191	souring agent added; it is not
	Fat	18.0g	cream that has turned sour.
	Protein	2.6g	
	Carbohydrate	3.9g	
CRÈME FRAÎCHE	Energy KJ	1567	Milk is treated with a culture
	Kcal	380	that gives acidity; used
	Fat	40.0g	extensively in French cooking
	Protein	2.3g	and now available in Britain.
	Carbohydrate	2.8g	
SMETANA (Smatana)	Energy KJ	540	A soured cream orginally from
	Kcal	130	Russia and Eastern Europe;
	Fat	10.0g	will curdle when subjected to
	Protein	4.7g	high heat. Add at end of
	Carbohydrate	5.3g	cooking time.

YOGHURT

There are many different types of yoghurt:

TYPES OF YOGHURT	NUTRITION per 100g		INFORMATION
NATURAL	Energy KJ	333	Can be used as 'starter' if
	Kcal	79	making yoghurt at home;
	Fat	3.0g	differing consistencies depend
	Protein	5.7g	on containers used for
	Carbohydrate	7.8g	incubation.

cont.

LOW-FAT	Energy KJ	177	Made from concentrated
	Kcal	41	skimmed milk; fat content
	Fat	0.2g	varies from about 0.5–2%;
	Protein	4.3g	available plain or fruit
	Carbohydrate	6.0g	flavoured.
GREEK, Greek-style	Cow's		Ewe's milk rich, creamy, 6%
	Energy KJ	477	fat; cow's milk variety often
	Kcal	115	strained to produce
	Fat	9.1g	concentrated flavour; will
	Protein	4.3g	curdle when subjected to high
	Carbohydrate	6.0g	heat; add towards end of
			cooking; can be stabilised with
	Ewe's		flour and cornflour.
	Energy KJ	442	
	Kcal	106	
	Fat	7.5g	
	Protein	4.4g	
	Carbohydrate	5.6g	
FRENCH, French-style (low fat)	Energy KJ	344	Low fat homogenised milk;
	Kcal	81	available natural and fruit
	Fat	0.9g	flavoured.
	Protein	4.1g	
	Carbohydrate	14.2g	
GOAT	Energy KJ	262	Suitable for those with lactose
	Kcal	63	allergies; does not curdle when
	Fat	3.8g	heated.
	Protein	5.8g	
	Carbohydrate	3.9g	
SOYA	Energy KJ	304	Available in some
	Kcal	72	supermarkets.
	Fat	4.2g	
	Protein	5.0g	
	Carbohydrate	3.9g	

BUTTER AND MARGARINE

TYPE	NUTRITION per 100g		INFORMATION
BUTTER Salted and unsalted	Energy KJ Kcal Fat total Sat. Mono. Poly. Protein Carbohydrate	3031 737 81.7g 54.0g 19.8g 2.6g 0.5g trace	Salted butter has minimum of 3% added salt; 2.5% and lower may be unlabelled although some packets may say 'slightly salted'.
MARGARINE – Hard (Animal and vegetable fat)	Energy KJ Kcal Fat total Sat. Mono. Poly. Protein Carbohydrate	3039 739 81.6g 30.4g 36.5g 10.8g 0.2g 1.0g	Made from hydrogenated fats.
MARGARINE – Hard (Vegetable fat)	Energy KJ Kcal Fat total Sat. Mono. Poly. Protein Carbohydrate	3039 739 81.6g 35.9g 33.0g 9.4g 0.2g 1.0g	
MARGARINE – Soft (Animal and vegetable fat)	Energy KJ Kcal Fat total Sat. Mono. Poly. Protein Carbohydrate	3039 739 81.6g 26.9g 37.2g 13.8g 0.2g 1.0g	Unhydrogenated fats; unsuitable for pastry.

cont.

MARGARINE – Soft (Vegetable fat)	Energy KJ	3039	Unsuitable for pastry.
	Kcal	739	
	Fat total	81.6g	
	Sat.	25.0g	
	Mono.	31.0g	
	Poly.	21.8g	
	Protein	0.2g	
	Carbohydrate	1.0g	
MARGARINE – Soft (Polyunsaturated fat)	Energy KJ	3039	High water content; only suitable for spreading.
	Kcal	739	
	Fat total	81.6g	
	Sat.	16.2g	
	Mono.	20.6g	
	Poly.	41.1g	
	Protein	0.2g	
	Carbohydrate	1.0g	
SOYA	Energy KJ	3060	Suitable for spreading; use creaming and melting methods to make cakes and biscuits.
	Kcal	744	
	Fat total	82.7g	
	Sat.	18.0g	
	Mono.	31.0g	
	Poly.	33.0g	
	Protein	0.0g	
	Carbohydrate	0.0g	

SOFT FRESH CHEESES

These cheeses are barely ripened, if at all.

TYPE OF CHEESE	NUTRITION per 100g		INFORMATION
COTTAGE	Energy KJ	558	Heated cow's milk causes curds to form characteristic lumps; strained, washed and coated with cream; used in cooking and eaten fresh.
	Kcal	132	
	Fat	5.4g	
	Protein	18.6g	
	Carbohydrate	2.7g	
CREAM (Full fat)	Energy KJ	2168	Used in cooking and eaten fresh.
	Kcal	528	
	Fat	56.8g	
	Protein	3.6g	
	Carbohydrate	0.09g	

cont.

CURD	Energy KJ	735	Lactic starter added to cow's
	Kcal	176	milk to produce curds and
	Fat	12.0g	whey, curds drained and salted
	Protein	17.0g	and sold separately; used in
	Carbohydrate	0.1g	cooking or eaten fresh.
FROMAGE FRAIS	Energy KJ	633	French curd cheese; not to be
	Kcal	153	confused with crème fraîche;
	Fat	9.6g	sometimes enriched with
	Protein	9.3g	cream; used in cooking and
	Carbohydrate	7.8g	eaten fresh; available natural
			or fruit flavoured.
MASCARPONE	Energy KJ	1666	Italian cream cheese; rich,
	Kcal	404	dense, smooth; used as double
	Fat	40.3g	cream.
	Protein	5.5g	
	Carbohydrate	4.8g	
MOZZARELLA	Energy KJ	1146	Italian; traditionally made
	Kcal	276	from water buffalo milk, also
	Fat	21.7g	more commonly available
	Protein	18.2g	made from cow's milk, which
	Carbohydrate	2.0g	can be bland and rubbery
			when eaten raw; stored in
			whey; stringy when cooked.
RICOTTA	Energy KJ	540	Italian whey cheese;
	Kcal	129	traditionally made from ewe's
	Fat	9.9g	milk though available made
	Protein	8.4g	from cow's milk; used in
	Carbohydrate	1.8g	cooking and also eaten fresh
			with fruit.
QUARK	Energy KJ	293	German curd cheese,
	Kcal	70	sometimes enriched with
	Fat	0.2g	cream; generally used for
	Protein	9.3g	cooking (cheesecakes, pâtés)
	Carbohydrate	4.1g	rather than eaten fresh.

MAIL ORDER ADDRESSES

FOX'S SPICES, Aston Cantlow Road, Wilmcote, Stratford-upon-Avon, Warwickshire CV37 9XN (0789 266420) Spices, herbs, mustards, peppers and oriental spices.

FIDDES PAYNE LTD, The Spice Warehouse, Pepper Alley, Banbury, Oxfordshire OX16 8JB (02295 253888) Herbs and spices in all forms and essential oils.

JULIAN GRAVES Ltd., Unit 18, Delph Road Industrial Estate, Delph Road, Brierley Hill, West Midlands DY5 2IP (0384 480493) Dried exotic fruits.

L'AQUILA, 40 Caledonian Road, King's Cross, London N1 9DT (071 278 0309) Truffles, dried mushrooms and saffron.

LINA'S, 18 Brewer Street, London W1 (071 437 6482) Home-made pasta, beans, olives, Italian breads, pastries, salamis, cheeses, dried mushrooms.

STEAMBOAT ORIENTAL FOODS, P.O. Box 452, Bradford, West Yorkshire BD4 7TF (no phone no.) Thai, Indian, Pakistani, Chinese and Japanese foods.

TAYLOR & LAKE, 44/54 Stewarts Road, London SW8 4DF (071 622 9156) OR Park Farmhouse, Sandford St. Martin, Oxfordshire OX7 7AH (0608 683366) Salted capers, sun-dried tomatoes, fine oils and specialist foods.

WILD OATS, 210 Westbourne Grove, London W11 2RH (071 229 1063) Health food shop; organic foods.

WING YIP, 395 Edgware Road, London NW2 61W (081 450 0422) Japanese, Chinese and Thai foods.

YAOHAN PLAZA, 399 Edgware Road, Colindale, London NW9 OJJ (081 200 0009) All types of fresh and canned Japanese foods.

INDEX